Your
Yorkshire Terrier's

Also Available

ELAINE WALDORF GEWIRTZ

Joanne Howl, D.V.M., Series Editor

Your
YORKSHIRE TERRIER'S
Life

Your Complete Guide to Raising Your Pet from Puppy to Companion

THREE RIVERS PRESS • NEW YORK

Published by Three Rivers Press, New York, New York.
Member of the Crown Publishing Group, a division of Random House, Inc.
www.randomhouse.com

THREE RIVERS PRESS and the Tugboat design and YOUR PET'S LIFE are registered trademarks of Random House, Inc.

Originally published by Prima Publishing, Roseville, California, in 2000.

Interior photos by Kent Lacin Media Services
Color insert photos © Isabelle Français and Tara Darling
Chapter 6 illustrations by Pam Tanzey

Special thanks to the beautiful dogs who appear in this book and their wonderful owners: Munchkins and Ginger, owned by Mary F. Greggain; Scooter and Shorty, Bonnie Sustich; and Demi Brown, E.S. Brown.

Printed in the United States of America

Library of Congress Cataloging-in-Publication Data
Gewirtz, Elaine Waldorf.
    Your Yorkshire terrier's life : your complete guide to raising your pet from puppy to companion / Elaine Waldorf Gewirtz.
        p. cm. — (Your pet's life)
    Yorkshire terrier. I. Title. II. Series.
    SF429.Y6 G48 2000
    636.76—dc21   00-031369

ISBN 0-7615-2535-1

10 9 8 7 6 5 4 3

Contents

Introduction

The Yorkshire Terrier is a big surprise in a little package who turns heads wherever he goes. A diminutive but spirited Toy with a tidy topknot in the middle of his head and a long, silky coat that shimmers blue and gold, the Yorkie brings a smile to the face of everyone he meets. And a Yorkie does meet a lot of people.

I remember once standing in a long line waiting to buy tickets for a play when a woman walked to the end of the line and put a duffel bag on the ground next to her. Inside were two mounds of long steel-blue hair with two sets of alert black eyes staring up. The huddle belonged to two four-pound Yorkies, John and Tessie, and they watched everything around them intently. With red bows perched on their topknots, they looked as impish as could be, yet seemed perfectly happy to just sit there and observe the crowd. As people began noticing them, the owner took one out of the bag and set her on the floor. Instantly she began investigating everything around her and had everyone's attention. The owner said, "They always liven things up and insist on coming along so I never go anywhere without them."

Here's a breed that's light enough to be portable yet won't be ignored. The Yorkie is cute and affectionate, and a lively bundle of energy always ready to take charge. Feisty and cuddly at the same time, the Yorkie acts ten times bigger than he really is. Imagine a dog slightly smaller than a five-pound sack of flour striking an indignant pose and standing guard over his household. By sounding off a series of short, shrill yaps, the Yorkie scares off two- or four-legged intruders who don't belong there. Minutes later he's happy to bed down and snuggle cozily into his owner's lap.

Weighing only three to seven pounds, the tiniest member of the Terrier family is one of the most popular Toys, but his appeal isn't simply that he is a lap warmer. Playing catch, investigating the garden, and zipping around the house are some of the Yorkie's favorite activities, as the Yorkshire Terrier has an adventurous spirit and is curious about the world around him. He likes to explore his surroundings, and going for long walks and hikes in the great outdoors—as much as six to nine miles in a single outing—is his ideal exercise once he has built up endurance. For the child who treasures having a playful, furry companion, the Yorkie is perfect. For the person who enjoys being active or the one who suffers from back problems, a Yorkie is a practical companion. Seniors will find Yorkies especially appealing because they can be protective and devoted at the same time. An owner who wears a hearing aid during the day can depend on his Yorkie's sharp hearing when he takes his aid off at night. A Yorkie can sound the alarm when the smoke detector goes off or the phone or doorbell rings.

Besides being a fun and loyal dog, a Yorkie is a flexible fellow with other attributes. As long as he gets out for exercise, he's fairly easy to keep in a small apartment, but is just as happy living in a house with a small yard. The breed is bright and thrives on visual stimulation and is often very happy to just stay at home and watch the world go by. As an indoor pet, he's not much to pick up after as he does not shed twice a year like most dogs do. He leaves no dog hair on your clothes or all over the house and, unlike other breeds, has no doggie odor. Despite his long, silky tresses and the fact that he must be combed and brushed every day, the single coat is easy to groom and maintain. Because Yorkies shed very little and are easy to groom, some dog-allergic people find them much easier to live with than other breeds.

If the Yorkshire Terrier sounds appealing so far, read on. There is more to learn before making the decision that this is the breed for you.

An Overview of Yorkshire Terrier Ownership

The elegant dog with the long, majestic coat may look far too fragile to be courageous, but at heart the Yorkshire Terrier is a scrappy working-class dog who likes to express himself with a series of sharp barks. Because this boldness can get him into trouble, you may have to take extra care to protect him from danger and possible injury. The person who values a strong and independent character in a small dog frame will have a loyal companion for many years to come. Like any dog, however, this breed will need some time each day devoted to routine care. Be prepared to spend a minimum of ten minutes brushing and combing your Yorkie's silken coat and another ten or fifteen minutes each day taking him for a walk.

What It Means to Have a Yorkshire Terrier in Your Life

Life with this breed is never dull. A Yorkie can amuse his owner for hours with his lively personality, intelligence, and cute antics. Yorkies are even capable of recognizing many words, including the names of different toys when they are called out. A high energy level usually goes along with the breed's cleverness, and they are always ready to accept a challenge and do appreciate attention.

The Yorkie has a serious side, too, and his keen sense of hearing allows him to hear someone coming long before the visitor gets to the door. This very people-oriented breed likes to greet the public and has strong territorial instincts that make him an instant alarm system and a menacing watchdog the minute the doorbell rings. Usually a Yorkie won't bark without reason, but he'll need reassurance from you that the intruder is welcome. His take-charge personality will require firm guidance and consistent training.

Because he is cute and little, you'll be tempted to spoil him. Once a Yorkie comes to stay, though, you'll need to establish who's in charge. If not, your Yorkie can become the supreme ruler of the house. A hunter by nature, Yorkies will stalk, catch, and kill small rodents, bugs, and other small game; and they can be just as aggressive toward other dogs. Because the Yorkie wants to please his favorite owner, he makes a great pet for a single person or a couple, but this sweet dog cannot be forced to do anything he doesn't want to do. Don't count on him to always be a lap dog, either, because if something more interesting comes along, he'll be off to investigate.

Watch him carefully to make sure he doesn't get himself into trouble. Living with a dog this tiny may present a challenge for young children or anyone who has difficulty walking because it's hard to avoid stepping on him. If you acquire a puppy, it's best to shuffle your feet to gently nudge the youngster out of the way rather than risk stepping on him. After a few little bumps, he'll learn to watch out.

The Yorkie is often too delicate for rambunctious children to handle and can easily slip out of their hands and become injured when they try to hold him. Like most Toy breeds, the Yorkie is prone to knee troubles and should not be allowed to jump from furniture onto the floor.

Why Choose a Yorkshire Terrier?

Many people want a Yorkshire Terrier because they think carrying their dog everywhere they go would be fun. And they want a lap dog. They also think training will be easy and cleanup minimal with a dog so small. A tiny Toy is appealing because he won't knock children or seniors over and is too small to cause much damage by chewing or digging.

Don't underestimate the responsibilities of having this active breed, however.

Talk to people who have Yorkies and ask them how much time and energy they put into caring for their dogs. Find out whether their relationships with their dogs have been positive or negative, and ask how much they spend every year on grooming, bedding, veterinary care, and high-quality dog food. Even though a Yorkie will probably eat a scant half to one cup of premium kibble every day, evaluate whether you can afford to spend $20 to $30 for a 20-pound bag of dog food to feed him, plus another $15 to $30 for a professional groomer to bathe, dry, and brush your Yorkie if you prefer to have someone groom your Yorkie for you.

You will learn from other Yorkie owners that some training is still needed and that not every place welcomes dogs. One owner discovered she could not keep potted plants inside her home on the floor because her Yorkie would jump into the pot and dig out the dirt, sending a mess onto the carpet.

Dog Ownership: The Many Sacrifices, the Many Joys

Having a cute little Yorkie for a pet may seem like a good idea, but it's important to realize that having any dog, even a small one, is a large commitment. This Toy is no mere plaything, but a live companion animal who needs at least one special person to care for him for the 12 to 15 years of his life. If you work long hours during the week away from home and like to get away most weekends, your Yorkie will need someone to supervise and care for him in your absence. A dog is not like a piece of furniture sitting in the corner that you can ignore or forget about.

Give some thought to how you like to spend your leisure time and whether you have enough time to spend petting and playing with your Yorkie. Owning this breed may involve rearranging your schedule and devoting special time just for your dog. Ask yourself whether you can do that. Other questions to consider are: Can you provide a safe, enclosed environment for your Yorkie so he won't be able to leave your premises in search of adventure? Can you protect him from larger dogs or from careless children who may drop or step on him? Are you willing to spend at least ten minutes every day combing and brushing him, and another 15 minutes taking him for a walk? If you can do all these things with a willing heart, without considering them a burden, then the Yorkshire Terrier may be the right breed for you.

You'll be rewarded by having an intelligent, independent yet loving dog greet you every morning and snuggle against you every evening. He is a perfect friend who will not pass judgment on you and is always eager to sit with you even when you're performing the most boring task. Once your Yorkie gives you that loving look from those bright shiny eyes of his, you will forget any inconvenience.

So, You Want a Yorkshire Terrier

In This Chapter

○ What Makes a Yorkshire Terrier Special?
○ Keys to Your Yorkshire Terrier's Happiness
○ Where to Find the Perfect Yorkshire Terrier for You

If you have already decided that a Yorkie is for you, this chapter will give you an idea how the breed evolved and for what purpose, and will provide information about the standard appearance of the Yorkshire Terrier. Keeping this feisty terrier healthy and happy will require your learning some new skills and dedicating yourself to each task. You'll also gain valuable information about how to raise a well-behaved and contented pet, and where to go to find the perfect Yorkshire Terrier for you. Good dogs don't just happen by accident. They're a combination of good genes, lots of positive experiences with the people around them, and consistent training.

What Makes a Yorkshire Terrier Special?

The Yorkie is a natural charmer wherever he goes. His doll-like good looks and curiosity make it easy to understand why owners enjoy taking this lightweight dog along on quick errands, for a day at the office, or on a week's vacation. Tiny Terrier Pasha lived at the White House with owners Richard and Pat Nixon. Bubba Zo and Lilliput are regular travelers to book signings and other engagements with their owner, novelist Amy Tan. Comedian Joan Rivers seldom left home without her Yorkie, Spike, and there have been Yorkies sitting in baskets alongside their owners in dress shops, theaters, classrooms, and interior-decorating shops since Yorkies first became a fashionable pet in the late Victorian era and even before.

Breed Overview and History

Unlike some breeds whose history is lost, Yorkie origins can be traced. His now-extinct ancestors, the Paisley, Clydesdale, and broken-coated Scottish Terrier went to work alongside their Scottish owners who were weavers and craftsmen in the mills in the late 1700s. Once they left their homes in England's northern cities of York, Manchester, and Leeds during the Industrial Revolution, these terriers were far from pampered because they lived with their working-class owners in squalid conditions. Aside from being companions, terriers were used to hunt rats and other vermin and were entered in ratting contests, a popular pastime.

> Aside from being companions, terriers were used to hunt rats and other vermin and were entered in ratting contests, a popular pastime.

The weavers, accustomed to spinning fine cloth, interbred a combination of the various terriers to produce their finest product—

SMOKY
Champion Yank Mascot SWPA 1944

In World War II, Army Corporal Bill Wynne bought a four-pound Yorkie from an army friend who found the dog abandoned in a ditch in New Guinea. An aerial war photographer, Wynne named the dog Smoky and trained her to respond to obedience commands and do tricks to amuse GIs. Living with Wynne in the army tent, Smoky was fed soldier's rations and taken everywhere her master went, including on combat flights. In Manila, where sand fleas were a major problem, Wynne gave Smoky a daily bath in his helmet. Her head was the size of a baseball and she was no taller than her owner's army boots, yet Wynne had a coat blanket made for Smoky that said, "SMOKY Champion Yank Mascot SWPA 1944."

Smoky performed her best trick, though, when she pulled 70 feet of wire through an eight-inch-high underground tunnel under an airstrip. In some places she was left with only four inches of headroom in the dark tunnel, yet Smoky trusted Wynne so much that she listened as he encouraged her to keep going to the end. Although she wasn't trained to do the job, Smoky required less than two minutes to navigate the pipe, a task that would have required soldiers several days to dig a trench, lay the wires, and replace the airstrip. Smoky's wire-pulling feat established communication to the combat squadrons and made her a famous war dog and a hero.

When the war ended, soldiers were not permitted to bring any dogs home with them. Wynne smuggled Smoky aboard ship anyway, and the pair became even more famous by entertaining adults and children and eventually starring in their own television show.

the early Yorkshire Terrier, which had a long, silky coat of blue and gold. The Paisley Terrier, which was no heavier than 16 pounds, contributed a silky coat in shades of blue, and the Clydesdale Terrier from the Glasgow region on the river Clyde added a long and straight coat that was neither curly nor wavy. The ten-pound Waterside Terrier added its silky coat, small size,

What's the American Kennel Club?

Founded in 1884, the American Kennel Club (AKC) is a non-profit organization dedicated to the advancement of purebred dogs. Composed of over 500 dog clubs from across the nation, the AKC's objectives include maintaining a registry of purebred dogs, promoting responsible dog ownership, and sponsoring events, such as breed shows, field trials, and performance events that promote interest in and appreciation of the purebred dog.

To be eligible for AKC registry, a puppy must be the offspring of individually registered AKC parents, and the breeder must obtain the proper paperwork before the puppy's sale. Once registered, a dog is eligible to compete in AKC-sanctioned events and, if bred with another AKC-registered dog, to have his or her offspring registered.

The AKC approves an official breed standard submitted by the parent clubs of each of the 147 breeds currently eligible for registration. The standard is written and maintained by each individual breed club. An attempt to describe the "perfect" dog of each breed, the breed standard is the model responsible breeders use in their efforts to produce better dogs. Judges of AKC-sponsored events and competitions use the breed standards as the basis of their evaluations.

Because of the AKC's emphasis on excellence and high standards, a common misconception is that "AKC registered" is synonymous with quality. However, while a registration certificate identifies a dog and its progenitors as purebreds, it does not necessarily guarantee the health or quality of a dog. Some breeders breed for show quality, but others breed for profit with little concern for breed standards. Thus, a potential buyer should not view AKC registration as an indication of a dog's quality.

and blue and tan pattern. The Skye Terrier added a long, hard, flat coat and an undercoat; and the rough-coated black and tan English Terrier were also bred with the Yorkie between the 1860s and 1870s.

A dog named Huddersfield Ben, born in 1865, is said to be the sire of the breed now recognized as the Yorkshire Terrier. In his first few years, this father of the breed is said to have produced all the best factors in the breed. Previously called Scottish Terrier, the breed was named Yorkshire Terrier by a reporter who claimed the breed was improved in York, England. Formally recognized in the United States in 1872, the Yorkshire Terrier began to look more like the breed seen today when English and Irish imports were added to the gene pool.

The breed was first recognized by the AKC in 1884, and today ranks among the top ten breeds registered by the AKC.

The Breed Standard

While computers, hairstyles, hemlines, music styles, and car models change and look different from year to year, Yorkshire Terriers have remained much the same since 1872. This is because conscientious breeders over the years have tried to consistently breed the same overall type of dog. They have followed a plan, called the breed standard, which is a detailed description, several paragraphs long, of what the ideal Yorkshire Terrier should look and act like. (The AKC Official Breed Standard for Yorkshire Terriers is listed in full in Appendix B.) If breeders didn't follow the breed standards, before long the Yorkie would lose his distinctive appearance and look like every other terrier.

Reputable breeders follow the standard when choosing sires and dams for their breeding programs. They estimate what qualities these dogs can reproduce so the resulting puppies will look like the Yorkie described in the breed standard. They take the breed's general appearance and every attribute into consideration, including such details as texture and color of the coat, the dog's weight (which should be no more than seven pounds), and the dog's overall balance, size, temperament, and personality.

The Yorkshire Terrier's pride and joy is its coat, (the attribute to which the Scottish weavers paid great attention), but these luxurious tresses should never detract from the fact that this dog is a wonderful companion. The standard calls for a long-haired Toy Terrier with a blue and tan coat that is parted on the face and from the base of the skull to the end of the tail and hangs evenly and straight down each side of the compact body. Well proportioned, the Yorkie should carry his head high to indicate his confident manner and exhibit his aura of self-importance. Small size does not mean his body is frail or fragile.

The standard is very specific about how the dog's coat should look. The quality, texture, and quantity is very important and should be shiny, silky, and dark steel-blue (never silver-blue) with rich golden tan. Darker at the roots than in the middle, the tan hair fades to a lighter tan at the ends. No black hair should appear in any of the tan. Perfectly straight (never wavy or woolly), the hair should hang down evenly on each side of the body. The blue portion should extend over the body, from the back of the neck to the root of the tail, and should have highlights of golden tan on the hair that falls from the head, at the ear roots and on the muzzle, ears, chest, and legs. The hair on the end of the tail is a darker blue.

Small and flat on top, the head should not be too round and the muzzle not too long. The hair on the head (called the headfall) is a rich golden tan with a deeper color on either side of the head.

It is usually long and tied with a bow in the center of the head or parted in the middle and tied with two bows. There shouldn't be any tan on the back of the neck. The Yorkie's muzzle hair is also long.

Yorkie puppies are born black and tan and have a darker body color with black hair intermingling in the tan that lightens when the pups begin to mature to adulthood.

Dark, medium-sized eyes that sparkle with intelligence and small, erect, V-shaped ears set not too far apart make the Yorkie distinctive and give the breed its typical, alert expression. The ears resemble radar dishes that signal the Yorkie's curiosity about everything around him. Though tipped over on young puppies, the ears should stand erect by the time the dog is three months old. A long neck is important to help the Yorkie carry his head high and look elegant.

Underneath the long crowning glory of his coat, the Yorkie's body is strong and athletic, built for an active life. Besides being able to go for long walks, play catch, or chase small animals, the Yorkie's body should be strong enough to participate in dog sports such as obedience, tracking, and agility. He should be able to do the same things a medium-sized dog can do, only on a slightly smaller scale.

The Yorkshire Terrier should be well proportioned with a short, level back. The height of the dog should be the same at the shoulder as at the hips. The back legs have moderately bent knees. Front and rear legs used to support this tiny dog with a magnificent coat need to be straight, and his feet should be round and have black toenails. Breeders generally remove dewclaws from the forelegs and from the hindlegs if there are any there. Yorkies are born with a long tail, which should be docked to a medium length. When the dog walks or runs around, you should see the tail carried slightly higher, above the back.

Personality

While Yorkies might look alike, they don't act alike. All dogs, like all people, are individuals and have their own unique personality with different behavioral and emotional traits.

Did You Know?

The wolf, from which dogs are descended, was the first animal to be domesticated.

How Little Should a Yorkie Be?

While the average weight of a Yorkshire Terrier is between four and seven pounds, some irresponsible breeders who think smaller is better have created a trend by specializing in "tinies" or "Betty Boops." These Yorkies, two or three pounds when full grown, are rejected by reputable breeders because they are novelty items.

Yorkies weighing up to 12 pounds once competed in the show ring, but over the years the standard has been changed and the breed can no longer exceed seven pounds. As Yorkies downsized, even smaller puppies were born who became oddities. Overly animated and adorable, these tiny Yorkies appealed to many people, particularly those wanting to make money without regard for what's best for the future of the breed.

While prospective owners may think that having a pet they can fit in their pocket would be fun, the reality is that tiny Yorkies are very expensive, ranging in price from $800 to $2,000, and are health nightmares. A tiny two-pounder cannot maintain the appropriate blood sugar level and becomes hypoglycemic very easily. These smaller dogs have other serious problems, such as enlarged hearts and hydrocephalus (water on the brain), which is fatal. Should these tiny Yorkies require surgery, veterinarians have a very difficult time operating on them. Simple medical procedures such as drawing blood or inserting a catheter are nearly impossible.

If you are unsure how big a Yorkie should be when you are shopping for one, take a food scale with you. A normal-sized 12-week-old Yorkie will double his weight plus add a pound by the time he is full grown, while an eight-week-old will triple his weight plus another pound. The minimum weight for a Yorkie is 3 to 4 pounds.

A Yorkshire Terrier should be just small enough to live a long and healthy life as a companion.

When you are choosing a Yorkie, think about what kind of personality type you are comfortable being around. Does an active, fun-loving dog make you feel happy? Do you prefer a quiet, more reserved presence in a dog? Is a sweet, easygoing nature

What Will It Be—Puppy or Adult?

Do you want a puppy Yorkshire Terrier or an adult Yorkie? They're all so cute! But depending on your lifestyle, one might be a better choice than the other.

Let's face it. Puppy Yorkies are so tiny and adorable! Have you ever seen such a face? But the flip side of the cuteness factor is puppies are a lot of work. It takes time to teach puppy the ropes—housetraining, manners, socializing. If you're home a lot—maybe you work from a home office or you're a stay-at-home parent—a puppy could be a good bet. Of course, you also must be willing to put in the time to teach your Yorkie the ways of the world.

Why not consider adopting an older Yorkie? There are plenty of rescue organizations who can place a wonderful Yorkshire Terrier in your home. With an older, adult dog, you're past housetraining, crying, jumping (maybe), and chewing.

Don't rule out a puppy or an adult dog. Figure out which one might best suit your lifestyle. Then decide.

more your cup of tea? Some Yorkies are just born to misbehave, while others live to please.

Whether your Yorkie is a big nine-pounder or a tiny four-pounder, his personality is the most important reason to own a dog. If you are annoyed that he barks every time a car comes up in the driveway or someone rings the doorbell, your relationship with your dog will not be a happy one. If your little fellow would rather sit and watch the world go by, but a constant stream of noisy people step over him all the time, he's likely to be unhappy.

Yorkies are intelligent and can often recognize names of different toys and even know in what rooms to find them when they are told where to look. Some apartment-dwelling owners say every Yorkie they've had has been able to tell who is coming up in the elevator before the person actually arrives on their floor.

While some people want a dog this smart, others may not relish spelling everything out or talking in code so their Yorkie can't understand.

As when you search for the perfect human companion, try to match your Yorkie's personality with your own. To help select a dog you'll be comfortable with later, tell the breeder what you enjoy doing in your spare time. Such hints will help the breeder match your personality with the right puppy. If you are very active and like spending weekends going for long walks or taking day trips and want to take your dog along, share that information. Or, if you have a calm nature and prefer doing quiet pastimes indoors, or if you like gardening or messy household projects and don't mind getting yourself and your dog dirty, let your breeder know.

When choosing a puppy, describe your ideal Yorkie and what you think that dog might be like when he grows up. This will give the breeder an idea of the right pup for you. After watching them grow and develop for several weeks, the breeder knows her puppies very well and can guess their personalities. The breeder also knows the parents' natures and can tell you cute stories about the sire and dam's favorite antics.

Temperament

The Yorkshire Terrier standard gives breeders a blueprint by describing the breed as having a confident and self-important man-

ner. This encourages breeders to produce dogs who are not fearful, shy, or mean. A well-bred Yorkie should be sure of himself and outgoing without being insecure, but not every pup will be like that. This is only a guideline of what you should look for in the breed's natural temperament.

When most people see a Yorkshire Terrier propped on his owner's lap, perched on fancy pillows at home, or at a dog show, they find it hard to think of Yorkies as brazen and wanting to take on the world. With their flowing blue coats fanning out around them, Yorkies look so delicate and passive that it's easy to assume every Yorkie is a living, breathing, pampered statue. Nothing could be further from the truth.

Instead of being bold, some Yorkies are timid or nervous. These characteristics are partly inherited from parents and partly due to the way they were raised. Puppies need to be exposed to new sights and sounds and frequently handled. It can take a long time for them to make up for a bad start in life.

Four-year-old Sweet Max weighs four pounds. His nickname is Teddy Bear because he is very cuddly and loves to be held and rocked. A little on the shy side and somewhat standoffish with strangers, Sweet Max is not eager to let people he hasn't met before pet or fuss all over him. When they approach, he backs up or crouches down and shakes.

"Once he gets to know someone he's okay, but that can take awhile. He just needs some time to relax and feel comfortable around new people," said his owner, Mary O'Neill of San Francisco.

This timid personality may be embarrassing to an owner or may be no problem at all. Whatever the human reaction, patience and good, solid training are required to help such a dog gain confidence. His owner must be willing to overlook Max's hesitancy because he is so loving and realize that Max will not suddenly turn into a confident, outgoing dog without some help.

Another aspect of the Yorkie's temperament is his tenaciousness, a trait his

Did You Know?

The word for "dog" in the Australian aboriginal language Mbabaran happens to be "dog."

ancestors needed to hunt rats underground. Some owners call this dogged determination when the dog is dead-set against doing something you wish. If a Yorkie is given a new toy, for example, he might persist in shaking or chasing it even though you're ready to leave the house and want to take him with you.

To understand a puppy's temperament before you make the final decision, look at the temperaments of his sire and dam. If the mother avoids you and barks, the puppies are likely to have inherited that behavior or learned that response from the time they were born until they leave her side at eight or ten weeks. Or if she shows interest in meeting you and approaches you with her tail up in a welcoming attitude, she's passed that on to her puppies.

> To understand a puppy's temperament before you make the final decision, look at the temperaments of his sire and dam.

The confident Yorkie will fit right into a home with gentle children or adults who appreciate his behavioral traits. He'll be the doll in the doll carriage or the canine running alongside a young soccer player, trying to steal the ball.

Life Expectancy

You don't realize how time sneaks up on a dog's life until you begin to notice your Yorkie has slowed down and may have developed a few problems due to old age. Suddenly he is an old dog. A Yorkshire Terrier can live to age 12 and up to 15 years or longer if he has excellent health care. Often energetic and happy into his senior years, a Yorkie begins to slow down between eight and ten years of age. Be sure to keep up his daily walks, although you may need to make them a little shorter. His vision and hearing aren't as sharp as they once were, and you may notice that he sleeps a little more than he used to.

Your older Yorkie may become more attached than ever before to his favorite person so avoid leaving him alone for long. He may also need more visits to the veterinarian. Begin saying your goodbyes and be sure to thank your Yorkie for all the wonderful times you have shared with him.

Keys to Your Yorkshire Terrier's Happiness

Before your new Yorkie enters your home for the first time, be prepared to accommodate his needs. This may involve adapting your environment and lifestyle to make sure he will be happy. You will need to evaluate the amount of space you have for a Yorkie, set aside the right amount of exercise time, provide the proper training and companionship, and estimate how he will get along with other pets already in your home.

How Much Space Does a Yorkshire Terrier Need?

A dog who can fit in your pocketbook isn't going to take up very much room in your house. While any dog would love to take up residence and roam around a ten-acre parcel of property, a Yorkshire Terrier is happy wherever his owner is. This includes living contentedly in a condominium or a two-story house. Yorkies don't need much space at all. As long as they are well cared for, a high-rise apartment will fit their needs just fine. Because Yorkies are intelligent, they can be trained to go potty outside or inside on special pee pads.

How Much Exercise?

While it may be tempting to carry your Yorkie around with you wherever you go, he does need to spend some time with all four of his feet touching the ground. While a Toy dog doesn't have the same need to run as a big dog does, a Yorkie will enjoy the opportunity to get outside for at least ten minutes a day. A mature Yorkie can walk for 30 minutes while a puppy or a senior will benefit from spending 15 minutes on an outing. If your Yorkie is going to compete in agility competition, he will need to run least 45 minutes a day. If there is a safe, fenced-in area he can run off-lead, so much the better. Once properly conditioned, a Yorkie is capable of running six to nine miles a day. He likes to go exploring, and going outside provides mental stimulation as well as physical exercise. Going for a walk in the neighborhood or to the park will help your Yorkie keep up good muscle tone and will prevent him from becoming overweight. Because he is small, this dog can get enough exercise just staying inside the house. Running back and forth when the doorbell rings or circling the coffee table in pursuit of a ball will give your Yorkie a marathon workout. If an owner throws a ball down the hallway, the Yorkie will happily run after it, returning often for a repeat game of fetch.

> Going for a walk in the neighborhood or to the park will help your Yorkie keep up good muscle tone and will prevent him from becoming overweight.

Encouraging your Yorkie to play games is another way to add some exercise into your Toy dog's life. Throw rings, small rubber and rope toys, things that squeak, and balls that have bells inside will delight and amuse your Yorkie for hours if you show interest in tossing them around. He likes to be kept busy, and the more often you offer different activities, the more physically and mentally fit he will be. You can also play hide-and-seek or tag with him. Such games also strengthen the bond between you and your dog. You'll know when he's tired of playing when he flops down with a look of contentment on his face.

How Much Training?

A small Yorkshire Terrier may not seem to require much training at all, but you need to establish a few rules just as you would with a bigger dog. It's easy to spoil a Yorkie and let him have his way. The first 18 months will require some training time, and starting good training practices early—before there is a problem—is best.

Once she has her basic vaccinations, make sure your Yorkie is well-socialized by being introduced to careful children, different adults, and a variety of public places to build her self-confidence and help her form a good bond with people later in life. With lots of positive reinforcement and plenty of treats given for good behavior, your Yorkie will strive to please you.

It's also a good idea to take your Yorkie to a puppy kindergarten or an obedience class. If you have never trained a dog before, one session may not be enough—two or three is the average. It may take you a while to realize your Yorkie is not so frail and fragile that he will crumble if you insist that he sit and wait until you tell him it's okay to get up. He will respond to practice and consistency on your part. You have to remember you are the head of the house, not your Yorkie.

A Yorkie is a good agility and obedience competitor if you vary the routines during practice and make him think the exercise is his idea. Many Yorkies have earned advanced obedience agility and obedience titles.

Can My Yorkie Stay Home All Day Without Me?

Toy dogs thrive on human companionship. They look forward to having their special person around the house with them and can become sullen, destructive, noisy, and lonely if left alone too much. Although you don't have to be home 24 hours a day and spend every waking minute with your dog, she does need you there several hours a day.

Give your new Yorkie plenty of time to adapt to his new surroundings with you around before leaving him alone for the first time. Many breeders recommend that new owners who work pick up their puppies on a Saturday morning so that the dog has two days with you before Monday morning workday comes along. During that first weekend, try to leave your new Yorkie alone for 10- to 15-minute periods. If you work during the daytime but are home during the evenings and weekends, your Yorkie should be fine. During that time he should have bathroom access, a clean supply of water, and a crate to snuggle in. A crate is a secure environment owners often leave their new, tiny Yorkies in until they are old enough to navigate the empty house by themselves. Remember that Yorkie pups are at high risk for hypoglycemia and thus should have food left down all day if left alone. By six months or so, this practice can be discontinued. Perhaps a friend can look in on your Yorkie once or twice during the day. Or if you have an understanding boss who doesn't mind a three- or four-pound free employee at the office, you might consider taking him to work with you.

Having a second Yorkie or another Toy dog will also help ease the separation anxiety your single Yorkie might feel when you are gone. They will amuse each another and keep one another company, but will both demand your attention when you come home.

Will My Yorkshire Terrier Get Along with Other Pets?

If you already have another pet, evaluate her needs and personality very carefully before bringing in a new Yorkie. Many big dogs will automatically think of a Toy dog as small game to hunt down. Remember that Yorkies think they are big dogs, too, and will think nothing of going after a larger dog if she invades their territory. Since you can never know exactly what any dog will think of another, be cautious when you introduce a second pet into your home. A lot depends on the sex of the two animals and the reliability of their characters. There are definite rules between animals, so letting your Yorkie experience other dogs when she is still a young puppy is best. She will learn how to behave around other dogs as long as all dogs are kept on a leash. Usually older dogs will recognize that she's a puppy and will not harm her, but be ready to pick up your Yorkie if you sense a problem.

> Remember that Yorkies think they are big dogs, too, and will think nothing of going after a larger dog if she invades their territory.

Dogs usually find out whether or not they like one another by first sniffing noses. Then they'll move to checking out the other's rear end where the anal glands are located. Dogs can tell a lot about one another from these scent areas and will soon figure out who is higher in the dog pack.

If a Yorkie grows up with a cat, the two will most likely get along, but it may take time and fighting some predatory instincts. Some cats are natural hunters and might think the Yorkie should be caught. Even if the cat just wants to play with the Yorkie, those feline sharp claws can be dangerous and may permanently injure a Yorkie's eyes. Or if you have an adult Yorkie and add a kitten to the household, remember that Yorkies were originally

Surefire Ways to Make Your Yorkshire Terrier's Life Unpleasant

Lack of attention, inadequate health care, and the wrong environment can make your Yorkshire Terrier very unhappy. When his unhappiness is constant, he will begin having behavior problems and become disruptive. Or he may become physically ill and you could lose him to a careless mistake. A dog this tiny can get in to all sorts of trouble so he is a constant responsibility. Once you know what dangers lurk, you'll be able to predict his needs. He deserves the best you can offer him.

bred to kill rats and have a predator instinct. Pet birds, hamsters, and domesticated mice are not safe around a Yorkie. Be sure to supervise your Yorkie around any animal.

What a Yorkshire Terrier Simply Cannot Live With

Adaptable as little Yorkies are, there are a few situations to which they should never be subjected.

Rough Children Who Don't Treat Him with Respect   Rough, rambunctious, or mean-spirited children may think the Yorkie is an action figure brought to life, but nothing is further from the truth. The Yorkie is not a toy for them to handle and use whenever they wish. He is a live animal capable of becoming injured very easily. Just in the normal course of moving around the house, active children can step on a Yorkie and break one of his legs. Young children are still developing their motor skills and are not always aware of things even smaller than themselves. Children of all ages should be supervised if the dog is around, but adults need to watch even more carefully when children three years of age and younger are in the room with your Yorkie.

Another Pet Who Thinks Your Yorkie Is Small Prey   Any dog with a strong instinct to hunt and prey or originally bred to hunt small game can make a Yorkie's life miserable. Some large cats also pose a threat to a new Yorkie. If your Yorkie has to live in fear that another dog is thinking of eating him, it's wise to place one of the dogs with someone else. Otherwise, your Yorkie is likely to meet an untimely death.

Being Left Alone Outdoors   A Yorkshire Terrier is an indoor dog. Although he relishes going for a walk every day, he cannot live outside or even be left unsupervised in a yard for long periods of time. Weighing in at less than eight pounds, the Yorkie can be easily carried off by very large birds, large cats, raccoons, opossums, or coyotes. In some neighborhoods, people think nothing of stealing a small dog. While a backyard may seem to be a safe place, there are always dangers to small dogs so low to the ground. For example, a Yorkie can easily fall into a spa or a swimming pool, even one that has a cover on it. A Toy dog can slip beneath the plastic cover and drown in seconds without making so much as a splash. Wood splinters can become imbedded into the Yorkie's throat or coat, and insecticide or sharp wires can mean sudden death.

Indoor Dangers   Yorkies, especially puppies, are curious and like to investigate interesting smells or objects around the house. Detergent, cleanser, and insecticide boxes or plastic containers should be placed up high, out of range of curious critters who like to chew on the edges of such objects. Keep

garbage cans and medicines out of the way and avoid keeping potted plants that might be poisonous within the Yorkie's reach.

Being Ignored A Yorkie demands your constant attention. If you're not looking at him when he wants you to, he'll make sure you notice him. He has to be the center of attention and acts as if the household revolves around his needs. When he does act independent, it's because he chooses that activity, not because you want him to be that way.

Being Fed Table Scraps Treating your Toy dog to people-food leftovers may seem harmless, but greasy, high-fat foods are too rich for a Yorkie and can trigger a condition known as pancreatitis. The vomiting and diarrhea that result will necessitate a trip to the veterinarian. Sometimes the reaction is so strong that the dog cannot be saved.

Things a Yorkshire Terrier Simply Cannot Live Without

Besides food and shelter, your Yorkie requires a few other things to be happy.

Good Medical Care Because they are so tiny, Yorkies can easily become dehydrated or hypoglycemic (when the blood-sugar level drops; the reverse of diabetes). Owners need to develop good observational skills to spot a problem before it becomes a serious problem. If your dog seems lethargic, is off his food for more than two meals, and fails to urinate, seek medical attention immediately.

Love   Yorkies deserve owners who think their dog is the most important creature on earth and are willing to devote their time, energy, and care.

Physical and Mental Exercise   A Yorkie has an active, intelligent mind and thrives on examining new and interesting sights, sounds, and smells. He does best when given a challenge. If left inside all the time without any mental stimulation, he will become bored and develop behavioral problems.

> Owners need to develop good observational skills to spot a problem before it becomes a serious problem.

A Special Bond with His Owner   A Yorkie is a companion animal who thrives on being around his human family. Many owners say that their Yorkie is like a Velcro dog—sticking to them as they move from room to room as though they're joined to their hip.

Maybe a Yorkshire Terrier Isn't the Dog for You

You've no doubt spent a lot of time deciding a Yorkie is the right breed for you and have just gone through a long process to locate and select the right puppy. Choosing toys, bedding, feeding dishes, and a collar and a leash has been a fun experience, and bringing home your new Yorkie puppy has been exciting. You've probably told all your friends and family and invited them to come see the new baby. Yet now that the novelty of owning a Yorkie has worn off, you realize that having a dog is a big commitment. It will take a few weeks, months, or even years to know exactly what your Yorkie wants and needs, but in the meantime you have to watch him constantly and feel as though you have no time for yourself.

If you think a Yorkie isn't the best breed for you but are anxious to make the relationship work, here are some things you can do some things to make living with him easier:

Realize Your Yorkie Is Still a Puppy   All puppies require constant supervision because they often get into trouble. Problems such as chewing and getting underfoot will go away as your puppy matures and learns how to get along in your household. All dogs begin as mischievous puppies and mature into well-behaved adults after they have had consistent training.

Call Your Breeder   This is one reason you bought your dog from a reputable breeder. That person can answer the questions you have and give you suggestions to help resolve any problems you are having.

Place Your Yorkie in His Playpen or Crate   Put your Yorkie in his playpen or crate for short periods. When you know your puppy is safe, you'll be able to relax and have some free time.

Seek Advice from Other People Who Have Yorkies   Contact your national breed club, read books about the breed, or log onto the Internet to find out whether other Yorkie owners have the same problems you do.

Sign Up for an Obedience Class   Even if you have had another dog before (even another Yorkie), this one is different. Now's the time to teach a new dog some old tricks. It may take a few sessions for some of the benefits to show, but in time you'll be glad you made the effort.

Relax, Relax, Relax Because of his size, you might think your Yorkie is frail and delicate and needs to be handled with kid gloves. When you comb out his coat for the first time and he cries, don't become intimidated and stop. Otherwise the next time you pick up the comb, he'll cry before you get started. He's trained you to be afraid of him. Learn how to do the combing correctly, take a deep breath, and try it again. Remember that underneath that long, glossy coat is a dog with a spirit and a will to take over your household. Don't be afraid to assume the leadership and take charge.

> Remember that underneath that long, glossy coat is a dog with a spirit and a will to take over your household.

Where to Find the Perfect Yorkshire Terrier for You

The small dog with the big attitude is very popular so you can find Yorkshire Terriers almost everywhere. After you decide whether you want a puppy or an older dog, your next decision is whether to buy from a breeder, purchase at a pet shop, or adopt from an animal shelter or a rescue group. You will live with this big decision for 12 to 15 years, so take your time rather than scoop up the first cute Yorkie that comes your way. People often bring home a dog because they believe the dog picked them, but that is seldom a good reason to choose a pet. The goal is to locate that special Yorkie who is healthy, has a good temperament, and is a good representative of the breed.

Puppies Versus Older Dogs

If you're choosing between a puppy and an older dog, consider the type of training and care that each will require. While few people can resist smiling when they see a puppy, taking one home and raising him is practically a full-time commitment, while an adolescent or an adult dog takes a little longer to bond with but less time to train.

A puppy will enter your life like a sponge, waiting to soak up all the training you can give him. Chewing only when appropriate, housetraining, walking on a leash, and sleeping through the night are lessons you'll teach your puppy in the beginning. Puppies have either two cycles of activity—full speed or sound asleep—and someone must stand watch during both times. While a Yorkie can't do much damage to objects up high, he can still find lots of things to chew at his level—chair legs, wood molding, your best shoes, or the edge of the rug. You'll need to protect such areas with a bitter-tasting spray or place chewable items out of reach. A Yorkie puppy also requires a few more meals throughout the day than an older dog does and has to be house- or paper-trained. A few visits to the veterinarian for vaccines will also be necessary.

> A retired adult dog makes an incredible companion because she already has basic training and has a better attention span than a new puppy.

Despite the work, a puppy is very entertaining and you'll have a lot of fun watching your new Yorkie grow up. If you think you'll miss something important by not starting with a dog early in its life, then a puppy is the right choice for you.

What to Ask a Breeder

○ What are common health problems found in Yorkshire Terriers?

○ Are your dogs routinely screened for heritable diseases?

○ What health certifications can you show me for parents and grand-parents?

○ What are the most positive and negative characteristics of the breed?

○ What kind of temperament should I expect from a Yorkie?

○ How long have you been breeding dogs?

○ Can you name five other breeders in this breed you'd recommend?

○ What do you expect of potential puppy owners?

○ What type of guarantee do you provide?

○ Will you take back this puppy at any age, for any reason?

○ Do you require limited registration and/or spay/neuter contracts on pet-quality puppies?

Getting an older Yorkie has advantages, too. Many Yorkshire Terrier breeders will place a retired show dog or a female after she is past the breeding age of five or seven years old. A retired adult dog makes an incredible companion because she already has basic training and has a better attention span than a new puppy. She may already be housetrained or be through with the chewing stage, and knows how to walk on a leash. An older dog may have acquired a bad habit or two along the way, but once you realize what the weaknesses are, you can begin correcting them. It's not true that you can't teach an old dog new tricks. But, the older a dog gets, the harder he is to teach. There's also no guessing about what an older Yorkie will look like when all grown-up because his adult coat will already have turned its final color.

Buying from a Breeder—Pros and Cons

Anyone can call herself a Yorkshire Terrier breeder, but only a special person with a passion and an unselfish commitment to the welfare of the breed and to raise healthy, well-adjusted puppies is a true breeder. If you just want a pet-quality Yorkie and are not interested in a show dog, buying your dog from an experienced breeder with a good reputation is even more important. A pet Yorkie who will be a member of your family should come from a well-socialized environment and be of the healthiest stock available.

A "hobbyist breeder" is a person who has raised Yorkies for many years, is a member of the Yorkshire Terrier Club of America, and knows a great deal about the history of the breed and how to deal with health problems unique to the breed. Hobbyists may breed only one litter a year, but treat the dogs in their homes as members of the family.

Being a breeder is not easy. A good breeder understands the basics of genetics and selects the sires and dams of her puppies only after carefully evaluating their pedigrees and screening for any health problems. Testing is expensive, which is why a puppy from a reputable hobby breeder is more expensive than buying one from a casual breeder known as a backyard breeder.

Every breed of dog is predisposed to certain health problems, and Yorkies are no exception. They are prone to liver shunt, Legg-Calve-Perthes (LCP), luxating patellas, heart problems, hernias, and hydrocephalus (each of which will be discussed in detail in Chapter 5).

A reputable breeder is honest and should be able to discuss any of these genetic weaknesses openly with you. However, while common, these problems are not normal, and you should take any genetic weakness seriously. The Yorkshire Terrier

Club of America is addressing these problems and many breeders are trying to rid their lines of them. A breeder who says her dogs do not have any genetic weaknesses is probably not telling you the truth.

Generally, a reputable hobbyist breeder has owned some dogs in the pedigree and has known many others, plus has a long history of producing healthy, personable Yorkies often going back four or five generations. The parents of the puppies are usually show dogs and have been evaluated by other Yorkie breeders and judges. Once the puppies are born, a breeder of this caliber spends a lot of time handling the puppies to make sure they are accustomed to people and confident with new sights and sounds. Most reputable breeders do not sell Yorkie puppies until they are at least 12 weeks of age and many wait until the pups are 16 weeks old. Whatever money a breeder makes from the sale of puppies usually reimburses the cost of quality food, clean bedding, veterinary bills, and information packages for new owners. Once the puppy goes to its new home, the breeder is available to answer any questions the new owner has regarding health and training. If the new owner discovers she cannot keep the new addition, the breeder should happily take the pup back.

> A breeder who says her dogs do not have any genetic weaknesses is probably not telling you the truth.

For a well-bred, well-socialized, pet-quality Yorkie with a health guarantee and return policies, expect to pay anywhere from $400 to $800; for show-quality prices, expect a range from $700 to $2,000.

A reputable breeder will also ask you questions concerning how much experience you have with dogs and what you already know about caring for and training a Yorkie. Questions will also cover what dogs you had before, what happened to them, and who will be responsible for this Yorkie's care. You will also have to agree to spaying or neutering your pet-quality Yorkie. The breeder isn't being nosy or demanding, but wants to make sure the dog she raised so carefully will be well taken care of for his lifetime.

A reputable breeder is very different than a casual breeder or a backyard breeder who decides to breed his Yorkie and sell the puppies to make some extra money, or breeds a litter to keep a puppy from his current Yorkie's litter, or does it so his children can experience the miracle of birth. The backyard breeder doesn't discover how much work is involved in caring for a nursing mother and her litter of puppies until it is too late. Many backyard breeders aren't concerned with what kind of home the puppies go to or what happens to them in the future as long as they leave the premises as quickly as possible. There is no return policy or guarantee about the pups' health either.

> The backyard breeder doesn't discover how much work is involved in caring for a nursing mother and her litter of puppies until it is too late.

The inexperienced breeder is unfamiliar with the Yorkie's predisposition to certain health problems and pairs a sire and dam together whether or not they have genetic weaknesses that might be passed on to their progeny. The puppies are often left unattended, may not be kept clean, and are rarely handled or exposed to different learning experiences. Usually the casual breeder raises puppies in conditions that are less than sanitary. Such breeders are often anxious to get rid of the puppies as quickly as possible.

The pups are sold before they can be properly socialized, often right after their mother weans them at six weeks of age, and usually for less money than a reputable breeder will charge. Cash is often the only form of payment such breeders will accept for the puppy; or if a check is accepted, you must provide a guarantee that the check will clear the bank.

Backyard breeders typically give little, if any, information about the puppy's care or training to the owner, and they seldom take any responsibility for the puppy's welfare once he leaves the breeder's premises.

It may seem like a lot of work to find a good breeder, but remember that you will live with this decision for 12 to 15 years. To find the best puppy, be patient and select the breeder with whom you feel most comfortable. You may even select your breeder before she has any puppies to sell since some breeders have a waiting list of buyers for litters planned in the future. Visit a few different breeders before you make the final decision.

To locate a good breeder, ask people who already own Yorkshire Terriers for the names of breeders they recommend. Visit dog shows and talk to Yorkshire Terrier breeders about their dogs and ask whether they are expecting puppies. Although there are no puppies for sale at the dog shows, attending these events is a great way to learn more about the breed. Also contact the American Kennel Club (AKC) either online or in your city's information service and ask for their breeder referral service and breeders in your city. Usually these breeders are members of Yorkshire Terrier regional clubs and the AKC does not recommend any in particular. AKC dog clubs are another good source for referrals. This is a network of local conscientious breeders.

Buying from a Pet Shop—Pros and Cons

The only advantage of buying a puppy from a pet shop is that you're able to do it on the spur of the moment and can charge your purchase on a credit card. You can also take the puppy

home immediately. The pet-store clerk will not ask you any questions about why you want this puppy or whether you can take care of it. The only reason they would refuse to sell you a dog is if the bank won't approve your check. Unfortunately, the salesperson at the pet store will not be able to give you any health or training information about the breed, or the sire and dam. Pet stores also charge exorbitant fees for inferior-quality puppies and typically do not give you any written information about housetraining, behavior, or what living with a Yorkshire Terrier is like.

Something else to consider is that pet-store puppies are often confined to their crates, and don't have the opportunity to be socialized or handled a lot. The pet store may give you a proof of vaccinations and worming and a health guarantee that is good for only one or two days. If you change your mind about keeping the puppy after this brief guarantee expires, a pet store will seldom take a puppy back, or will only give you store credit when they do.

Adopting from an Animal Shelter— Pros and Cons

Purebred dogs, like mixed-breed dogs, can sometimes be found at animal shelters, but not very often. Those who wind up in a shelter are usually victims of bad circumstances and are seldom at fault. Other than possibly having a bad habit or two, these Yorkies rarely have anything wrong with them. They come from owners who moved to a housing unit that didn't allow pets, families who decided they couldn't handle the grooming or otherwise care for them, or caretakers who passed away. If you want a Yorkshire Terrier and don't mind adopting one that used to belong to someone else, check your local public or private animal shelters.

The chances of finding a purebred Yorkie puppy at an animal shelter right away are slim. If you're not in a hurry, check back with the shelter staff periodically, and they may call you next time they have a Yorkie puppy who needs a home.

Getting an adult purebred Yorkie may be easier. Once you do find one, ask if you can take him out of the small cage and spend some time with him in a larger room or outdoors. Observe how he reacts to you and whether he seems highly fearful or somewhat confident. Although most dogs are naturally frightened when they first arrive at a shelter, beware of the Yorkie who is so afraid of people that his tail is between his legs or he tries to grab your arm with his teeth. This dog has probably never been away from home before or been around people other than his owner. Most likely the Yorkie will feel depressed because he is away from his familiar surroundings. Don't rush at the dog or try to pick him up right away. He's probably not accustomed to a noisy, crowded environment full of unfamiliar people. Ask shelter staff members to tell you anything they've noticed about the dog's temperament since they have taken care of him.

Look for a temperament that ranges from outgoing to slightly cautious. The staff may also be able to give you information about the Yorkie you are interested in, such as his age, why he was given up, and with what family members or other pets he might have lived. Hopefully he will have a health history.

Check the dog for any physical signs of distress. Despite the disadvantages of

Did You Know?

The United States and France have the highest rates of dog ownership in the world (for countries in which such statistics are available), with almost one dog for every three families. Germany and Switzerland have the lowest rates, with just one dog for every ten families.

knowing nothing about his parents or the physical problems he might have had in the past, you can enjoy the satisfaction of giving a Yorkie the chance for a new life.

Adopting from a Rescue Group—Pros and Cons

Your chances of finding a purebred, pet-quality Yorkie—either a puppy or an adult—are the greatest through a rescue group. Reputable breeders often communicate with rescue groups in their area if they need to find a new home for well-bred puppies. Rescue workers are volunteers who feel passionate about Yorkshire Terriers and are willing to be responsible for making sure all Yorkies find good homes. Often these Yorkie lovers take in dogs who have been abandoned or need homes on the spur of the moment. Owners generally place Yorkies with rescue groups for the same reasons they take them to shelters. They don't want them or can't have them anymore and need to find new homes for them immediately. Rescue organizations have very dedicated volunteers who use their own facilities and resources to take in the dogs they save.

Sometimes, rescued dogs have a bad habit or two and may need extra time to adapt to a loving environment. When rescue volunteers acquire a Yorkie, they evaluate the dog's temperament to make sure he is not aggressive, then they implant a microchip. If the dog gets lost, stolen, or becomes homeless again for any reason, the rescue group will be able to trace and retrieve the dog so they can return him to his family or find a new family.

Before a dog is ready for adoption, a veterinarian will vaccinate him and make sure he doesn't have heartworm before they give him a clean bill of health. Expect to pay a fee to adopt a rescue dog,

The Yorkie Express State to State

Mary Elizabeth Dugmore of Nashville, Tennessee, heads the national Yorkie rescue group known as YESS (The Yorkie Express State to State). When a puppy mill raid uncovered 450 dogs kept in deplorable conditions, Dugmore took 27 Yorkies into her home and kept them for over a year until they were socialized and cleared of health problems. Even though good homes were only available out of state, YESS volunteers transported the dogs by car instead of shipping them on airplanes. Meeting at rest stops and coffee shops along highways, these dedicated Yorkie fans have moved rescue Yorkies from state to state. In one rescue, 19 drivers relayed four Yorkies from Idaho to Oregon. In another effort, three Yorkies were driven from Michigan to Virginia by nine different drivers.

usually less than you would pay to buy a puppy from any breeder. The rescue group wants to make sure each home is the best one and volunteers screen adopters to make sure the match between the Yorkie and new owner is the best one possible. You will be asked to spay or neuter the dog and return him if he doesn't work out. The goal is to make sure the rescue home is the last home the dog will ever have to go to.

Both male and female Yorkies have good temperaments, can be equally loving, and be just as much fun as the other sex. Either will be ready for a car ride or just as content to nap by the window. Although some breeders say males tend to be slightly sweeter, many females can be just as adoring. Other breeders claim that a female Yorkie will bond more closely to the male in the household and that a male Yorkie will bond with the female of the house. As with people, Yorkie personality types in both males and females are acceptable, although hormonal cycles will

A Boy or a Girl?

After you've decided which breed to buy, the next big question is whether to get a male or a female Yorkshire Terrier. Prospective owners always ask breeders which sex is better, but neither is superior to the other. Both males and females appeal to different people for different reasons.

When Melissa Curran of Dover, New Hampshire, wanted to get a Yorkshire Terrier, her husband, Stephen, a six-foot, four-inch college basketball coach, was worried that everyone would make fun of him for having such a small dog. Melissa convinced Stephen that a Yorkie would make a wonderful companion by promising him she would select a male and would let Stephen pick the name.

"Today you would never guess that Stephen loves our little five-pound Kobi (named after Los Angeles Laker basketball star Kobe Bryant) more than I do," Melissa said.

affect the sexes differently. Generally, females can have a few more mood swings even if they have been spayed.

Females should be spayed and males should be neutered if they are not going to be show dogs. If not spayed, a female will come in season every six months for about three weeks. The bloody discharge can be very messy if she has the run of the house, and she will need constant supervision so she doesn't run out of the house in search of a willing mate. A pet female Yorkie weighing anything less than three-and-a-half pounds should be spayed before she reaches her first season and never bred. She is too tiny and her life would be endangered.

When males reach maturity, they are likely to hump anyone or anything they can find and may lift their leg to urinate on things in the house. Some unneutered males may become more territorial or aggressive when they are out exercising.

Hormonal urges and instincts influence both unaltered males and females and detract from their ability to pay attention during training sessions, which may interfere with their ability to be good pets. No doubt if you spay or neuter your Yorkshire Terrier, either a male or a female will make a wonderful pet.

How Do I Choose the Pick of the Litter?

Now that you've settled on either a male or a female and have found a responsible breeder you trust, your next step is to choose the best puppy you possibly can from a good, quality litter. Don't just rush out and pick the first cute Yorkie who gives you kisses!

To get a sneak preview of what the puppies will look like when they are grown-up, ask to see the sire and dam. If the sire doesn't live with the breeder, ask to see pictures of him. If you are not allowed to see the dam, choose another breeder because something must be wrong.

Assuming you like the temperament of the dam and the sire, discuss with your breeder what the responsibilities of having a pet or a show dog are. Ask yourself what you envision doing with your Yorkie—showing, obedience, companionship, going for long walks? A show puppy must come as close as possible to the breed standard so if that's what you want, your breeder will probably have to select a puppy for you since he or she is more familiar with what show puppies look like at 12 weeks of age. Make sure you understand the difference between a show puppy and a pet puppy, and be honest with your breeder about which appeals to you so he or she can help you make the best selection.

If the parent is a show dog, be prepared to not get the pick of the litter. Reputable show breeders always keep these dogs to show themselves. Breeding and raising a litter is a tremendous amount of work and giving away the best result of several generations to someone new to the breed doesn't make sense, no matter how much money you might offer.

But if you want the first pick of the pet-quality puppies, your breeder should be able to accommodate that request and help you select the best pet. A breeder with a good reputation often has people waiting ahead of you for puppies so you may only be offered one or two.

If you do have a choice, look at the whole litter to make sure all the puppies look healthy and active. A responsible breeder will only offer healthy puppies for sale, but be on the lookout for even one sick puppy because that often means the rest will come down with whatever that puppy has in a matter of time. Avoid that litter until all the puppies look vigorous. Other physical signs to look for are clear eyes, ears, and nose. None of the puppies should have a discharge from these areas, and eyes should be bright and not in-flamed. Coats should be shiny and not tangled and dirty. Pay attention if a puppy keeps scratching at his ear, as this could mean an ear infection or a severe, waxy buildup. There shouldn't be an odor around the dog's ears. If you

> All reputable breeders should permit you to take the puppy to your veterinarian 24 to 48 hours after you take him home.

can sneak a peak into the puppy's mouth, check his gums to make sure they are pink and healthy-looking without being pale. Hopefully the body will be fairly firm and somewhat muscular, although many puppies need time to grow into their coats. The puppy should also walk evenly without hunching its back, and its belly should not be bloated, which may mean worms.

Hopefully the area in which they spend their time is very clean, but if any of the puppies do have a bowel movement, make

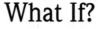

What If?

It can and does happen. You've acquired a Yorkie, maybe even done a tad of research about the breed beforehand, but after living with the dog for a month or two, you realize maybe it's not the dog you thought you wanted.

Don't panic. And don't immediately see getting rid of your Yorkshire Terrier as a solution to the problem. Make sure you exhaust all options, such as training or neutering, before you decide to give up your dog.

Know that this can happen no matter what breed you bring home. It's rare for anyone to initially have the "perfect" canine companion. Rather, good companions are partly created, which means they're the result of your efforts. If you put some time, energy, and effort into a puppy or dog, chances are you'll have a suitable companion.

It's true you might not have exactly what you wanted. But who has everything they want, all the time? For example, maybe you've found your Yorkie's size and demeanor is not what you were looking for, or training isn't going as you planned. Seek guidance from a professional trainer. Make a list of unwanted behaviors or dislikes about the dog and take the list to someone who can help you work through them.

The answer to solving the problem is your willingness to work on it, not getting rid of your Yorkie.

sure it is not a loose, runny stool, and that it contains no blood. If you see wiggling worms that resemble strands of spaghetti, the puppy has roundworms. Not good. The rectal area should be clean without showing any signs of diarrhea. All reputable breeders should permit you to take the puppy to your veterinarian 24 to 48 hours after you take him home. If a licensed veterinarian finds anything wrong with your puppy, you should be able to return him with no questions asked. Make sure this is stipulated in writing on your sales contract.

Once you've selected a healthy puppy, pay attention to his personality. You want an alert Yorkie who bounds up to greet you, not one who acts shy and shivers in the corner. Avoid choosing a puppy because you feel sorry for him. The reason could be a temporary problem such as an upset stomach or something genetic that causes the puppy to feel frightened around people. If the puppies are a little cautious when you first approach them, that's okay; but they should get over that and become interested in sniffing you and wanting to play. Think carefully, too, about the Yorkie who simply must reach you despite others being in his way. He may require more discipline when he grows up. For those who welcome such a challenge, this may be the puppy for you; but if you want a dog mainly for company, this bold little fellow would not be a good choice.

Your breeder can give you hints about the puppy's personality, but careful observations can reveal a lot about a dog's nature and whether a particular puppy will fit into your household or even with your personality. Whatever personality type you select, quiet or rambunctious, remember this: You will live with this Yorkie for 12 to 15 years.

Watch how the puppies interact with one another. You can easily see when one is dominant by his continual jumping on or picking on another. This one may be a lively choice, but he may constantly challenge your authority at home. The most dominant puppy is rarely a good choice for the first-time owner. A submissive Yorkie does not exactly fit the breed standard, may lack confidence later in life, and may develop a behavior problem and submissive urination (urinating every time he gets excited or anxious). The ideal puppy is one who takes turns jumping and dominating, as well as being bottom-dog. This shows confidence and a willingness to fit into the pack.

When you pick up one of the puppies, notice his reaction. If he squirms and wants to get away, that's probably okay as long as he doesn't try to bite your hands if you don't release him. If he looks happy about being picked up, that's a good sign he'll enjoy being around strangers.

Sit on the floor in the middle of the puppy area and watch the puppies' reactions to you in their space. If they climb all over you, that's wonderful; but if a puppy acts frightened and backs away instead, you should probably avoid choosing that puppy.

Ask the breeder if you can take the puppy to an area the puppy hasn't been in before. If so, put the puppy down and walk away but encourage him to follow you. If he follows, that

> **A**sk the breeder if you can take the puppy to an area the puppy hasn't been in before.

means he is willing to please. Being inquisitive by nature, chances are that a well-adjusted Yorkie will just take off exploring so don't take it as a reflection of what he thinks of you. Some puppies love to retrieve objects, so wad up a piece of paper into a ball and toss it in front of the Yorkie pup. If he runs after it but is soon distracted, it means he has a short attention span at this age. He'll need time to mature and maybe some instruction before becoming a go-getter. Another puppy may happily run after it and try to bring it back to you. If he drops it halfway and prefers coming into your arms, you've probably got a lover there. Still another pup might pick up the paper ball after you've tossed it and tear off in another direction with it. That shows confidence and retrieving ability. Your challenge with that puppy will be trying to convince him he really wants to bring it back.

Handle every part of the puppy's body. If you press gently between the Yorkie's toes, you will get an idea of the dog's touch tolerance or how much physical correction he will need later in life.

Does banging a pot with a metal spoon frighten the puppy? Or does he listen to it but soon resume what he was doing before he heard the sound? This test determines your puppy's sensitivity to sounds and will answer the question for you whether or not this Yorkie will be absolutely terrified of thunder when he grows up or basically ignore it.

If your puppy has a bad reaction to any of these tests, return to the breeder's another day at another time to test again. None of these predictors are 100 percent foolproof, and results can change from day to day. They're designed to be a guide and can be interpreted in many different ways. Certainly your breeder is your best resource for predicting behavior.

A Yorkie's size should be the last factor to consider. For a single person or a family with well-behaved children older than toddlers in the home, a larger male makes a wonderful companion. The tiniest Yorkies do not make good pets for small children.

Sometimes people just know the right puppy when they see it. Sometimes a magical bond takes place during the evaluation process. If you are lucky enough to experience that, go with it.

If you cannot find any medical problems in the puppy you like, and his temperament is what you are looking for, you have found your pick of the litter.

2

Welcome Home!

In This Chapter

❍ Preparing for Your Yorkshire Terrier's Arrival
❍ Yorkshire Terrier-Proofing Your House and Yard
❍ Which Supplies Do You Really Need?
❍ Homecoming Day for Your Yorkshire Terrier

One of the most memorable times you will have with your Yorkshire Terrier is when you pick her up from the breeder, animal shelter, or rescue organization and introduce her into your home for the first time. In later years you'll reflect back on this time and recall the beginning of your great adventure with your Yorkshire Terrier. Bringing a new puppy home can also be stressful. You may experience moments of confusion when you won't know what to do about a problem; but by planning ahead for your Yorkie's first day home, you'll have the best possible start.

Preparing for Your Yorkshire Terrier's Arrival

Before your Yorkie comes into your life, it's a good idea to decide what you will allow her to do and what you will not. If you don't want her sitting on the furniture, for example, set the rules now rather than waiting until someone puts her up there and she looks too cute to put back on the floor.

Call a meeting with all family members living in your home and discuss how the new dog will be treated and cared for. If everyone knows the rules beforehand, the training will be consistent and your Yorkie will know what's expected of her. You also need to talk about who will be most responsible for your Yorkie and who will perform the important support duties. Sometimes it takes a whole household to raise just one little five-pound dog the right way.

> If everyone knows the rules beforehand, the training will be consistent and your Yorkie will know what's expected of her.

"When my husband first brought our Yorkie, Gina, home for me, we never agreed on what she should be doing," says Kim Weston, of Woodland Hills, California. "It didn't take long for Gina to become very confused so we had to make some new decisions. Once we made some rules, she behaved much better."

Setting Boundaries—Decisions to Make Before Bringing Your Yorkie Home

Dogs are creatures of habit, and once they figure out the routine, they do the same thing all the time. Yorkshire Terriers like consistency so setting boundaries the first minute the puppy comes into your home is a good idea. The cute things she does at this stage may not be so cute when she is an adult dog. While most dogs can learn anything at any age, it's much easier to teach your Yorkie correctly the first time rather than having to change bad habits into the desired behaviors later on. Start setting your boundaries by answering these questions:

How Do You Want Your Adult Yorkie to Behave?   Start training your puppy to act the way you want your adult Yorkie to act, and you won't have to change the rules on her later. Do you want a free spirit or a miniature canine robot? Discuss what everyone in the household thinks the ideal Yorkie behavior should be like. Chances are good that if everyone in the house agrees on what they expect from their Yorkie before she comes home, everyone will work toward that goal and she will grow up exactly as planned.

What Area Will Your Yorkie Use for Housetraining?   Select an outdoor potty area to which you will consistently take your Yorkie, then decide whether you will also designate a potty area inside the house. Many Yorkie owners who live in apartments will paper-train their puppies to eliminate in the same specified area of the house. If this is what you plan, start taking your puppy to this area the minute she arrives at your home.

In Which Rooms Will Your Yorkie Be Allowed?   Any children at home will probably want the puppy to be wherever they are. Because children are naturally excited to have a playmate, it's important that you explain to them that your Yorkie will need to be supervised until she is older. It's much easier to keep an eye on your Yorkie if you limit her environment to the one or two rooms in which you spend most of your time. These rooms shouldn't have the expensive carpet or the heirloom furniture and might need baby gates to secure them. If you can't watch the puppy, she needs to be confined in a safe location.

Where Will Your Yorkie Sleep?   Putting your Yorkie in a puppy crate is the safest place for her at night. Some owners like having their pup in bed with them. As cozy as this might sounds, it's not safe. The dog can easily fall off the bed during the night and break her leg or back. One compromise is to place the puppy crate in your bedroom so you both feel close to one another, and you can hear when your Yorkie needs to go outside during the night. Owners usually have strong feelings about where their Yorkie will sleep so deciding this before you get the puppy home and certainly before the evening arrives is a good idea.

Where Will You Feed Your Yorkie and Place Her Water Dish? Some owners do not like seeing a dog dish with dog food in their kitchen, while others aren't bothered by it. Discuss this with other family members before the first meal. Your Yorkie will quickly learn where her next meal will be served and will often wait there if she knows supper's on the way. While you'll want to be sure your puppy's water dish isn't underfoot, you won't want it so far away (perhaps in the laundry room or garage) that you won't notice when it's empty. You should empty and wash the water dish every day before refilling it.

Will Your Yorkie Be Allowed on the Furniture?   That's up to you and others in your household. One advantage of owning a five-pound dog is that she doesn't take up much room on the couch. A member of the Toy group, the Yorkie was bred to be small enough to be easily petted or carried around the house. But once she claims the furniture as her playground, your Yorkie will have a hard time adapting to the floor should you change your mind later on. Another word of caution: Visitors don't always like to sit next to a dog when they come for a visit—even a small, beautiful Yorkie.

> One advantage of owning a five-pound dog is that she doesn't take up much room on the couch.

What Training Method Should You Use?   Everyone has a different idea about how to correct a dog if she makes a mistake. Do some homework and learn about different training methods, such as using positive reinforcement involving food, using punishment, putting the dog outside, or ignoring bad behavior, then discuss them with the household.

Will You Give Your Yorkie Table Scraps?   This decision is really a health issue. Besides encouraging a lifelong begging pattern every time you sit down to a meal, your Yorkie may reject her own well-balanced dog food and hold out for people food. Because human food is much higher in fat than dog food is, table scraps are not healthful for Yorkshire Terriers. If you insist on giving her a treat that doesn't come in a dog-food bag, try giving her tiny bits of cheese, raw fruit, raw vegetables, or tiny bites of lean cooked steak. Cooked eggs, baked or broiled potato, and green beans are also acceptable. These should not be fed directly from the table but should always be placed in her dog dish, and given only sporadically. Get in the habit of saving these healthful delicacies from a meal to use as spontaneous treats for good behavior. Your Yorkie will appreciate this more than food thrown from the table on a nightly basis.

Where Will Your Yorkie Stay While You Are Away?   If you're just leaving the house for only an hour or two, a dog crate is the

What Do You Mean It's My Turn?

Divvying Up Dog-Care Responsibilities

Often, parents buy a dog "for the kids" and end up taking on all the responsibilities of caring for the pet themselves. Even couples have been known to purchase a puppy with the understanding that they'll share dog-care duties, only to find one spouse doing the majority of the work once the pup arrives. When family members shirk their responsibilities, it not only can cause resentment, it can also prove detrimental to the puppy's care. To avoid these problems, call a family meeting before bringing your new dog home and divide all dog-care duties among family members. Keep in mind that, although children should be given some responsibilities related to puppy care, you may want certain jobs, such as obedience-training an adolescent or adult Yorkie or food and water responsibilities, to be handled by an adult. Grooming and games such as fetch are two excellent responsibilities for children. Also, clearly spell out during the meeting the boundaries you expect the dog to follow, so all family members will be consistent in their dealings with your new pet.

Questions you should answer include:

❍ Who will feed the dog?

❍ Who will walk the dog?

❍ Who will clean up after the dog?

❍ Who will groom the dog?

❍ Who will housetrain the dog?

❍ Who will obedience-train the dog?

❍ Who will play with the dog to ensure he gets to release his energy and doesn't become bored?

❍ What kind of games are okay to play with the new dog and what kind of games should you avoid?

❍ Who will take the dog to the veterinarian for his regular checkups and shots, as well as if he becomes sick?

❍ Where will the dog sleep at night?

❍ Where will the dog stay during the day when people are home? Once he has learned the rules of the household, will he have free run of the house or be confined to a crate or certain rooms?

❍ Where will the dog stay during the day when no one is at home?

❍ Will the dog be allowed on the furniture?

❍ How will the dog be contained in the yard?

❍ What kind of treats will you give to the dog? Will you give people food to the dog occasionally, or never?

❍ How will you correct the dog when he makes a mistake?

safest place for your Yorkie, whether she's a puppy or an adult dog. Other options include a baby playpen once she has become accustomed to it, a safe room with a door that closes securely, or a baby gate that has been dog-proofed.

Day-to-Day Care

It's amazing that one little dog can create so many job opportunities! Unless yours is a one-person household, or one person wants to be responsible for everything, give everyone in the household who is old enough or capable enough to share the joys of raising a Yorkie a job in caring for your Yorkie. While some jobs aren't as exciting as others, all are necessary to raise a healthy, happy dog. Some families rotate the jobs on a regular basis or have various members who specialize in specific chores. Whatever the system, remember that small children should be supervised while doing whatever they are capable of so they can feel part of the puppy-raising experience, too. Even with a household of helpers, one person with the most dog experience needs to be in charge to make sure everything gets done and to be on the lookout for health problems that may arise. Not only do young children need to be supervised to make sure they are taking care of their dog duties, older children must be checked-up on, as well. One missed meal or walk can cause problems with your Yorkie. Here is a list of all the dog-care responsibilities:

Feeding You'll need to feed puppies three or four meals a day and adults two meals. The dog dish needs to be thoroughly washed after every meal. As your puppy grows, the amount of food needs to be increased according to the breeder's guidelines. Keep an eye out for any feeding problems that

might occur, such as a poor appetite or vomiting. You may need to change the type of dog food, such as switching from puppy to adult food as the puppy grows.

Keeping Fresh Water Available   Once a day the water dish needs to be emptied, thoroughly washed, and refilled with cool, clean water.

Bathroom Responsibilities   If you have enough helpers, you might divide this category into two tasks—getting the dog to go to the bathroom and cleaning up after she has gone. Immediately after a puppy eats or wakes up and before bedtime, she needs to be taken outdoors or to the designated indoor potty area. Watch to make sure she has eliminated. Then clean the outdoor area and dispose of the waste. While your Yorkie puppy is awake, she needs to be supervised and taken to the potty areas every 15 to 20 minutes if possible. Any accidents need to be cleaned up immediately. Those responsible for taking the puppy to the bathroom and cleaning up must be on the lookout for any bloody or loose stools, worms, or straining, and report it to the person in charge, who in turn needs to report it to your Yorkie's veterinarian.

> While your Yorkie puppy is awake, she needs to be supervised and taken to the potty areas every 15 to 20 minutes.

Exercise   Yorkies need to be taken for a 15 to 20 minute walk at least once a day.

Grooming   These tasks can also be divided, depending on the number of helpers, into combing and brushing, bathing and cleaning, and clipping. Yorkies must be first combed, then brushed once a day for about 10 minutes. Nails should be trimmed once a week and teeth brushed and ears cleaned regularly as needed. The eyes, ears, and nose should be checked for any discharge or redness. Bathing should also be done on a regular basis.

Training   If you decide to take your Yorkie to obedience or puppy kindergarten classes, at least one person needs to take the dog and be in charge of the training. While not everyone has to go to the classes, all household members should know what the rules are and abide by them.

Health   At least one person needs to take the Yorkie to the veterinarian for regular vaccinations and when any health problems arise. Any suggestions the veterinarian makes should be relayed to other household members.

Yorkshire Terrier-Proofing Your House and Yard

Count on a puppy to find every little thing you don't want her to. According to the standard, Yorkshire Terriers are curious creatures who love to investigate their surroundings, and Yorkie puppies fit this standard especially well. Once they've located something particularly interesting, they simply must sniff it, chew it, dig it out, or pull it apart. These little four-pound puppies have an uncanny ability to find anything and everything that can be destroyed, often surprising their owners with the amount of damage they can cause.

"When we first moved into our home I didn't even give it a thought that a small, loose piece of wallpaper along the floorboard would be endangered when I left our Yorkie, Sally, in that room when I went to the store," remembers Kris Nelson, of Topeka, Kansas. "I came home an hour later and Sally had pulled the little corner of paper up and the whole panel of wallpaper had come off with it."

How Your Yorkshire Terrier Sees Your Home

Dogs do not distinguish between something valuable and something ready to be discarded. The whole world is a canine treasure that must be sniffed, chewed, dragged, or pawed. They also don't realize that one good bite of your antique coffee table can ruin the object forever. To protect your furniture, try spraying legs and edges with a bitter-tasting substance such as Bitter Apple (available at pet-supply stores). It's harmless to both dogs and furniture, but doesn't last long and must be re-applied.

Don't underestimate the trouble this tiny dog can get into. Your new Yorkie will notice every little thing in your home that's slightly above floor level, including things you'll never notice—unless you check every room from a Yorkshire Terrier's point of view, which is about eight to ten inches above the floor.

House-Proofing

Get on your hands and knees, then crawl along the floor through every room of your house, noting what's loose, valuable, and life-

threatening if puppy teeth or paws were to encounter it. Try to imagine everything as a potential play toy or danger zone for your Yorkie. You'll want to move these items out of reach. Check also for anything sharp or protruding that might be hazardous to your dog.

Before Shelly Smith, of San Diego, California, brought her first Yorkie home, she worried about dangling wires and fallen objects.

"I ran all of my electrical cords through PVC pipe along the walls. Not very cute but effective," Smith said. "I also vacuumed the floor really well and get down on all fours and crawled around looking for things the dogs might get into."

Kitchen   Check to see if any cabinet doors open easily. If they swing right open, your Yorkie will use his agile paws and little, but very determined, muzzle to knock over and sniff and lick cleaning solvents or poisonous bottles stored beneath the sink. Install baby locks inside to prevent your Yorkie from helping herself to whatever she finds inside. Yorkies are also smart enough to figure out how to jump from a chair to a kitchen counter in two seconds flat if something smells particularly tasty up there. It's best not to leave food on the kitchen counter when you're not around to watch it, but if you must, be sure the chairs are far enough away. Garbage cans have a special allure to Yorkies because their contents smell so wonderful. If your puppy climbs into the trash or knocks it over, she'll want to chew things such as poultry, meat, fish bones, twist ties, spoiled food, and plastic wrap—all of which can be deadly. Either store the trash in a cabinet with a baby lock on it or choose a container that has a secure lid.

Do you have any precious kitchen towels hanging from the drawers or a rack? Your Yorkie can pull them down and have a great time gnawing them or dragging them around the house.

Bathrooms   Bathrooms are danger zones. Items such as razor blades, dental floss and

Did You Know?

The smallest dog ever documented was a Yorkshire Terrier measuring 2.5 inches tall by 3.75 inches long fully grown and weighing only 4 ounces.

dental floss holders, sanitary napkins, and tampons—whether dropped or retrieved from the trashcan—can be deadly to your Yorkie should she swallow them. These can slice or obstruct her intestinal tract and cause pain and death. Discarded Q-tips, cotton balls, partially filled medicine bottles, hair, and staples from packages—anything small enough for your Yorkie to pick up in her mouth and ingest—are all hazardous.

> To be safe, put child locks on bathroom cabinet doors to keep your investigative Yorkie out of your household cleaning products, hair dyes, and unused sanitary items.

The cool, fresh water from an open toilet can be alluring to a thirsty Yorkie. She's also smart enough to figure out how to jump up on another object to test the water but may fall in and drown instead. Keep the toilet lid closed at all times.

To be safe, put child locks on bathroom cabinet doors to keep your investigative Yorkie out of your household cleaning products, hair dyes, and unused sanitary items. Portable heaters, blow-dryers, and curling irons with dangling cords invite your dog to pull them down on her head.

Bedrooms Well-worn shoes, socks, and underwear are special chewable attractions to your Yorkie, though any clothing carrying your scent is a chomping paradise. Not only can your clothes be ruined, but your Yorkie can choke on pieces of elastic or a sock, for example. Nylons and rubber bands are especially dangerous if swallowed because they can become entangled in or block the intestine. Here's your opportunity to become a neater person! Keep all clothing picked up and stored in closets, drawers, or laundry baskets. Keep jewelry, coins, paper money, checks, and other items that are too tasty for your Yorkie to pass up out of sight.

Electronic equipment such as computers, phones, stereos, and televisions have cords that your Yorkie may want to chew or pull on. To protect your dog from this electrical danger, put electronic equipment as close as possible to the outlets and block electrical cords with heavy pieces of furniture or securely tack them down along the baseboard. No one knows why, but some puppies like to lick outlets. If she gets that area wet enough, your dog could receive an electric and deadly surprise. Therefore, keep open outlets hidden with child-proof outlet covers.

Children's Bedrooms   If your Yorkie is left to wander in rooms filled with dolls and toys, there's no telling what she might swallow or destroy. Dogs love to chew marking pens, which can ruin carpeting or a beautiful Yorkie coat. If you can't keep a child's room immaculate, keep the door closed as often as possible.

Living Room, Office, Den, Entry   Hobby and fun items such as books, magazines, puzzles, games, models, paint, and sewing materials are just as much fun for your Yorkie to get into and chew on but a lot more dangerous. Remote controls, snack foods, correspondence, potted plants, treasured pillows, and anything with fringe can become Yorkie toys the minute you leave them unattended.

"I couldn't leave Dillon alone with our houseplants that were in big pots on the floor because he would jump up into the pot and dig out the plants, scattering dirt everywhere," said Kim Thomas, of Westlake Village, California.

Yard-Proofing

Your yard may be fenced, but unless it's solid concrete, dangers still lurk everywhere outdoors for a

Common Household Hazards

- Small toys, dolls, children's hair ornaments, shoestrings, rubber bands, staples, twist ties, paper clips, thumbtacks, push pins
- Razor blades, sanitary products
- Medication, including aspirin, acetaminophen, ibuprofen
- Suntan lotion and beauty products, including makeup, nail polish, and nail polish remover
- Household cleaning solvents
- Garbage, including plastic bags, spoiled food, bones, and broken bottles or can lids
- Poison and mousetraps
- Toxic houseplants
- Antifreeze, motor oil, brake fluid
- Sewing supplies, including pins, needles, buttons, snaps, thread, ribbon, or string
- Electrical cords or uncovered outlets
- Fragile glass collectibles
- Tall, wobbly items that can fall over if knocked off balance

little dog. Once a day check your backyard for holes in the fence that your Yorkie might decide to use as an escape route. Sharp protrusions around patio furniture or fencing, poisonous mushrooms or plants that might suddenly appear can be deadly if your Yorkie finds them before you do. Keep an eye out for surprises such as plastic bags that may blow into the yard on a windy day, and for dangerous objects such as rusty nails, broken glass, any sharp or rusted tools or gardening implements, and any toxic chemicals left out by mistake.

If you have a pool or a spa, make sure it is securely fenced at all times. Pool covers are particularly dangerous if a dog happens to fall into the pool and land on top of the cover. Attempting to get a foothold on the slippery cover is impossible and a dog may drown trying to get out of the pool.

Common Poisonous Plants

This list contains some, but not all, of the common plants that can harm your dog. Consult a plant book or a nursery if you have any doubts about a plant in your home or yard.

Alfalfa

Aloe vera

American yew

Angel's trumpet

Amaryllis

Apricots

Arrowgrass

Asparagus fern

Azalea

Beach tree

Bird of paradise

Bittersweet

Black-eyed Susan

Black locust tree

Boxwood

Buttercup

Caladium

Calla lily

Carnation

Castor plant

Chinaberry

Chrysanthemum

Coriandrum

Crown of thorns

Cycas Revoluta (Sago palm and Japanese fern)

Daffodil

Daphne

Datura

Delphinium

Dieffenbachia

Dumb cane

Easter lily

Elephant's ear

English ivy

Eucalyptus

Euonymus

Foxglove

Hemlock

Henbane

Hibiscus

Honeysuckle

Horse chestnut

Hyacinth

Hydrangea

Iris

Ivy

Jack-in-the-pulpit

Jerusalem cherry

Jessamine

Jimsonweed

Kalanchoe

Lantana berries

Lily of the valley

Lupine

Mistletoe berries

Monkshood

Monseed

Morning glory

Mountain laurel

Nightshade

Nutmeg

Oak trees (acorns)

Oleander

Onions

Oxalas

Paspalum

Peaches (peach pits)

Periwinkle

Philodendron

Podocarpus

Poinsettia

Poison sumac

Potato plant

Pothos

Precatory bean

Privet

Pyracantha

Ranunculus or buttercup

Rhododendron

Rhubarb leaves

Schefflera

Skunk cabbage

Toadstools

Tobacco

Tomato vines

Tulip

Umbrella plant

Voltaren

Wandering Jew

Water hemlock

Wild carrots

Wild parsnip

Wild peas

Wisteria

Yew tree

For the avid gardener who doesn't want to see the fruits of his labor eaten by a Yorkie, fence off fruits, vegetables, and flowers with a small white picket fence. Or put an exercise pen or a dog run into the yard in which your Yorkie can spend a limited, but safe, amount of time.

Keep your Yorkie away from rotting organic material or compost. These produce toxins that are very harmful to a small dog. Because lawn-care products and pest-control sprays and pellets can be lethal, be sure to read the labels of these items and follow their suggestions for keeping your dog off the lawn or patio areas after they have been applied.

Your yard fencing and gates should also be secure enough that no other dogs, cats, or wild animals can gain access. Even if you think your neighborhood is a safe one, make sure your yard and Yorkie are not visible to passersby. Dog theft is a problem in many areas.

Which Supplies Do You Really Need?

When you look at all that's available on the market for dogs, you can easily become overwhelmed by all the products retailers try to convince you are necessary. While shopping for your new Yorkie can be fun, it can also be expensive. You may want to take your time in order to make choices within your budget rather than go overboard on a shopping spree before your puppy even comes home.

Most reputable breeders will give you a list of items or show you Yorkie supplies you'll need with the sizes and shapes recommended. Some doggie items will be needed the first day while others can wait a bit.

Supply Checklist

Food and water bowls (ceramic or stainless steel)

Crate (plastic, wire, or both)

Dog bed or crate cushion, if you are sure he won't chew it

Doggie/baby gates

Outdoor kennel or secure perimeter fencing

Doghouse

Collar

Leash

ID tag

Enzyme cleaner

Grooming supplies (pin brush, slicker brush, Greyhound comb, shampoo, dental and ear-cleaning supplies)

Safe toys

Once you know exactly what you need, check at various pet-supply stores, pet-supply catalogs, or the Internet.

May I See Your ID?

Within the first few days of having your new dog, she should be given a form of identification. She's yours now, and once you've started the bonding process, you don't want to lose the momentum by having her disappear from your life by being lost or stolen.

Your dog should be easy to identify at all times. You never know when a curious Yorkie will go exploring and wander away from you. Even if you decide to just pop her in the car for a short ride down the street, an accident can separate the two of you. Or if you have someone else take care of more than one Yorkie, your dogs' identification tags will enable the dog sitter to tell them apart.

Three forms of safe identification are available for dogs: an identification tag, a tattoo, or a microchip. Each has advantages

High-Tech Identification Protection

Identification tags are your dog's first line of defense if she ever gets lost. Many a dog has been quickly reunited with her family because she was wearing a tag with the owner's phone number. However, what if your dog's collar comes off or is removed? How will your Yorkie find her way back home? Two other forms of identification can supplement the ID tag: tattooing and microchip implants.

With tattooing, a series of numbers or letters, or a combination of numbers and letters, is imprinted onto your pet's body, and the code is then recorded in a database. If someone finds your precious Yorkie, they can call the toll-free number to a tattoo registry, which maintains a database record with your name and phone number, corresponding to your dog's tattoo ID code. The toll-free number usually is provided on a tag that attaches to your dog's collar. Advantages to the tattoo is that it is a permanent and visible means of identification. One disadvantage is that, if your dog loses her collar, whoever finds your pet may not know who to call. If your dog won't let a stranger near her, the person who finds her may not be able to get close enough to read the tattoo. Also, horror stories exist of stolen dogs who have had a tattooed ear removed to keep them from being identified. To prevent this, it is safer to tattoo your dog's inner thigh.

Like tattoos, microchips contain a unique code, which can be read by a handheld scanner that is passed over the skin of the animal where the chip was inserted. The code corresponds to information in a database, such as the owner's name and phone number. An advantage to microchips is that they, too, are permanent. The microchip itself is composed of non-toxic components sealed in biocompatible glass. The chip, about the size of the lead tip of a pencil or a grain of rice, is fitted into a hypodermic needle and injected under the skin of a dog between her shoulder blades. A disadvantage is that not all scanners read all microchips. Humane societies usually have only enough money to invest in one scanner, at best, and if that scanner can't read the chip in your dog, it's useless. Again, if your dog is uncomfortable with being handled by strangers, she may be hard to scan.

Tattoos and microchips are gaining popularity as permanent means of identifying your pet. However, the standard ID tag that dangles from the collar of your pup remains an invaluable tool for helping to return your lost pet to you.

and disadvantages, but no single method is foolproof. By using two together, your dog will have even greater protection.

Almost everyone is familiar with an identification tag including your address and phone number that hangs from your dog's collar. Another alternative is to tag the dog's collar directly. Today you can choose from metal, plastic, and reflective tags in all different shapes, sizes, and colors, and new tag styles debut all the time. This is a tried-and-true method that provides quick and easy identification if your dog is lost or stolen. Many dogs are reunited with their owners when the people who find them read the identification tag. Imprinted tags are readily available in most pet-food stores, pet-supply catalogs, and mail-order locations.

If you move or change your phone number (even an area code change), be sure you get a new tag with the correct information.

Consider buying two tags so if one is lost or broken, you have another right away. Check the tag about once a week to make sure the ring holding it to the collar isn't bent or loose. As time goes by, check the imprint on the tag because it can wear thin and become unreadable. If you move or change your phone number (even an area code change), be sure you get a new tag with the correct information. Keep an eye on your metal dog license tag that your local county animal control department gives you. Because it's worn next to an ID tag, the constant rubbing can eventually erase the engraved letters and numbers.

This system isn't foolproof, however; if the collar is removed or comes off, the ID is lost. Because Yorkies are so close to the ground, many owners are reticent to use a tag, which can catch on objects sticking up and choke the dog. Many owners are using tattoos for identification. A unique set of numbers is safely imprinted onto a small area of your pet's skin, preferably on your dog's inner thigh or belly. If the tattooer is experienced, this procedure shouldn't take longer than 20 minutes if your Yorkie cooperates by lying on her side and keeping still. A tattoo isn't painful so most dogs hardly react.

If your dog is registered with the American Kennel Club, you can choose to tattoo her AKC number on her, or you may select any other set of numbers, such as your social security number, for identification purposes. The permanently tattooed number is registered with one of the two or three national tattoo companies. Whoever finds your Yorkie can call the tattoo registry and then her number will be matched with yours.

As a second precaution, the registry also provides a tag with the dog's ID number and the registry's toll-free phone number, which the dog can wear on his collar.

Another form of identification is a microchip, which has become very popular because it is also permanent. About the size of a grain of rice, the microchip must be placed by a veterinarian who loads it into a special needle-like apparatus and inserts it under the skin between the dog's shoulder blades. It's a painless procedure that lasts for the dog's lifetime. A tag with the microchip number is also given to the owner to attach to the dog's collar if desired.

Each microchip has a unique code that can be read by a handheld scanner. The scanner is passed over the dog, and the number instantly appears on the scanner. The code is located in a database, which registers the owner's name, address, and phone number. If the dog changes owners, the database information can be changed for a nominal fee, but the microchip number inside the dog always remains the same. It's important to remember to notify the registry if you move or if your dog passes away.

Unfortunately, different microchip registries have different scanners, and not all animal shelters and veterinarians have every scanner because of the expense. The Home Again registry gives a scanner to all shelters and veterinarians.

For very little effort on your part, you can protect your Yorkie from ever becoming lost and a statistic at an animal shelter.

Dinnerware for Your Dog

Your dog will need a water bowl and a food dish the first day she comes to your home, but fortunately her dining needs are simple. Rather than a complete china service, all she needs is a water bowl and a food dish. Yet when you look in a pet-supply catalog or go to a pet store, you'll be overwhelmed by dinnerware choices. You'll find dog bowls in all shapes and sizes made from collapsible canvas, plastic, ceramic, and stainless steel. You will find water containers that keep refilling the dish the minute it's empty and a divided food dish with a timer and individual covers that pop up at certain hours.

Purchase one water bowl and one food bowl. Skip the one-unit servers with two dishes and choose separate dishes instead. Even though you have a

Did You Know?

Researchers are almost positive that dogs dream. If you look at a sleeping dog, sometimes you'll notice his eyes move beneath his eyelids. Because this is what humans do when they dream, researchers believe it is an indication of dreams in dogs, too. No word yet on what they dream about.

little dog that doesn't eat or drink all that much, the temptation is strong to just use people bowls from your kitchen cabinet. These are not made to sit on the floor and can tip over easily and frighten your dog enough so she may not want to eat from that dish again.

Ask your breeder what size bowl to purchase. There's no sense buying a bowl a Great Dane could use nor one so tiny that the food overflows. Your Yorkie can use the same size food bowl throughout her lifetime. Since dogs prefer cold water, select a water bowl that's deeper and larger than the food dish. Or if you and your Yorkie spend enough time outdoors, a second water bowl for outside is convenient. If you plan to take your Yorkie on daytime or overnight trips, a second smaller food bowl left in your travel bag will come in handy.

Plastic bowls are cheapest but not the best choice. Some Yorkies like to lick their bowls after the food is gone or chew on plastic bowls. Eventually, small slivers of plastic will start appearing, which will irritate your Yorkie, possibly inside and out. It's also difficult to get rid of food odors or to thoroughly clean plastic. A slight residue will build up if bowls are not cleaned thoroughly every day, and your Yorkie's water or food will become contaminated. Another disadvantage to plastic bowls is that teeth marks leave holes in the plastic where bits of food can become lodged and spoil. In addition, a rambunctious Yorkie puppy can pick up a plastic bowl and carry it around the house.

> Stainless steel bowls are the most expensive but well worth the investment.

Ceramic is another choice (but don't drop it!). Ceramic bowls come in different colors and can sometimes be hand-painted with your dog's name or breed. Avoid ceramic bowls that are made in foreign countries because they might contain lead. If in doubt about lead content, you can purchase a quick test from your home improvement store. Ceramic bowls are also heavier when you place them on the floor. If your Yorkie is extremely anxious to get to her food, you could accidentally set the heavy bowl on a paw and injure it.

Stainless steel bowls are the most expensive but well worth the investment. They will be around for your children's and grandchildren's Yorkies because they last several lifetimes. They're very easy to clean with a sponge, or you can pop them into the dishwasher. Water stays the coldest in these bowls—except when left in the hot sun outdoors. Stainless steel bowls are sturdy and not too heavy for you to move around, yet not easy for your Yorkie to pick up. Your Yorkie won't want to bite into steel, and if you drop these bowls they won't break.

Collars, Leashes, and Leads

Within a few days of acquiring your new Yorkie you'll need to get him a collar. To get the correct measurement, take him to the pet-supply store and, holding him in your arms the whole time, try collars on to see which fits the best. Or measure your dog's neck at home with a tape measure and add two inches. Get a collar that fits with only a little bit of growing room. Don't buy a German Shepherd–sized collar that you think your Yorkie will grow into because a collar that's too big may slip off or catch on objects and choke your dog. Plan on buying a few collars as your Yorkie grows. For a first and a second collar, some Yorkie owners prefer a nylon buckle model that's adjustable. When your Yorkie is older and you think he is done growing, a leather buckle collar will last his lifetime. Avoid cat collars or harnesses because they can be restrictive to a Yorkie.

Leashes come in a variety of colors and textures. Be sure to check the swivel and the safety snap to make sure they are sturdy and cannot easily unhook. While the nylon leashes are more colorful, they can also slice through your hand if your Yorkie makes a mad dash after a cat on the street. Leather is the best material for a leash and will also last a lifetime. Just make sure you don't leave it lying around where your puppy can chew it. Dogs think leather leashes have a great aroma and are just right for chewing. If your Yorkie insists on biting on the leash when you go for a walk, you can spray it with a bitter-tasting but harmless spray product such as Bitter Apple.

Skip the chain leashes entirely. They make too much noise and are hard to hold in your hand. Leashes also come in a variety of lengths, widths, and weights. Choose a lightweight but sturdy leash that feels the best in your hand. A four-foot length is all your Yorkie needs.

A lead is a one-piece combination of the collar and leash together. This works well on tiny three-pound and under Yorkies or puppies. The lead is usually made out of lightweight nylon that won't hurt the smallest of the breed. They also come in waxed linen with a clip that can loosen or tighten. The advantages to this type are that it won't damage the neck or the coat and it is very strong. If the lead feels stiff when you first use it, try washing it or boiling it in water to soften it up a bit.

Avoid retractable leashes. While they can extend to 12 feet and are great for exercising a dog when no other loose dogs are around, they can be dangerous if you take your Yorkie for a walk around the block. Once your dog is at the end of his leash, you can stop him, but you cannot get him to come back to you unless he wants to. If a large dog darts out at your Yorkie ten feet ahead, there's little you can do to save him. You have virtually no control of your dog if you use a retractable leash.

Crates Are Great!

Have a crate ready for your Yorkie as soon as he comes home. If you have never used a crate before, it will take some getting used to. Once you have used one you'll wonder how you ever raised a dog without one before. Descendants from wolves who used dens for security, dogs welcome this portable bedroom as a safe haven once they become accustomed to it. If unruly children visit your home, your Yorkie will appreciate being settled in his crate, away from their poking and prying. A crate can be a nighttime bed for your Yorkie, or a safe place when you cannot watch him for a short time. You can also use a crate to aid you in housetraining your Yorkie and as a safe way to transport your dog in an airplane or an automobile.

> A crate can be a nighttime bed for your Yorkie, or a safe place when you cannot watch him for a short time.

Several different crate models are on the market. If you plan to take your Yorkie traveling, be sure to purchase an airline-approved crate. You will only need one crate unless you want an extra one for your car or another room of the house. Wire crates are cooler for your Yorkie in hot months but are often too cool during the winter.

Ask your breeder what size crate is just right for your Yorkie. While crates big enough for calves to fit into are available, your Yorkie's certainly shouldn't be that big. Your Yorkie's crate should be high enough for her to stand up in without bumping her head and allow enough room for her to turn around.

When you purchase a crate, check the spring-loaded latch to make sure it works properly. Fit the door on the crate before you buy it and be sure it clears the top and bottom easily. If there is a handle, verify that it is strong enough to bear weight.

Once your Yorkie is tucked inside, check the air vents around the crate to make sure ventilation is adequate, and never leave the crate in the hot sun next to a window or directly in front of air-conditioning. If your puppy is not a chewer, add a few comfy blankets and certainly some favorite toys, and your Yorkie will think she's in hotel heaven.

Bedding

Bedding is pretty important the first night your Yorkie spends in your home. If she has a nighttime environment similar to what she had at her previous home and is comfortable, her transition to your home will be an easy one. While some owners insist that their Yorkie sleep in bed with them, that isn't the safest choice. You can roll over on top of that tiny body in the middle of the night and crush her. Or she can miscalculate the edge and fall off and break a leg or hit something and cause even more injury to herself.

Dog beds for Yorkies needn't take up much space. A fluffy, oversized dog bed or pillow with a cover you can remove and machine wash is just fine for your dog. Avoid wicker baskets because your Yorkie will love to gnaw on the pieces and can choke on them. Metal beds last a long time but are more expensive and may be drafty. A crate makes an excellent bed as well.

Grooming Supplies

One look at that shiny magnificent Yorkie coat and the word "grooming" sends chills through a first-time owner's mind. This need not be the case. Have your grooming supplies ready the day your Yorkie arrives. The sooner you begin using them, the sooner your Yorkie will learn to enjoy the process.

It's important that you begin brushing your dog's teeth as soon as her permanent teeth are in. Toy dogs have weaker gums and bacteria tends to build up quickly. This leads to a higher incidence of dental disease, which can progress to heart infections and kidney problems.

If your dog has bad breath, it usually means her teeth are not being brushed regularly. Veterinary experts recommend brushing your Yorkie's teeth at least three times a week. If you can do this more often, that's even better.

Use a canine toothbrush and toothpaste. There are several brands available that you can easily to find in pet-supply catalogs or pet stores.

Getting those Yorkie ears to stand up is easy if you keep the hair trimmed every two weeks. The weight of just a little extra hair can cause the top half of the ear to drop forward. Cut a triangular paper pattern and hold it up on top of your dog's ears. This makes it easier to cut the hair around the ears. You'll need a sharp pair of grooming scissors to do this correctly.

Good grooming also means cleaning out the insides of your Yorkie's ears. The breed is prone to getting ear mites and infections, but if you keep the ears clean, you'll prevent the problem from beginning. You'll need ear-cleaning solution and separate Q-tips for each ear, and your veterinarian can tell you how and when you need to clean your Yorkie's ears. Cleaning too often or too vigorously can create infections rather than help avoid them.

Be sure to clean your dog's eyes if you notice any tearing. Using a washcloth or a cotton ball and warm water, place these in the inside corner of the eye and wipe to the outside corner. Use a separate washcloth or cotton ball for each eye. You might need to repeat this for several days to clean the eyes. Eyes that have a lot of discharge, especially over a period of days, often indicate a problem with the eye or a sick dog. Make sure to visit the vet if you find yourself frequently cleaning your Yorkie's eyes.

A Yorkie coat can be wooly, cottony, and wiry with a few different combinations of each. To make sure your dog's coat doesn't mat, you'll need a brush, comb, hair-dryer, towel, a good quality dog shampoo, conditioner, and detangler spray. Many breeders start detangling their Yorkie's coat with a pin brush. A second, fine slicker brush will catch any tiny mats the pin brush misses. A metal comb with even spacing works great for getting rid of mats and snarls. You may end up buying several different kinds of combs and brushes until you are satisfied with the tools you have.

> You may end up buying several different kinds of combs and brushes until you are satisfied with the tools you have.

The Joy of Toys

A Yorkie likes to be a busy dog and should have a number of toys to go with her active personality. Otherwise she will begin looking at your good furniture and find other mischief to get into. You'll have no problem finding toys to buy for your puppy, and they will be the most fun items to purchase. Squeaky toys, soft stuffed toys, hard rubber chews and rope tosses make great playtime companions for your Yorkie. After your Yorkie has lived with you for awhile, you will gain a sense of what she likes best. Not every

Removing Doggie Stains and Odors

If you have purchased a puppy, you must accept the fact that you will probably encounter a housetraining accident or two, no matter how diligent you are, until your dog is fully trained. Even if you have adopted an adult dog, there may come a time when you find a mess on your carpet, whether that mess is urine, feces, or vomit. Even the best-trained dog may not be able to control himself when he is sick.

Not only must you remove the stain and odor you can smell, but more important, you also need to remove the odor your dog can smell. Remember, a dog's sense of smell is much more acute than ours. Therefore, you'll need to use a product designed specifically for pet-odor removal. Never use an ammonia-based product. Since ammonia is present in urine, your dog will actually be more attracted to urinate there again.

If your dog has an accident, first clean up any solid waste that is present. Next, apply an enzyme-based stain and odor remover. Any pet-supply store carries such a product. Follow the directions carefully to ensure the cleaner does its job. If you are applying the cleaner to a carpeted area, test it in an inconspicuous spot first to make sure it won't change the color of your rug.

toy is suited to every dog. When you buy toys, make sure there are no small, detachable pieces. Today many stores hang toys with plastic hooks that are inserted into the toy itself. Cut these off before giving the toy to your dog as they can be easily swallowed and lodge in the dog's intestines. As your Yorkie works on her toys, check them frequently to see that the noisemaker inside isn't ready to pop out. Because they smell and taste good, your dog may swallow the noisemaker, which can cause intestinal blockage or necessitate emergency surgery. As the stuffing begins to come out of your Yorkie's new furry friend, sew it back up or discard it before your dog begins ingesting the filling.

Other Items

Here are the essential items you will need when your dog is carried through your front door.

Doggie Gates   These are invaluable if you want to confine your Yorkie to a particular room and keep the rest of the house off limits. They attach easily inside a door frame and can be removed whenever you want.

Puppy Pens   When you cannot watch your Yorkie, a pen is a safe area to put him into. Place a few treasured objects in there with him and give him a biscuit when it's time for him to go to his pen.

Outdoor Shelter   Your Yorkie should not be left outdoors for long periods of time. However, if he must be left outdoors, a permanent tent placed over a corner of your fenced-in yard will protect him if the weather is either very hot or very cold.

Puppy Cleanup Supplies   These are a must. Even though your Yorkie may become very adept at housetraining, there will inevitably be the occasional accident in the house. Enzyme-based cleaners are effective for cleanup. Citrus sprays come in handy for a fresh smell following cleanup.

Homecoming Day for Your Yorkshire Terrier

The day has finally arrived! It's time to bring home your new Yorkie and introduce him to his new home and family. If you work outside the home full time, arrange to take off at least a few days to help your puppy adjust. If possible, schedule his arrival for early in the day to give him time to fully investigate his new environment before bedtime.

If you are picking up your puppy, rather than having him delivered to you, prepare for a less-than-smooth ride home. Unless the breeder has already taken your puppy for short trips, this may be his first car ride. Bring along several old towels in case your pup drools excessively or vomits. The most important thing to do if your puppy whines or cries is to act like nothing is wrong. Don't ooh and ahh over your nervous pup—otherwise, you'll just reinforce his fear of car rides. Instead, act calm and even businesslike. Sing along with the radio, or talk to your puppy in a matter-of-fact tone. For now, you'll just want to get through this first car ride as quickly as possible!

As soon as you get home, take your puppy outside to the area you want him to use as his bathroom. Chances are, after his exciting ride, he will need to go right away. Pick a phrase such as "go potty" or "hurry up" and use it when your dog starts to eliminate. Timing is extremely important. If you issue the command before your dog goes, in your dog's mind it may take on the meaning of something else that your dog is doing at the moment, such as "sniff the tree" or "chew on grass." Once your dog understands the command by associating it with the action, you can use the command to elicit the behavior. Each time your puppy eliminates outside, remember to praise, praise, and then praise some more! You must help the puppy realize from the beginning that pottying outdoors is the goal. If he doesn't go right away, bring him inside and put him in his crate for half an hour, then take him out to the designated spot again. Once he has relieved himself, you can bring him inside and let him explore the house. Remember, you'll need

to keep a close eye on your pup so that you can correct any mistakes he may make.

Resist the temptation to have all your friends and relatives over to see your new addition; too many people on the first day can be overwhelming for your new dog, whether he's a puppy or an adult. Instead, enjoy a private, getting-to-know-you first day with your pet. Although puppies do need lots of rest, you may want to try to wear your Yorkie out on his first day home to help him sleep through the night! This doesn't mean going on marathon runs around the neighborhood; simply playing with your pup and letting him explore your house and yard should do the trick.

After the first few days, when life has settled back to normal and you return to work, either come home at lunch to let your puppy out or have a neighbor or friend drop in. Remember, a crate is a wonderful tool that shouldn't be abused. It's a good idea to pick a certain indestructible toy, such as a Kong stuffed with treats, that the puppy gets only when he is crated. This gives your Yorkie something to look forward to when you leave and helps keep him from feeling bored and lonely.

The First Night with Your Yorkshire Terrier Puppy

As nervous as you might be about your Yorkie's first night in your home, your puppy is probably more anxious. Try to bring her home

as early in the day as possible so she has plenty of time to become accustomed to you and her surroundings. Although she will miss her mother and familiar surroundings, keeping her occupied with attention and play will help. Avoid inviting all the neighbors and extended family to come visit the first few days. This will give her a chance to feel comfortable with just the immediate family.

Allow enough time to become settled at bedtime. Hopefully you didn't bring her home on the night before you have an important engagement early the next morning. After the last trip outside for a potty break, settle your puppy down gradually by first lowering the lights and putting her in her crate or pen in your bedroom when you are ready to go to bed. Put a stuffed animal that feels a little like her littermates in with your puppy so she can feel another furry body against her own, but only do this if your little Yorkie isn't a chewer or the stuffed toy is indestructible. After the lights go out, your puppy may cry or yelp. Using your voice to quiet her, reassure her that you are there.

> Avoid inviting all the neighbors and extended family to come visit the first few days.

Making an Older Yorkshire Terrier Feel Welcome

An older Yorkie will feel just as disoriented in his new home as a puppy does. Instead of being very active the first day, an older dog may want to sit back and observe his new surroundings and new owners. This is a very acceptable transition so just give him time to adapt. Stay close by so he knows you haven't abandoned him and be ready for play if he becomes suddenly interested. Be sure to put his bed in your bedroom so he can feel secure if he awakens during the night. An older dog may require more time to feel comfortable in his new home than a puppy does. Be patient, and you'll find your wait worthwhile.

3

Food for Thought

One of the most overwhelming choices to make when you bring your new Yorkshire Terrier home is what to feed him. Pet-supply stores and supermarkets overflow with dry dog food bags, with all different brands, sizes, types, and prices stacked on shelves. Neat rows of various canned foods line shelves above the bags. If that's not enough to confuse you, there's also a dizzying array of boxes and small packages of treats and snacks. All you have is one four-pound Yorkie, yet there's enough dog food to feed every Yorkie in the country. It's easy to be confused.

So let's talk about your dog's nutritional needs and what he really needs to live a long and healthy life.

Why Nutrition Matters

Gone are the days when all dogs were wild and had to forage for their own food in order to survive. While they might have stayed alive on scraps and small game, they didn't live long or healthy lives. Coats were sparse, teeth quickly decayed, and eyes were dull and hollow.

Good owners have been taking care of their dogs' nutritional needs for a long time, but today it's not enough to pour your leftovers or whatever's on sale at the grocery store into your dog's bowl. Because more is known than ever before about good canine nutrition, you have the opportunity to make sure your dog has the right food to maintain a good immune system, build strong bones, and provide for proper growth.

If your dog doesn't have all the essential nutrients at the right stages in life, he will suffer from being under- or overweight, or have skin problems, bowel dysfunction, bone loss, or digestive upsets. Your Yorkie's body needs a combination of protein, carbohydrates, fats, vitamins, minerals, and water in order to stay healthy.

Protein, the first ingredient listed in most premium dog foods, is usually beef, chicken, turkey, lamb, or duck. Other  sources include meat meal, fish, fish meal, liver, eggs, milk and milk products, wheat, corn, rice, soy, and barley. Protein is responsible for your dog's metabolism, growth and development, digestive and reproductive functions, blood flow, and repair of body tissues.

The Importance of Water

Water is important to every living creature, and your Yorkie is no exception.

Water makes up around 60 percent of your adult dog's body and even more of your puppy's constitution. Dogs need water to help their cells function properly and to aid in proper digestion. Basically, dogs need water to live. Without water, a dog will die within only a few days.

The water in your dog's body needs to be replenished on a regular basis, since it is routinely lost through respiration, digestion, and urination. On hot days or when exercising heavily, your dog needs even more water to keep his body running smoothly.

To keep your Yorkie at optimum health, provide him with constant access to plenty of cool, fresh water.

Carbohydrates are usually the second or third ingredient listed in most quality dog foods. Corn, rice, wheat, and oats are common carbohydrates that give your Yorkie the energy he needs to be so active. Carbohydrates are also a source of fiber, which helps digestion and elimination.

Fats—specifically oleic and linoleic acids—are also necessary in a balanced nutritional program because they provide energy. Fats provide energy, keep your Yorkie's skin and coat healthy, are important in hormone regulation, and make your dog feel satisfied.

Vitamins help the body fight diseases and maintain the critical balance between constructive and destructive cellular changes. Vitamins themselves must be properly balanced since excesses or deficiencies of vitamins, or interference between vitamins, can cause serious health problems. The fat-soluble vitamins A, D, K, and E are stored in the liver and fatty tissues. Since they can be maintained in the body, an excess intake of these vitamins can easily become toxic. Water-soluble vitamins, on the other hand, are flushed from the body daily and must constantly be replaced. Both plant and meat sources contain vitamins, plus manufacturers often add vitamins to dog food during processing.

Minerals are needed for the body's metabolic processes and to keep the proper level of salts in the bloodstream. They also are an essential part of your dog's bones and teeth. Canines need seven major minerals and 15 trace minerals. Like vitamins, all minerals, especially trace minerals, need to be properly balanced or they can be toxic. And, as with vitamins, deficiencies or excesses can contribute to myriad health problems, from anemia to hip dysplasia. Minerals are present in both vegetable matter and animal tissues, or are added by the manufacturer during processing.

> The best way to keep your dog fully hydrated at all times is to always give her access to plenty of clean, fresh water.

Water is the most essential nutrient of them all. It is necessary for the proper working of every living cell in your pet's body. Since water is constantly being used up or excreted through normal body function, dogs need to continually replenish their supply. The best way to keep your dog fully hydrated at all times is to always give her access to plenty of clean, fresh water.

Choosing the Best Food for Your Yorkshire Terrier

When it comes to choosing a dog food for your Yorkie, you have many choices. While everyone would rather pay less, the cheapest dog food isn't always the best for your dog—nor is the most expensive or the most heavily advertised meal.

Like people, every dog has unique nutritional needs, depending upon his size, activity level, and other factors. Add in specific likes and dislikes and you'll have even more food choices to think about. Look for a food that provides balanced nutrition, contains the best ingredients, is highly digestible, and is appetizing to your Yorkie. Start by looking at the label. Dog food labels consist of two parts: the main display label and the information panel. The main display label states the brand name, flavor of the food, life stage the food is meant for (puppy or senior, for example), and weight of contents. The information panel is where you need to look to determine the quality of the food. It lists a number of items: the guaranteed analysis (the minimum levels of crude protein and fat and the maximum levels of fiber and water); the ingredient list (listed in descending order by weight); and a statement verifying that the food has undergone feeding trials by the Association of American Feed Control Officials (AAFCO) and provides complete and balanced nutrition. If the label doesn't include this statement, do not buy the dog food, no matter how highly recommended it may be by your breeder or neighbor down the street. Once you have found a food that meets these guidelines, it is time for the final test: whether or not your Yorkie will eat it! You can give your dog the best diet available, but if he doesn't eagerly gulp it down, it isn't the best diet for your Yorkie.

Toy dogs, and Yorkies in particular, do not require the same food that medium or giant breeds do. Size-wise, dry dog food for a small dog should come in little pieces, not in big chunks. The ingredients should also be different for a tiny breed than they are for a small, medium, or large dog. When compared to other dogs, a tiny breed has a higher metabolism and needs more calories per bite of food or per pound of dog.

What's on the Label?

The wide variety of cans, bags, and boxes of pet food shelved in shops throughout the nation has at least one thing in common: labeling. True, the colors, pictures, and words used on individual foods vary, as do the diets within. But all labels must by law contain specific information.

Pet food labels give basic information about the diet's ingredient content, nutrient guaranteed analysis, feeding instructions, net weight, the name and address of the manufacturer or distributor, and additional facts about the product. No, pet food labels don't tell everything about a product. But they do give a savvy consumer a good way to begin comparing foods.

At the federal level, pet food labeling and advertising claims are regulated by the Food and Drug Administration, the U.S. Department of Agriculture, and the Federal Trade Commission. State feed control officials determine regulations to which pet food manufacturers in individual states must adhere. Another organization with an important role in labeling pet foods is the Association of American Feed Control Officials (AAFCO). The association is made up of officials from the United States, Canada, and Puerto Rico. Although the AAFCO has no regulatory authority (state and federal officials do), it does set forth guidelines, or "models," for feed and pet food regulations that individual states are encouraged to adopt. A large number of states comply with the suggested laws and guidelines. The AAFCO also provides nutritional guidelines for dog and cat foods called nutrient profiles and guidelines for testing foods.

Pet food companies that sell diets that don't meet the label guarantee are subject to a warning, a fine, removal of the product, or cancellation of the product's registration.

Pet food labels contain several elements:

Look for the percentage of ingredients listed on every bag of dog food. The minimum and maximum amount of crude protein, crude fat, crude fiber, and moisture will show what your dog is eating. Manufacturers will change formulas so it's a good idea to check each bag before you buy it. For Yorkie pup-

The product name must be placed on the principal display panel, that part of the label most likely to be seen by consumers.

Certain nutrient guarantees—guaranteed analysis—are required on all pet food labels: crude protein (minimum percentage), crude fat (minimum percentage), crude fiber (maximum percentage), and moisture (maximum percentage).

The package must include an ingredient listing of all the ingredients used to make the food; they must be listed on the label in descending order of predominance by weight.

Additives must be noted. That includes nutritional additives such as vitamins and minerals, antioxidants such as BHA or BHT, chemical preservatives, flavoring agents, and coloring.

The net weight must be placed on the principal display panel.

Manufacturer information, the name and address of the manufacturer, packer, or distributor, must be included on the label.

The label must state in the nutritional adequacy statement whether or not the product provides complete and balanced nutrition and if it is appropriate for all life stages or one particular life stage.

The amount of food required, or feeding directions, must be printed on the label.

The caloric statement, which is the calorie content of the product, must appear away from the guaranteed analysis and be under the heading "calorie content."

Last but not least many pet food packages include a toll-free consumer information number. This isn't mandatory, but it's a good resource for owners wanting to learn more about the product they're feeding their pet.

pies the protein level should not be higher than 28 percent, and for adults it should be around 22 percent. The protein content on some foods may be as high as 32 percent, which may be suitable for a working dog, but not for an active Yorkie. If you fed your tiny dog this much protein, his kidneys would have to work overtime to process this much energy, which could be harmful.

Premium Foods Versus Grocery Store Foods

Dog food commercials and advertisements tout premium, high-quality food for your dog. This type is usually found in pet-supply stores while grocery stores generally avoid stocking premium dog foods in favor of moderately priced, popular brands as well as cheaper brands for penny-pinching owners. Breeders, owners, and veterinarians have different opinions about what you should feed your dog. The answer is whatever your dog does the best on. No single dog food is perfect for every dog.

Since Yorkies eat so little, each bite is important and should offer the best nutrition possible. If you compare ingredients on both premium and non-premium foods, they may appear very similar. On closer inspection, premium food has more natural and whole-food sources with a higher quantity of meat-protein ingredients, while the non-premium includes by-products or vegetable products, such as ground corn, cereal grains, and fillers. Your little Yorkie does not need fillers.

Premium foods also have more digestible nutrients that are more easily absorbed than the non-premium foods have. This means your dog will be eliminating more often and you will have to feed more non-premium food than you would a more expensive brand. In the long run, feeding a better food is usually cheaper.

The cheaper brands don't include extra additives to enhance a shiny coat, either. With a breed like a Yorkie, whose pride and joy is his coat, this is an important factor to consider when purchasing food. Another difference between a less expensive dog food and one that costs a little more can be the addition of a natural plant source that neutralizes stool odors. Yet another difference is the addition of vitamin E as a preservative, which is important for food that may be left on a shelf or stored in a warehouse before it actually reaches the consumer.

Despite claims made that grocery store foods equal premium foods, most veterinarians recommend the better quality varieties.

Canned Versus Dry

Pet owners want to give their dogs a food they will like. Dry food seems boring to most pet owners while the canned food resembles a hearty stew-like treat. There are advantages and disadvantages to both. Canned food is usually more expensive and contains more moisture (70 percent water by weight). You can't leave it in your dog's bowl for very long and must refrigerate it if your Yorkie doesn't consume the whole can in one meal; otherwise, it will spoil. For dogs whose teeth are always in need of a cleaning, the dry food gives them more chewing action and may aid in keeping teeth tartar free. Dry food also is more easily digestible and helps maintain healthy gums as chewing stimulates salivation. While canned food looks meatier than dry food, pet owners worry about the type of meat used in the canned food. Some has a foul odor when you open the can and may give a dog diarrhea.

But for many dogs who have dental decay, are elderly, are finicky eaters, or are recuperating from surgery, canned food is often the answer. Canned food comes in a variety of different flavors and has an interesting smell that people

Did You Know?

Veterinarians estimate that between 30% and 50% of today's dog population is overweight.

don't like, but which entices dogs. Cans are easy to take with you if you are traveling with your Yorkie. Some companies sell the food in small cans, often just enough for a meal or two for your Yorkie. Select a premium-brand canned food. Remove whatever is left over from the can and store it in the refrigerator.

Another choice is the semi-moist or soft dog food resembling individual bags or patties. This type comes frozen or contained in resealable packages or plastic wrap. This type lasts a long time and usually has less odor, but can be quite expensive. Such prepackaged foods usually contain a high amount of corn syrup or other sweeteners that can be harmful, especially to a Yorkie.

Most breeders and owners prefer dry food because it doesn't spoil, is less expensive (especially when they have several dogs to feed), and can be added to other ingredients such as vegetables or fruit or a small amount of canned food.

Cost Differences—Why They Exist, What They Mean

There are dog foods made to suit every different type of dog and every owner's pocketbook. The difference between a grocery store dry food and a premium-quality food can vary as much as $10 for a 20-pound bag. A few dog food manufacturers are aware that some people simply cannot afford to feed their dogs a higher-priced food so they produce several different varieties with varying prices from which you can choose. In the long run, the less expensive food may cost as much as the premium food because you have to feed your dog more of it.

> In the long run, the less expensive food may cost as much as the premium food because you have to feed your dog more of it.

To figure out how much it actually costs to feed your dog, divide the cost of one bag of dog food by the number of cups fed and track how long it takes to use all the food in the bag. You can compare results of feeding grocery store with premium-brand foods. Canned and semi-moist food is more expensive per pound (partly due to higher water content) and you have to buy more of it to feed your dog. The larger the quantity you purchase at one time, the more the price goes down with both grocery store and premium foods. However, Yorkies are small and don't eat large quantities. The more food you purchase the greater the risk for spoilage. It is best to buy in smaller quantities for such a little dog, or at least freeze uneaten portions.

The reason a food is priced higher is because quality ingredients are used. A brand containing all-natural products with no artificial colors or preservatives is also more expensive than a food that contains man-made chemicals and dyes.

The price difference also depends upon the type of ingredients used. A premium food might contain lamb, venison, duck, or turkey rather than beef by-products or chicken meal, which is used in most grocery-store foods. Grain that isn't treated with pesticides, and contains additional vitamins and omega oils for healthy skin and coats is also more expensive. A premium food should not need any vitamin supplements because everything the dog needs is contained inside.

Veterinarians recommend premium foods because grocery store brands have been known to slow growth and produce poor skin condition and coat quality. Fewer visits to the veterinarian should also be a consideration as a cost-saver when you purchase a better quality food.

All-Natural Foods

As people have become more health-conscious about what they eat, they have also become more concerned about what their dogs eat. The association between eating healthy and living a longer, more active life has been established for dogs as well as for people. It's no surprise then that natural dog food products have become popular in recent years—and natural kibble and canned food is no exception. Manufacturers recognized the trend and began producing dog food that does not contain artificial preservatives and food dyes known to cause cancer in laboratory animals. Advertisers' claims that a dog food is all-natural can mean anything is included, but it usually means that the dog food contains organic meats, grains, and natural preservatives with vitamin E or ascorbic acid. These premium foods are usually found in pet-supply stores, in natural-food markets, or via mail order. Some brands that feature all-natural ingredients are available only from the manufacturer and are shipped directly to the pet owner's home.

Preparing Homemade Meals for Your Yorkshire Terrier

While many of the premium foods on the market are adequate for a Yorkie's nutritional requirements, some breeders and owners prefer to make their own dog food. Many Yorkie breeders don't mind making their own dog food because Yorkies don't need much of it. These owners enjoy preparing homemade, fresh dog foods and

even raw foods incorporating bones. They feel the time spent is worthwhile when they can choose natural ingredients free of processing. Many veterinarians and some pet owners feel that a raw, homemade diet is better and far more healthful for their dogs than anything available commercially.

Some controversy exists over whether or not a homemade cooked or a raw diet is really good for

Food Allergies

It's not common, but some dogs develop food allergies. Digestive upset, itchy skin, or hair loss can be signs that something in the animal's diet is triggering an allergic reaction. What exactly is an allergic reaction? It's an exaggerated response of the immune system to something that's usually harmless; wheat, for example. What the pet is allergic to is called an allergen.

The way the body responds to that allergen is called a hypersensitivity reaction. There are two kinds of hypersensitivity reactions. The immediate type occurs within minutes of exposure and often produces hives, itching, and sometimes, trouble breathing or collapse; anaphylactic shock is an example of this. The delayed reaction produces itching hours or days afterward.

The most common food allergens are wheat, milk, soy, chicken, eggs, beef, fish, and corn. Dyes and preservatives may also trigger allergies.

Treating allergies usually begins with a diet trial supervised by a veterinarian. But not just any diet—preferably foods to which the Yorkie hasn't been exposed. Changing from one pet food to another doesn't work because many foods contain similar ingredients. Dietary restriction is the only way to truly determine what food(s) your Yorkie is allergic to. Once the offending agent is pinpointed, an appropriate diet can be started.

dogs, but owners who prepare such diets say this is the most healthful for their pets. If you decide to feed raw meat, make sure it has been frozen first and comes from a reliable organic meat supplier. Additionally, you must also be aware that raw meats do carry health risks, such as E. coli bacteria and various parasites that can make your Yorkie very ill. Use raw diets cautiously, and be aware that there are risks associated with them. Buy organic foods from health-food stores or from people who grow organic vegetables and grains. You can also incorporate treats such as raw fruit and vegetables, cheese, lean beef, cooked eggs, and potatoes.

To decide whether you want to prepare your own dog food, consider what time you have available and how much organization keeping the food stored fresh in your refrigerator or freezer will require. If you work all day, you may not have the time or energy to cook for your dog when you get home. Many of the items can be frozen or refrigerated ahead of time and wrapped in small portions that are ready to take out, defrost, and serve.

You should also make sure your dog receives all the nutrients he needs and be sure you provide the right combination of proteins, fats, and carbohydrates. Vary your Yorkie's diet and introduce the new food gradually to allow your dog's system to become accustomed to the new taste sensations. For a small fee, a board certified veterinary nutritionist will help you balance a home-cooked diet that suits your pocketbook, schedule, preferences, and your dog's specific needs. Some holistic veterinarians can offer specific recipes for your Yorkie.

> Vary your Yorkie's diet and introduce the new food gradually to allow your dog's system to become accustomed to the new taste sensations.

If you use chicken, be sure to use boneless, skinless breasts. Any pieces of bone left in the food can perforate the stomach and bowels and death can result.

Food for a Hypoglycemic Yorkie

Yorkshire Terriers may become hypoglycemic when their blood sugar level drops very low. This happens most often in young puppies whose livers are not yet mature enough to regulate energy between meals. Rarely does it occur in an older dog.

If your Yorkie is listless, unable to walk, and has loose stools, the dog may be hypoglycemic and has no fuel left to move his body. In this case, place a little honey or Karo syrup on your Yorkie's tongue, which will rapidly restore blood sugar. Follow by feeding him some plain steamed or cooked rice with boiled chicken. If your Yorkie takes the food within a few minutes, he will feel better as the balance in his body is restored. However, if he is not back to himself within 15 minutes, he should see his vet immediately.

Can My Yorkshire Terrier Go Vegetarian?

While a vegetarian diet is popular with many people, dogs need a variety of nutrients, and not all of them can be found in vegetables. Deficiencies may develop if a dog doesn't receive a few supplements along with an all-veggie diet. Be cautious about serving only veggies and keep an eye on your dog's coat and stool quality. Cooked vegetables are good for a Yorkie, but a diet solely based on vegetables is not well-balanced and will leave your dog less healthy than if he ate a well-balanced diet.

How Often and How Much Do I Feed My Yorkshire Terrier?

Depending on the size and activity level of your Yorkie, the amount you will feed him and how often will vary. Generally, puppies up to 12 weeks should be fed four times a day, and have dry food available at all times. Some puppies will not eat when they are teething because their gums and mouth hurt. Keep an eye on a puppy who skips a meal or two. Something besides teething might be going on, so alert your veterinarian.

After 12 weeks and until he is 24 weeks old, your Yorkie should eat three meals a day. From six months on, your Yorkie should have two meals daily, though some do fine on only one.

Many breeders will keep dry food out as often as possible for puppies under six months because some Yorkies can be nibblers. They'll grab a few bites here and there between activities. Other breeders like to place the food down one time and pick it up after ten minutes if the dog does not finish it. Consult with your veterinarian as to which method you should use. Puppies that have had hypoglycemic episodes are best left with dry kibble available at all times.

The Importance of a Feeding Routine

Dogs don't have to have an alarm clock to know when feeding time is; they seem to have their own internal clock. Their bodies tell them when they are hungry. If you become distracted and forget to feed your Yorkie, he will paw at you and yip to remind you. To avoid a panic, establish a set feeding schedule at the same time each day so that your Yorkie will know when he will be fed. Choose a time that is convenient to you so you don't have to rush.

Puppy Feeding Schedules and Amounts

Yorkie puppies have tiny tummies and it is best they have dry food available at all times. If you add a small amount of cottage cheese or canned food to the dry, do so about three or four times a day. The amount a Yorkie needs will vary from puppy to puppy,

but generally you can tell whether he is too fat or too thin by looking down at his body. If his weight is just right, you'll see a slight inward curve where his stomach ends and his rear begins. If he is too fat, that area will bulge outward. If he is too thin, the inward curve is very sharp. Increase or decrease the amount you feed him by only a few tablespoons at a time. Remember that a puppy is always growing and that his needs constantly change. Just when you think you're feeding the right amount and his weight is just right, he may suddenly look too long and too thin. He's taken a growth spurt and needs a little more food. You'll also notice he's a lot more active and will require more fuel for all that energy.

Feeding Your Adult Yorkshire Terrier

Adult Yorkshire Terriers do best on two meals a day—breakfast and dinner. The times can be adjusted to your schedule, but two meals are more easily digested by your dog than one, larger meal, although some Yorkies do well with once-a-day feedings. Two- or three-pound Yorkies will appreciate being fed every four to six hours. They have a very high metabolism and just a little bit of room in their stomachs to hold food. You should feed these small Yorkies as much as you would feed bigger Yorkie puppies. It's also a good idea to switch over to the adult formula of food with both tiny and larger-sized adult Yorkies by the time they are a year old. Although Yorkies will obtain their full growth by 12 months, they will continue to fill out until they are 18 months of age.

When you begin the process of switching from puppy food to an adult recipe, do so on a gradual basis, mixing in a little of the puppy recipe with the adult. This will make an easier transition for your Yorkie's digestive tract. Sometimes the dog food will give a recommended daily serving size. Use this as a

Did You Know?

Dogs and cats in the United States consume almost $7 billion worth of pet food a year.

guide only because every dog's metabolism is different. It's easy to overfeed an adult dog so check him often to make sure he doesn't get fat. Being overweight is just as harmful to dogs as it is to people.

Is It Okay to Share My Food?

People who have never owned a dog often assume a dog is hungry because he is always looking for food. Because a dog can always eat, if you feed him every time he looks up at you with those pleading eyes and cute expression, he will become a blimp. Because of his small size, a Yorkie who is overweight can have severe health problems, such as an enlarged heart, kidney failure, and water retention. You would not want to lose your Yorkie because he has been overfed.

Once a dog figures out that you are eating food at the table and that a few morsels may come his way, you will never convince him it's not a good idea to hang around while you're eating. People food is warm, has a wonderful aroma, and has a variety of taste sensations to which kibble flavor doesn't even come close. It's no wonder that any dog would rather have human food than dog food.

> Because a dog can always eat, if you feed him every time he looks up at you with those pleading eyes and cute expression, he will become a blimp.

However, because human food is much higher in fat, it is too rich for most Yorkies. It also has different nutrients than dog food does. Feeding your Yorkie only people food will not provide him with the best nutrition. An occasional snack of a healthful treat is acceptable but limit the amount you give your dog, preferably between 5 and 10 percent of your Yorkie's daily caloric intake. Read the following section on treats to discover what your Yorkie will like.

Healthful Treats

Pet owners like giving their dogs a treat. Just to see the dog's happy expression with alert ears and shining eyes is worth the gesture. Some dogs will even cavort in circles or sit patiently at attention waiting for the tidbit. This showoff trick is sure to delight owners and entice them into handing out even more snacks. Resist the urge to give your Yorkie unhealthful treats (at least don't do it too often!).

Lisa Farmer, a Yorkshire Terrier breeder who lives in Oakwood, Georgia, is not a big fan of lots of treats. "Yorkies are small and thus have small tummies. Even a few small treats can end up being a large percentage of their daily food intake. I feed a good quality dog food and try to use praise and toys as rewards rather than a lot of treats."

If you must hand out snacks and can limit your offerings, give your Yorkie only tiny pieces and give them very sporadically, perhaps once every two weeks at different times and never from your dinner table. You can use the snack as a reward for a behavior when you are training or while you are preparing your own meals. The dog should be eating his normal kibble and should be in optimum health.

Treats can include small pieces of raw fruit and vegetables (especially cooked green beans and potatoes), tiny pieces of cheese, cottage cheese, cooked egg, and lean steak cooked rare or medium rare. Other special tidbits are dog biscuits, bite-sized dog food morsels, or premium dog food snacks. Don't forget to use kibble or a canine vitamin as a treat. When given unexpectedly, your dog will consider it a gourmet snack.

Toxic Treats—
Dangerous Foods for Dogs

A Yorkie named Sassy wanted a chocolate Easter basket filled with chocolate bars and bunnies left on the dining room table so badly that she jumped onto a footstool left near the table to get to it. When Sassy's family came home, they found an empty basket and a very sick Sassy. Luckily they were able to rush her to the veterinarian in time who was able to save her life.

Chocolate consumed in very large quantities can be very dangerous to dogs because of a chemical that can lead to vomiting, diarrhea, panting, restlessness, and muscle tremors. The caffeine contained in chocolate may also cause some damage to your dog's heart. While you might think a tiny piece of chocolate candy would not cause immediate danger, it's best to avoid giving your Yorkie any amount of chocolate. Even a little bit can be damaging to the tiny digestive system of a little Yorkie.

Raw or cooked onions should also be avoided since a tiny sliver can easily become caught in a Yorkie's small throat. In addition, a chemical in onions can cause hemolytic anemia, which destroys the body's red blood cells.

While the flavor of garlic is very appealing to dogs, when fed in large quantities its strong chemicals can reach toxic levels harmful to your dog's blood. For a picky eater, a dash of garlic sprinkled on dog food occasionally isn't going to hurt.

High-fat meat or meat with a lot of spices can also harm your dog because his digestive system cannot tolerate rich food.

Cooked pork, lamb, beef, poultry or other bones can also be deadly for a dog. They can splinter and perforate the dog's trachea or become lodged in their throats or perforate an intestine.

While many proponents of a natural food diet claim that raw turkey necks are good for a dog's digestive tract because they do not splinter, they may be infected with salmonella, E. coli, or other bacteria. If you decide to offer this treat, buy the meat from a highly reliable source and make sure it is very fresh when you give it to your dog. There is still no guarantee of safety, though.

Another harmful food item is anything stringy, such as celery. The strings are difficult to digest and can become lodged in a dog's throat. A fruit pit that is not chewable and digestible can be lethal. Apricot pits also contain a toxic chemical. Even an apple core can be dangerous to a tiny Yorkie tummy because it will not break down and can also easily lodge in the dog's throat.

What's All the Fuss About Supplements?

Hardly a day goes by without a notice in the news about the importance of people taking vitamins. Advertisements for new natural and herbal supplements claim to reduce stress, relieve arthritis, aid the immune system, and help people avoid heart disease and cancer. While such claims sound good, nutritionists believe that people can obtain everything they need to be healthy by eating a balanced diet of unprocessed food.

Since many commercial dog foods already contain acceptable percentages of vitamins and minerals necessary for a dog's good health, many veterinary nutritionists believe supplements are not necessary. They feel that dogs who eat a premium, well-balanced dog food do not need anything extra. Supplements can in fact throw the nutritional balance in a dog's system off and be harmful.

Does My Puppy Need Supplements?

Puppies should never be given supplements to their regular food unless your veterinarian directs you to do so. Your veterinarian may prescribe supplements if your puppy is ill or recuperating, for example. Hopefully your Yorkie puppy is already eating a premium, well-balanced food and receiving all the vitamins and minerals he needs. Extra supplements—such as calcium, which is sometimes given to a puppy during his vital growth period—can actually cause damage to his skeletal system.

What About My Older Dog?

When dogs age, they require a little more nutritional help. Bones become softer, coats become more brittle, and kidneys

cease to operate at their optimum efficiency. A senior dog's system cannot absorb the same amount of vitamins and minerals as easily as he once did. Your veterinarian might suggest a supplement such as vitamin B to help with your older dog's kidney function.

Ask your veterinarian about switching your dog's formula over to a senior recipe. Senior foods provide balanced nutrition with extra calcium already added for much-needed bone density. If your veterinarian does not prescribe additional supplements, your dog probably doesn't need them, especially if he is already eating a premium, well-balanced dog food. Everything he needs is contained in that recipe.

4

Medical Care Every Yorkshire Terrier Needs

In This Chapter

❍ Your Yorkshire Terrier's Veterinary Care
❍ Preventive Medicine
❍ Spaying and Neutering
❍ Sick Calls and Emergencies

T o ensure that your Yorkshire Terrier will have a long, active life, it's important that you provide her with good preventive health care. Careful observations of your dog's physical condition and her everyday behavior will tell you whether everything is all right. If you notice anything unusual, call or visit your veterinarian. The right veterinarian will take an interest in your Yorkie's health and be able to give regular exams, inoculations, and treat any illnesses that might come up.

Your Yorkshire Terrier's Veterinary Care

Besides yourself, a good veterinarian should be your dog's best friend. After you have selected a vet who is familiar with Yorkshire Terriers and is someone you can trust, regular visits for vaccines or checkups should be pleasurable experiences for both you and your Yorkie. If your dog does have an emergency, your vet is someone you can rely on to treat your dog using the latest veterinary information and medical equipment available.

Selecting the Right Vet

People usually look for a veterinarian when they get a new puppy or dog, have just moved into town, or are dissatisfied with their present veterinarian. The worst time to choose a new veterinarian is when your dog has an emergency. Therefore, begin your search when the need isn't immediate and you don't have to rely on a new doctor to make a life-or-death decision for your Yorkie.

Just as you would be very selective when choosing a doctor for yourself, the process of finding a veterinarian for your dog should be just as thorough. Although you'll probably find many vets listed in the phone book and perhaps a few whose offices are close to your home, it's important that you choose the right veterinarian. While having your veterinarian's office close to your home certainly helps if you have an emergency, don't choose your vet solely on the basis of convenience. The doctor should be someone you like and feel comfortable talking with, as well as someone who enjoys working with Toy dogs and has extensive knowledge about them.

To start your search for the right veterinarian, contact your regional Yorkshire Terrier club for a

Oh, So Special

What's a veterinary specialist? That term can be confusing to owners. A glance under the heading "Veterinarian" in the yellow pages reveals a wide variety of listings under the vets' names: general medicine, specializing in surgery, cancer treatments, cardiology, vaccinations, dentistry, internal medicine. But a veterinary specialist isn't a practitioner who limits her practice to dogs or is interested in a particular area of medicine, such as dentistry. A veterinary specialist is a veterinarian who is board certified by a specialty board approved by the American Veterinary Medical Association (AVMA).

To earn the title of veterinary specialist, the veterinarian must complete a veterinary school program approved by the AVMA, usually extends her education by completing a one-year internship and a two- or three-year residency program in a particular discipline. She must be licensed to practice veterinary medicine in at least one state.

Once the educational requirements are finished, the vet then has to pass a battery of rigorous examinations in her field. Only then can he receive official certification by a specialty board, such as the American College of Veterinary Behaviorists or the American College of Zoological Medicine. Certification requirements vary but are governed by the American Board of Veterinary Specialists (ABVS).

The Board has specific guidelines on how specialists may list names or practices. Veterinarians may not imply or infer that they're specialists when they aren't. The terms an owner should look for when seeking out a true specialist are board certified (board eligible or board qualified aren't the same and are considered misleading by the ABVS), diplomate, ACVIM (American College of Veterinary Internal Medicine), and ABVP. The board-certified veterinary specialist's name and title are usually listed like this: Mary Veterinarian, D.V.M., Diplomate American Board of Veterinary Practitioners, Board Certified in Surgery.

If your Yorkshire Terrier requires the services of a veterinary specialist, your general practitioner will usually give you a referral. If you want to contact a specialist on your own, contact your local or state veterinary association for a name or call the American Veterinary Medical Association at (800) 248-2862 for a listing of board certified vets in your area. If you live near a school of veterinary medicine, contact the college. Many specialists work at veterinary colleges.

list of veterinarians familiar with the specific health problems of the breed. The local and state veterinary associations also have a list of veterinarians available. Contact the American Animal Hospital Association (AAHA) to determine whether the animal hospitals you are considering are members of this organization. The standards set for medical procedures and hospital management for participating AAHA members are strict and establish that the facility is a cut above other offices who are not members.

Don't forget to ask your breeder for recommendations. If your breeder does not live close to you, he or she might know breeders who do live in or near your city. Another good method of finding a vet is to ask friends and neighbors who own dogs for their recommendations. Regardless of the praise someone heaps on a veterinarian, check him or her out yourself to make sure this one is the right veterinarian for you and your Yorkie.

There are a few different types of veterinary practices to consider. A veterinarian may operate his own practice as a sole practitioner, or several doctors can share duties within a larger facility. Other veterinarians work in a franchise operation, or if you're lucky enough to live near a major university with a veterinary department and a teaching hospital, you have access to these public hospitals.

> Regardless of the praise someone heaps on a veterinarian, check him or her out yourself to make sure this one is the right veterinarian for you and your Yorkie.

Call the offices of veterinarians you are considering and ask what days and hours they are open and what after-hours facility they recommend you call should your dog have an emergency when the office is closed.

Find out if you can schedule a consultation with either the office manager or the veterinarian and ask for a tour of the facility.

There may be a charge for the consultation. You will want to see the waiting area, the exam rooms, the laboratory, the operating room and any adjoining recovery rooms. Hopefully you will find clean areas without too strong an antiseptic smell. Since a dog's sense of smell is much greater than ours, a powerful odor can make your dog uncomfortable when he visits the doctor.

While a sole practitioner can really get to know you and your dog, be sure another veterinarian is accessible when the regular doctor is on vacation or is otherwise unavailable. Another question to ask the sole practitioner is how often he is able to attend continuing education seminars that teach new techniques and the latest advances in veterinary research.

In many large practices, it's not always possible to see the same veterinarian every time you take your dog in for a procedure. If you are not comfortable with this, ask whether you can request the same doctor. Some clinics offer other services such as training classes, grooming, and boarding, and sell supplies such as dog food. This is a plus if you also need these services and amenities.

Other information you will want to know is what the office fee schedule is for routine procedures such as regular exams and vaccinations, and prescription products you will need for your canine medicine chest, including ear cleaning fluid, antibiotic ointment, and heartworm and flea prevention medications. Be sure you ask how the office prefers you pay for services rendered. Is the entire balance due when each visit is over, or are timely payments acceptable?

When you meet with the veterinarian, ask where he practiced veterinary medicine before and what his area of expertise is. If he has treated several other Yorkshire Terriers in his career, that is a bonus. Ask what he thinks about your breed and how he treats breed-specific problems. Find out his

basic philosophy regarding general treatment—does he rely solely on traditional medicine or will he sometimes look to alternative therapy as a solution? If this veterinarian cannot treat a problem, will he refer you to a veterinary specialist who can?

Just for fun, ask the veterinarian if he has a dog himself and how long he has had that dog. If he has dealt with some of the same problems, he will be even better prepared to give sound advice.

The answers to these questions are important, but above everything the veterinarian who treats your dog should be someone you trust and who can communicate in terms you can easily understand.

Observe how the staff interacts with other patients and dogs who have come to see the doctor. All office staff members should be pleasant to you and appear comfortable around the dogs there for appointments. The last thing you want is a technician who is afraid of dogs. Technicians should be knowledgeable enough to answer general health questions yet should not dispense medical advice themselves.

Remove from your list the name of any veterinarian who appears rude or brisk when you ask a question or uses a lot of medical jargon you don't understand.

Check several different facilities to compare your impressions and evaluate the pluses and minuses of each professional office. When you have chosen a veterinarian, schedule a routine physical for your dog as a first visit.

Your Yorkshire Terrier's First Visit— What to Expect

The first time you take your Yorkie to see the veterinarian, bring in a fresh stool sample that can be checked for parasites. Once you and your dog arrive at your veterinarian's, expect your canine companion to act differently than he does at home. In the parking lot or in the waiting room, your Yorkie is likely to encounter other breeds and sizes of dogs that he has never seen before so may either act afraid or aggressive. Because dogs have a very strong sense of smell, your dog will sniff the air and detect odors of other dogs who recently visited the office. If those dogs were afraid, your dog will pick up on that particular scent. Most likely he, too, will act afraid—before he ever sees the veterinarian!

For your dog's first visit, schedule a time when you are not rushed, especially if you have to wait to see the vet. Your dog will pick up on your feelings of impatience or apprehension. If you feel confident, your dog will tend to be confident, too. Make sure your dog is wearing a collar that fits properly and walk her in on a leash. If she walks into the office instead of you carrying her, she will feel more secure in her new environment. If you are bringing a young puppy in for vaccines, however, she is still building up her immunity so it's best to carry her in so she does not come into contact with dogs who might have a communicable disease.

Bring whatever medical records you have from the breeder or from your previous vet. The office manager will probably ask you to fill out a questionnaire describing your dog's vital statistics such as her breed, age, sex; where you acquired her; whether she has any previous health problems; and what you are bringing her in for that day. Describe other pets your dog lives with and what her normal exercise routine is. Be sure to list what kind of food she eats and the amount, as this will help the veterinarian evaluate your dog's nutritional

Did You Know?

Shelters in the United States take in nearly 11 million cats and dogs each year. Nearly 75 percent of those animals have to be euthanized.

Questions to Ask Your Vet

○ How many other Yorkies have you cared for?

○ What do you know about the original purpose the Yorkie was bred for and what do you know about the breed's nature and personality? You want to make sure your vet is aware of the Yorkie's unique medical problems and is aware of the latest treatment procedures.

○ Whom do you consult concerning a medical problem you're not familiar with?

○ Do you perform your own surgical procedures?

○ Who monitors the dogs after surgery and where are they cared for?

○ How much veterinary education do you require your staff to have? If other veterinarians also see your patients, what is their medical background?

○ How often do you attend veterinary conventions to learn about new medical procedures?

○ Do you have your own laboratory in the office? If you send lab work to an outside service, where is it located and how long does it take to get results back?

○ What areas do you specialize in?

○ Are your dogs involved in any dog sports?

health. Be as honest as you can about your dog's lifestyle and habits so your veterinarian can make an accurate diagnosis. This is the beginning of your dog's medical history which will help your veterinarian keep track of your dog's health and any continuing problems.

An animal health technician will probably weigh your dog and take her temperature when you come in and will ask whether your dog is having any problems you want to discuss with the vet. Once the examining veterinarian enters the room, he should greet your dog in a friendly and comfortable manner. Either he will ask you to sit down and hold the dog in your lap or will prefer

What the Veterinarian Might Ask You

○ Have you had a dog before? Have you had a Yorkshire Terrier before?

○ When was the last time you took her to a veterinarian?

○ Are you having any problems with her training?

○ Do you plan to spay (or neuter) your Yorkie (if that has not already been done)?

○ How many hours a day do you spend with your dog?

○ What type of activities do you like to do with your dog?

○ Do you notice any problems with her eating or eliminating?

○ Do you use a crate?

○ Have you noticed any signs of illness, such as general lethargy, loose stools, poor appetite, excessive sneezing or coughing, or any discharges from the eyes or ears?

○ What are you feeding your dog and how much?

that you put your Yorkie up on the examining table. Some veterinarians will also offer a healthful treat to your dog to win her trust. Hopefully your vet will be able to take the necessary time to explain a vaccination or a treatment plan.

Your veterinarian will look at your Yorkie's overall appearance, including her beautiful coat, feet, head, eyes, mouth, teeth, and gums. He will look into your dog's ears with an otioscope to determine whether she has an ear infection, and use a stethoscope to listen to her heart and lungs.

This is also a good time to discuss having your Yorkie spayed if she isn't already (owners of male Yorkies will discuss neutering). It's also a good opportunity to find out anything special you should know about Yorkies, including keeping them fed properly so their blood sugar level doesn't drop too low and lead to hypoglycemia.

You also don't want to let your Yorkie get too fat. This is also a good time to discuss having your Yorkie's teeth cleaned on a regular basis.

Preventive Medicine

By being aware of weaknesses to which Yorkies are prone, you'll be in a better position to avoid some health problems before they begin. Working with your veterinarian will help you learn what to look for and how to treat problems if they do crop up.

Annual Visits

Dogs should have annual checkups just like people do. Each year your veterinarian will examine your dog and check her general health and give her a booster vaccine. There is yet another reason to take your dog to visit the doctor each year: Your vet will have the opportunity to detect problems before they are apparent to you and before they turn into full-blown emergencies. Your veterinarian is trained to see symptoms that many well-meaning and conscientious owners never notice. Often when a problem is detected early enough, you can do something before it is too late.

> Your veterinarian is trained to see symptoms that many well-meaning and conscientious owners never notice.

The annual exam is also a good time for the veterinarian to tell you the latest medical developments regarding your breed and to answer any questions you might have. It's also a good opportunity to teach your dog to trust her veterinarian and to let him examine her as needed. In case your Yorkie ever experiences real pain, she will understand the vet is not causing the problem and will allow him to touch her.

What to Expect   When you bring your dog in for her annual checkup, her weight and temperature will be taken. The doctor will also check her pulse and respiration rate and take a good look at her eyes, which can indicate problems such as anemia, jaundice, glaucoma, and other eye diseases. He'll look for any inflammation or odd discharge coming from your dog's eyes, ears, and nose, or any unusual change in shape or color of your Yorkie's nose and mouth. If the vet notices your Yorkie scratching at her body or shaking her head, or if he notices an unpleasant odor coming from the head area, he'll check for ear infection.

He will also feel your dog's major organs through her thick, silky coat to make sure they are not enlarged and that she has no tumors. The anal area will also be examined to make sure she doesn't have diarrhea, parasites, or anal gland infection. Feeling over the genital area will reveal any tumors or discharges. By putting his stethoscope up to your dog's heart and lungs, your vet will make sure she shows no signs of heart disease.

Assuming all is okay, you'll take your dog home with a clean bill of health. If the doctor does find something wrong, he may recommend laboratory tests, X-rays, a urine or a blood test, or an electrocardiogram. The office should have the results back to you as quickly as possible and your veterinarian should personally explain what the laboratory results signify.

Vaccinations

Dogs are susceptible to several deadly and crippling infectious diseases. With the exception of rabies, people will not get these diseases from dogs. Humans can, however, transmit them to other dogs, as viruses will cling to clothing, hands, and shoes. Fortunately, with the help of modern medicine, veterinary researchers have developed vaccines that can prevent these diseases from affecting your Yorkshire Terrier. Rabies, parvovirus, canine distemper, canine hepatitis, parainfluenza, and distemper are among the viral infections that are dangerous to dogs. The vaccines to combat these are given in a series with a booster application once a year or every other year.

> Rabies, parvovirus, canine distemper, canine hepatitis, parainfluenza, and distemper are among the viral infections that are dangerous to dogs.

When a vaccine is introduced into your dog's system, it stimulates her body's immune system to produce antibodies that fight infection. The antibodies remain in the blood system to repel disease. Puppies under the age of eight weeks do not need vaccines if their mother has been inoculated. Her immunity passes through the colostrum, a substance puppies get from the mother's first milk as they nurse. Sometime after eight weeks this immunity begins to fade, and puppies need extra protection in the form of the vaccine. A series of vaccines slowly builds puppies' immune systems.

Until the series is completed, many veterinarians recommend that owners not allow their puppy to interact with strange dogs and that they keep her completely away from public grassy areas until her immunity is built up. Because these spots attract stray dogs that haven't been vaccinated, a new puppy is most likely to pick up diseases in such locations. Many of these diseases are transmitted through infected feces and saliva excretions. If a puppy happens to step in these dangerous deposits and later licks her feet, she will ingest the dangerous substances. By the time a dog is 17 or 18 weeks of age, her immune system should be stronger, but you should always be cautious when taking your dog around neighborhood areas where stray dogs are likely to visit.

When to Vaccinate

Vaccinations should never be given to a puppy or a dog if she is not feeling her best. If your dog is having a bout with diarrhea, is vomiting or coughing, or has missed a few meals, her immune system is already too stressed to receive the benefits of a vaccine.

Make sure your Yorkshire Terrier puppy has had a meal before shots are given or at least right afterward. The stress of the experience can cause her to lose her appetite, which may contribute to the onset of hypoglycemia.

Be sure to avoid giving a vaccine right before traveling, as the excitement or stress of the experience can make your dog more susceptible to coming down with the illness itself.

Always watch your puppy for at least two to three hours after a vaccine has been given to make sure she does not have a reaction. If her gums are pale or gray, or if she seems weak and is trembling, or develops hives or red splotches, she is having a reaction. Other signs include swollen eyelids, excessive itching, coughing, vomiting, or diarrhea. If you see these symptoms, rush your dog to your veterinarian.

Recommended Vaccinations

Veterinarians usually recommend a series of three shots, each of which includes parvo, adenovirus 2, parainfluenza, and distemper. At about four to six months of age a rabies vaccination should be given. Some vets also vaccinate against adenovirus and

leptospirosis, depending on whether you live in an area where those infections are likely to occur. Your puppy should receive her first booster shot once she reaches a year of age. The booster should be repeated once a year or every two to three years, depending upon your own veterinarian's recommendation, and state law in the case of rabies.

Because opinions differ as to when these should be given, consult your veterinarian. He will make his decision based on current research, the prevalence of disease in your area, and your individual Yorkie's needs.

Other vaccines are available for the prevention of Lyme, bordetella, and coronavirus; however, these should only be given when the dog is at risk for these diseases. Bordetella is usually given if a dog is to be boarded at a kennel facility or is going to a dog show where she might be exposed to dozens of dogs.

Every area of the country has certain infectious diseases specific to that location. Usually the local university veterinary teaching hospitals will prescribe a vaccine protocol that veterinarians in the area can rely on. Tell your veterinarian if you plan to travel with your dog so he can recommend other vaccines your dog might need for the utmost protection.

While most veterinary offices keep track of your dog's vaccine schedule, this is also your responsibility. Keep a file folder with your Yorkshire Terrier's important information, and be sure to note the date and the type of vaccine your dog has been given. Know when the vaccines should be repeated and mark the dates on your calendar. That way, if your vet forgets to send you a reminder card or his computer system fails, you have your own records. This file is also a good place to keep the receipts your vet gives you when he administers vaccines. You may need to produce this verification later if you take your dog to be boarded at a kennel or travel out of state with her.

Spaying and Neutering

You have probably heard a lot about having your Yorkshire Terrier spayed or neutered and may wonder what those terms really mean.

As early as it sounds, puppies sexually mature between the ages of six to nine months. Their hormones begin to activate and the dog is capable of reproducing. Most females start their estrus or heat cycle when they are six months old and will repeat the cycle in another six months. The heat cycle, which is also called a "season," begins with proestrus, which is the bleeding people see most often. This can last anywhere from one to 15 days, depending upon the individual female. Sometimes the bleeding will taper off or stop completely with only a straw-colored discharge in some females, but this signals the start of the estrus cycle. During the estrus cycle, a female is the most fertile and likely to be more attractive to male dogs. She may flirt with males and lift her rear while twitching her tail back and forth. Females during this time may also be hyperactive or seem stressed. Although the total length of the heat cycle is different for individual females, the cycle is no longer than 30 days.

Once male dogs are sexually mature, they can breed females in heat at any time. Once male dogs have been bred a few times, they usually know when a

> **Did You Know?**
>
> Tests conducted at the Institute for the Study of Animal Problems in Washington, D.C., revealed that dogs and cats, like humans, are either right- or left-handed.

Myths About Spaying and Neutering

Myth: Spaying or neutering takes away my dog's personality.

Truth: This is simply not true. Since this surgery is usually done when a dog reaches adulthood and naturally stops acting puppyish, most people blame the procedure.

Myth: My Yorkie will get fat.

Truth: Some dogs do add some ounces after this surgery, but it's more due to a change in his natural metabolism. Make sure you cut the food slightly and add in more exercise.

female in heat is fertile—and that's without looking at a calendar! If a male is not neutered, he is constantly sniffing the air to locate females in season and frequently marks his territory on the chance that a female in heat is around. A once housetrained male can suddenly begin to lift his leg on furniture or draperies inside the house if he thinks a fertile female is near. Sometimes unneutered males will also grasp pillows or someone's leg and hump them as if they were a female in season.

Having an unspayed female or an unneutered male around the house is not relaxing. And it's no fun for the dog, either, unless he or she is allowed to roam and breed at will. Here's where spay and/or neuter surgery can make life with a dog a pleasure again.

Besides preventing pregnancies, spaying or neutering your dog can save his or her life. A spayed female is protected from uterine infections and uterine cancer, whereas a neutered male can avoid the threat of prostate disease and testicular cancer since both testicles are removed from the dog's scrotum during surgery. Dogs who are not going to be bred should be spayed or neutered. This is healthier for your dog and also helps to control pet overpopulation.

Neutering is also called orchiectomy, or castration. Recovery is quick and can be done anytime after the male is eight weeks old. It's best to neuter a male by the time he is six months old, the time he would be physically ready to breed.

In females the spay surgery is called an ovariohysterectomy and it ends the heat cycles and mood swings and removes the ovaries, fallopian tubes, and uterus.

Veterinarians perform both surgeries while the dogs are under a general anesthetic. The procedure is usually done in the veterinarian's operating room and it takes most dogs a few hours to feel like getting up and walking again. There is some pain but your veterinarian can recommend relief medication for your dog. Some vets prefer to keep the dogs overnight while some like to send them home at the end of the day. He or she probably won't feel much like tackling the household at first, but most dogs, especially feisty little Yorkies, are at full-steam within 24 hours. Most females can be spayed as early as four months, but the procedure should be done by six months and before the first season.

> Many county animal control districts offer low-cost spay and neuter surgeries and a reduced license fee for dogs who are permanently altered.

Many county animal control districts offer low-cost spay and neuter surgeries and a reduced license fee for dogs who are permanently altered. Spaying and neutering dogs also prevents many unwanted litters of puppies.

Breeding and Overpopulation

If you have purchased your Yorkshire Terrier to be a wonderful pet and companion and have no plans to exhibit your dog in dog

Myths About Breeding Your Dog

Myth: Breeding a litter of Yorkshire Terriers is a good way to make extra money.

Truth: When a conscientious breeder matches a Champion male with a Champion female Yorkie, she'll incur many expenses before any puppies are ever delivered. The stud fee, or the cost of sending your bitch to be bred may amount to a few hundred dollars. Responsible breeders make sure both the sire and the dam have been cleared of any health problems. This often involves expensive genetic screenings that can cost several hundred to two thousand dollars. Having both parents complete their championship titles can cost several thousand dollars. Once you've paid vet bills for an ultrasound to check the pregnancy and the number of puppies, an X-ray to determine position of the puppies, and the cost of a veterinarian if one assists in the delivery, you'll find you make very little, if any, profit. And that doesn't count puppy supplies such as a whelping box or exercise pens, which can be costly, or the cost of a premium puppy food, toys, blankets, cleaning supplies, first shots, and wormings. Many breeders actually lose money when their female Yorkshire Terrier has a litter.

Myth: We want to have a litter so our child can witness the miracle of birth.

Truth: Most small children (except those who live on a farm and have experienced many animals going through life-cycle events) are frightened by the pain your dog undergoes while delivering puppies. The Yorkie mother will not want a lot of commotion going on while delivering her babies so a small child who clamors for affection at the same time is not a welcome guest at a puppy birthing.

Myth: We love our female Yorkie so much that we want another just like her.

Truth: Forget it. It won't happen. It usually takes two or three generations before any puppies actually resemble their grandmother. Every dog is unique and it's rare to get anything close to a carbon-copy pet.

shows, she should be spayed (or he should be neutered). There is no reason to breed pet-quality Yorkies. Breeding is best accomplished with superior quality males and females who have obtained the American Kennel Club special designations as Champions. This doesn't mean that your dog isn't a great specimen of the breed. No doubt you have purchased her from a reputable breeder and can trace her lineage back four or five generations of quality Yorkshire Terriers, but that alone is not a reason to breed her.

Breeding a litter of puppies is a tremendous responsibility and not something to be taken lightly. Giving birth can often be fatal for your female, or if there is a complication, she may require emergency Cesarean section surgery to save her life and that of her puppies. This may cost you hundreds of dollars. Once puppies are born, you must constantly make sure the mother is feeding them properly. If she isn't, someone will have to supplement the mother's milk by hand-feeding the puppies around the clock from baby bottles filled with formula. Here again complications can occur because a nursing mother may develop an infection or a puppy may become sickly and require additional medical treatment.

Puppies also have to be frequently handled to make sure they become confident, social creatures, and the mother must also be watched all the time so she doesn't roll onto one of her babies and suffocate him.

Even if you know people who say they want to adopt a puppy, you could find yourself in a situation where you're unable to find homes for all of them. What would you do? Until adoptive owners step forward, you'll have to keep them all. Your responsibility as a breeder is to make sure your puppies are properly fed and cared for and never abandoned in an animal shelter. Remember, too, that contributing to the pet overpopulation problem is not being a responsible dog owner.

Sick Calls and Emergencies

Dog owners never relish the thought of rushing their dog to the hospital in an emergency. Hopefully you will never have such an emergency, but it's good to have a plan in case a crisis does come up. It's also helpful to learn basic first aid for your dog and know the difference between a real emergency and what you can do to help your dog.

When to Call the Vet

Because it's not always easy to know when to call your veterinarian, until your observation skills are sharpened you'd be wise to call when you're unsure. The following checklist includes a number of signs to look for before you rush your dog to the vet.

○ *Inability to move.* Your dog had an accident and doesn't respond when you try to move her.

○ *Constant coughing, sneezing, or gagging.* Your Yorkshire Terrier could have a collapsed trachea, or something stuck in her throat.

○ *Straining to urinate or defecate.* She may have a kidney problem, bladder infection, or blockage, especially if she frequently urinates but produces very little urine.

○ *Loss of appetite.* If your dog misses three meals in a row or consumes excessive amounts of water, she may have a serious illness.

○ *Swelling around the face and head.* She may be having an allergic reaction that affects her breathing. This can be fatal.

Signs Your Yorkshire Terrier Is Feeling Under the Weather

Do you suspect your Yorkie is a little under the weather? Below are some signs that may indicate your Yorkie isn't feeling well and needs to see her veterinarian:

○ Acts tired and sluggish and would rather stay in bed or even refuses to fetch a ball

○ Isn't hungry—refuses several meals in a row

○ Drinks an excessive amount of water

○ Throws up several times

○ Diarrhea or blood in stools

○ Whimpers when touched

○ Drools excessively

○ Loses weight but isn't on a weight loss program

○ Gums are very pale or very red

○ Coat looks dull and feels rough

○ Tummy looks bloated

○ Eyes or nose is runny

○ Scoots or bites or chews at rear end

○ Coughs and sneezes a lot

○ Limps or walks abnormally

○ *Bloody urine.* Your Yorkie may have a bladder or prostate infection. Visit the vet.

○ *Distended stomach.* This can be a sign of bloat, which is fatal if untreated, or a sign of parasites or heart disease. Bloat is an emergency.

○ *Neck or back pain.* Your dog yelps if she jerks her head or moves in a certain way.

○ *Abnormal discharge from the eyes, nose, and ears.* An infection might be present.

What to Expect if Your Yorkshire Terrier Is Sick

You may not have to rush your dog to the vet, but medical attention or a call to the vet is necessary. Although you'll usually know when something doesn't look right, these signs will help you know to look for and what they might mean:

○ *Diarrhea.* Several loose stools. Diarrhea that is very bloody and smelly may indicate a serious disease, like parvovirus, that needs immediate attention.

○ *Vomiting.* One or two meals may not have been digested all the way.

○ *Skipping a meal.* If it happens twice, call the vet.

○ *A scrape that turns puffy and swollen.* An infection has probably developed.

○ *Scratching.* Your dog may need an antihistamine to stop the discomfort.

How to Administer Medication and Pills

If your dog requires medication and pills, your vet will likely recommend the best method to give them to your dog. Your vet will tell you whether the medication must be given on an empty stomach or with food. If the medication comes in a liquid form, it is usually okay to mix it in with your dog's regular food or with a little cottage cheese. Check with your Yorkie's veterinarian.

Pills may also be combined with food. Hopefully your dog will love to gobble up a pill right from your hand. If she doesn't, you may have to hide it

Emergency Instructions
for the Boarding Kennel/Pet Sitter

What if your dog becomes sick or gets hurt while you are away? Before you leave your dog at a boarding kennel, ask if they have a veterinarian on staff or if they use one in the area for emergencies. In either case, it's a good idea to give them the name and number of your dog's veterinarian, especially if your Yorkie has a specific medical condition. If you have hired a dog sitter, leave an emergency list with your veterinarian's phone number, the phone number of the local emergency hospital, and the phone number for the National Animal Poison Information Center (800-548-2423). Also leave information on any medications your dog needs or any special medical conditions to watch out for. Prepare for the unexpected to ensure that your dog gets the care she needs should an emergency occur.

in a piece of cheese or beneath a mound of peanut butter. Ask your vet if you can pulverize the pill in a small food grinder then mix it with food. If that's not an option, and your dog spits the whole pill right out, you may need to open your dog's mouth, being sure to point it gently upward, and carefully insert the pill on the very back of your dog's tongue. Hold your dog's jaw closed for a few seconds while you stroke the underjaw at the same time. Continue to hold your dog in this position until you notice her swallowing.

Costs

It's hard to imagine that a tiny Yorkie can cost so much in veterinary bills, but her medical costs add up quickly. Your obligation as a pet owner is to care for your dog, and sometimes this isn't easy. An accident resulting in a broken bone can lead to a cost of several hundred dollars, a big bite out of anyone's budget.

Why Does It Cost So Much?

People think that because a Yorkie is an animal, veterinarians should charge less, and often they do. Most surgical procedures performed on animals, for example, cost much less than the human equivalent. When you evaluate how much rent, upkeep of medical equipment, and compensation for a professional office staff cost, you'll realize that operating expenses for a veterinary clinic are large. Most veterinarians have as much equipment for complicated procedures as they can afford. This includes X-ray machines, labs for analysis, medications, a fully stocked operating room, and after-care facilities. Attending seminars to learn about new procedures is also expensive. Insurance, lease expenses, long hours of staffing, and computers keep a veterinary office bustling and add to the cost of operating one.

How to Discuss Finances with Your Vet

Once you have established a bond with your veterinarian, you should feel comfortable discussing any aspect of your pet's care with him, including the bill. Because regular office visits, vaccinations, and dental care can add up to a few hundred dollars, and an emergency can rise into the thousands, it's important that you are able to talk about this.

Some people feel embarrassed if they cannot pay the entire bill all at once. If payment is an issue for you, bring up the topic when you are discussing treatment options. That way you'll be able to select a therapy that fits your budget. By discussing it prior to treatment, the office understands you have a problem and doesn't think you are avoiding dealing with the issue of payment. Most of us, at one time or another, receive a bill that doesn't fit nicely into our regular budget. No responsible dog owner should have to deny his pet proper medical attention in an emergency because the treatment is unaffordable.

Speak to your veterinarian and be frank about what you can pay. Find out whether you can make payments until your dog's medical bill is paid off. Many offices accept credit cards or are willing to spread the charges out into a few payments.

Sometimes your vet will be able to offer choices regarding your pet's care if payment is an issue. Ask to find out whether a less expensive treatment is available that may be appropriate for your pet.

Savings Plans and Insurance—How They Can Help

Pet insurance has been available for several years, but only 1 percent of pet owners carry it. Having pet insurance for an emergency may be the answer you need to budget concerns.

Although most pet insurance companies do not cover regular care such as vaccinations, routine physicals, or elective surgery, they do handle emergencies if your Yorkie breaks a leg and needs surgery or treatment for other conditions. Some pet-insurance plans include prescription medication and laboratory tests.

Before making the decision whether or not to purchase pet insurance, read all

Did You Know?

The Chihuahua is the world's smallest breed, while the Irish Wolfhound is the largest and the Saint Bernard is the heaviest.

the fine print and call the representative to discuss what is covered and what isn't. There's nothing worse than assuming the bill will be paid, only to discover when funds are short that it was not covered.

You might consider one of several different pet-insurance plans—such as an HMO or preventive program that includes vaccinations and teeth cleaning, for example.

Expect to pay a deductible before you receive any coverage. The amount of the deductible varies depending upon the plan you select. Some plans pay as much as 80 percent of the expenses. Some companies also offer discounts for multiple pets. The bottom line is that different plans have different benefits.

The one disadvantage to pet insurance is that coverage is limited. You may never need to use your policy or it may save you hundreds of dollars, but with pet insurance, you may be better able to choose the level of care your dog receives.

5

Common
Health Concerns

In This Chapter

○ Parasites, Inside and Out
○ Illnesses and Emergencies
○ Obesity
○ Health Concerns Specific to Yorkshire Terriers

Like people, some dogs may develop health problems that need medical attention. Often many of these ailments, such as parasites, can be completely prevented if you take precautions. Other medical emergencies can be abated if you are observant and spot a problem in the early stages. Here it helps to know what to do before you can get your dog to a veterinarian. In addition, every breed of dog is subject to certain genetic diseases and disorders. Learning the conditions to which a Yorkie is susceptible and how to avoid them can add years to your Yorkie's life.

Parasites, Inside and Out

Just the thought of your dog having external or internal parasites can make any owner worry. No one likes parasites, and they are the curse of every animal. Surviving by feeding off other animals' bodies, parasites are bothersome creatures that can make your dog's life uncomfortable at the very least to quite miserable or possibly fatal in extreme cases. Some parasites exist inside and others outside of animals. Fortunately, your dog doesn't have to feel the irritating bites of fleas or suffer the potentially fatal effects of heartworm once you learn about these dangerous pests and know how to provide preventive care.

External Parasites

Three external parasites can wreak havoc on a dog's body: fleas, ticks, and skin mites. A fourth skin irritant, ringworm, is actually a fungus. While infestation is not fatal to your dog, these critters can certainly make his life miserable. The best defense against these varmints is to keep an eye open for their appearance. If you see just one flea on your Yorkie, chances are high that there are more. Each of these troublemakers can be prevented and, should an outbreak occur, remedied. The sooner you recognize the specific parasite, the sooner you can start bringing your dog some relief.

> The best defense against these varmints is to keep an eye open for their appearance.

Fleas   The annoying predator needs a host to survive and presents health problems for both people and dogs. There are more than 2,000 different species of fleas in the world, several in the

United States. When your dog acquires even one flea, he will act as if he has all 2,000! Fleas are troublesome pests you'll wish you and your pet never encountered. Incredibly hardy, fleas are able to survive in almost any climate, but not at high altitudes. With the exception of high mountains, wherever you and your dog go, expect to find fleas. These tiny black or brown pests live for just three to four months, but during that time they reproduce, creating future generations that can make your pet miserable for years.

Besides scratching and biting at himself to get rid of fleas that have bitten him, your dog can suffer from long-lasting damage. Fleas carry diseases such as plague and typhus and can give your dog tapeworms. The flea saliva alone creates a strong allergen for many dogs and causes flea-allergy dermatitis. Your Yorkie's coat can actually fall out if he is allergic to the fleabites. Besides feeling very uncomfortable, a dog with severe flea-allergy dermatitis looks awful. Fleas crawl along the dog's skin, poking in and out of the fur looking for the right place to bite the host. Once they have a blood meal, they can begin to reproduce.

Just one female flea can lay 2,000 eggs during her life span. The eggs usually don't stay on your dog but will fall off and take up residence in your backyard or inside the house in your carpet, furniture, floor crevices, and bedding. When the eggs hatch, the new flea larvae will feast on debris buried deep in carpet pile or couch cushions where they will nest for up to a year. At that point insecticides cannot harm the larvae. When the weather is warm (65 to 80 degrees Fahrenheit) and the humidity is high (70 to 80 percent), the fleas become active again.

It's easy to tell when your dog has fleas because he will use his front teeth to bite closely at his own skin or will constantly scratch himself in an effort to rid himself of the irritating parasites. Rolling on the floor in an attempt to ease the discomfort is another sign that he has fleas.

Catching fleas is not easy. They are very fast and capable of hopping great distances relative to their body size, and usually jump from one area of the dog to another or from your pet's skin onto the carpet or furniture in search of another host. Even if you are able to grab a flea, it will squeeze out from between your fingers and hop into the air in search of another warm body. To find fleas on your Yorkie, look beneath her tail and hindquarters, underneath her forequarters, or in the groin area. Often fleas will be the same color as your dog's undercoat so try using a flea comb through the hair so you can spot them more easily. You may also see their white eggs or their excrement, which can resemble specks of brown or black pepper.

Once fleas find a comfortable environment on your pet and in your household, they can thrive for several years. Add to that a few grassy or sandy areas outside your home where they can also take up residence, and your flea population may number in the tens of thousands. Ridding your Yorkie of these hardy parasites will require a dedicated three-plan attack. Besides treating your dog, everything inside the house—including your carpets, bedding, and furniture—must be thoroughly de-flead. Your entire yard must also be treated.

Many different products on the market are designed to fight fleas that are present on your dog. These include prescription medications, topical remedies you can apply monthly between the shoulder blades, as well as over-the-counter dips, shampoos, powders, sprays, flea collars, and flea combs.

Flea control methods also include flea traps, mechanical removal with vacuums, high-audio frequency sound generators, and drying agents—all of which have been used with varying degrees of success. New advances in flea prevention products continually become available on the market. Many of these are advertised as being safer and more effective than previous treatments. Some of the chemical products, however, can actually harm your dog if used incorrectly or mixed with other products. Check with your veterinarian before administering anything; she can advise you as to the best remedy for your Yorkie.

Many advertisements extol the virtues of flea powders, dipping, and bathing; but the actual effectiveness of these treatments is short-lived. Sprays work for a brief time on a dog with a short coat, but will not penetrate the Yorkie's long, luxurious hair.

A dip can be used once every two weeks. The dog must be bathed first, then the flea dip is poured over him and cannot be rinsed off. A flea collar may prevent a few fleas from swarming near your dog's head, but won't do much to stop fleas from congregating near his hindquarters.

A better line of defense is administering a pill containing lufenuron, which prevents flea eggs from maturing into adults. Given once a month, lufenuron is only effective when a flea bites your dog. The drug is passed to the flea via your dog's bloodstream then affects her eggs, preventing them from hatching. Stray fleas that jump on and off without biting your dog will not be affected by lefenuron. Another disadvantage to this product is that your dog will still suffer from flea dermatitis.

Still another group of prescription products provides all-over protection for your dog and kills fleas on contact. These are a better choice for flea-allergic dogs,

Did You Know?

Dogs have extremely sensitive hearing and a sense of smell up to 1,000 times better than humans to compensate for their relatively poor eyesight.

as fleas don't need to bite to be affected. They are much safer for your dog than dips and sprays. Beware of over-the-counter imitations, though. These may contain toxic chemicals that can make your tiny Yorkie sick. Many people believe that filling your dog's bedding with cedar chips and feeding him garlic will prevent fleas from setting up residence. Garlic, in fact, will make your dog sick.

Still other products are designed to kill fleas in your dog's environment both inside your home and outdoors. These have to be used on the same day you rid your dog of his fleas. Otherwise they will hop off the dog and onto the carpet to set up residence. Vacuuming can remove flea larvae in carpeting and on furniture and prevents newly hatched fleas from beginning an infestation. Be sure to empty the vacuum bag carefully and quickly dispose of it. This will prevent fleas from hatching in the bag and getting back into the household.

> Many people believe that filling your dog's bedding with cedar chips and feeding him garlic will prevent fleas from setting up residence. Garlic, in fact, will make your dog sick.

Insect growth regulators (IGRs) will keep immature fleas from developing in the house, killing them before they mature. Used with a borate powder sprinkled on your carpet and in the corners of your floors, the IGRs are highly useful in your fight against fleas. Hopefully you've saved some time in your de-flea process to also treat your yard. Be sure to clean up any plant debris first, as fleas feed on this material. A spray-contained IGR will interrupt the flea's life cycle. Though safe for your pet, IGRs are dangerous to insects so use them sparingly in limited areas. For a good flea deterrent, keep grass and bushes trimmed.

Revolution is a new product that prevents and controls fleas, heartworm disease, ear mites, sarcoptic mange, and ticks. A topical application, it's given once a month and can be used safely on six-week-old puppies as well as adults. It is available through prescription.

Ticks   Another pest that is a dog's worst enemy is the tick. A dog who has a large number of ticks can become anemic or develop tick paralysis. Ticks are parasites that look like brown or black sesame seeds with eight legs attached. If they are engorged with blood they've siphoned from your dog, they will appear round and bloated. They love to congregate in shady, wooded fields and bushes, although they are also known to exist in grasslands and in every type of weather condition.

To become a host for ticks, all a dog has to do is visit a tick-infested wooded or forested area in spring or summer and pass next to or beneath a bush. These parasites will crawl on the dog and attach themselves immediately. Looking for a meal, they suck blood from a pet by digging in and grabbing hold of the dog's skin with their sharp mouth parts. Most of the time they can be found around the dog's head, neck, ears, and feet, and in the warm, soft areas between the legs and body.

By secreting a cement-like substance made of their own saliva, ticks bond to their hosts, making themselves very difficult to remove. It takes a special tick remover or tweezers to get them to let go of your dog. You should never remove a tick with your bare fingers because their saliva can infect you, too. Be careful not to break off part of the tick when you remove it. Dip it in alcohol or flush it down the toilet so it can't crawl back. Fortunately, ticks don't move very fast.

Ticks carry diseases that can affect both dogs and people. Their saliva can transmit Rocky Mountain spotted fever, ehrlichiosis, tick paralysis, and Lyme disease. They cause anemia, fever, depression, weakness, and wasting away.

Elizabethan Style

Although wearing an Elizabethan collar may sound stylish, its purpose is medicinal. Hopefully your Yorkie won't need one, but if she suffers an injury, a wound, or a skin problem that mustn't be scratched, bitten, or pawed, the Elizabethan collar will do the job. Named for the high neck ruff popular during the reign of Queen Elizabeth, this lampshade-like collar prevents your Yorkie from turning her head to chew and makes scratching nearly impossible. The size of the collar is tailored to fit the size of the dog.

The Elizabethan collar is effective, but it's not always well received by its wearers. It's a bit bulky, and certainly looks funny. Hopefully your Yorkshire Terrier will accept this with good humor.

Be sure to thoroughly examine your Yorkie after every visit outdoors. Separate the long strands of hair and check his skin. The best defense against ticks is to avoid them, and quick removal is almost as good. The sooner a tick is removed the less likely it is to spread disease.

Although many flea products will also rid your dog of ticks, they aren't as effective. The products should be used more frequently than when treating fleas. A permethrin spray or a broad-spectrum insect repellent is effective if you apply it before taking your dog for a walk into tick-infested areas. Other IGR products break the flea and tick life cycles. Several of the prescription topical remedies are quite effective against ticks.

Skin Mites (Mange)   Many reasons could account for your dog's frantic scratching, but if you do not see any fleas, he may actually have mites. You would expect to see some culprit by separating the strands of hair in your dog's coat, but you won't see anything if your itchy dog has mites. Mites are so small they can only be detected by skin scrapings done by a veterinarian. Looking at these scrapings under the microscope could reveal that several different types of mites are bothering your dog.

Sarcoptic mange mites, or scabies, can take up residence anywhere on your dog—most commonly around the elbows, hocks, ears, and face—where they dig under the skin to lay their eggs. Mites irritate the skin uncontrollably, causing "mange." The skin swells and forms pus-filled scabs, often preventing any new hair growth from taking root. Treatment is time-consuming and requires a regular cycle of dipping your dog with a veterinarian-prescribed insecticide and cortisone, a medication given by your veterinarian to ease some of the itchiness.

Demodex mites cause demodectic mange. Demodex mites live on almost all dogs and are passed on by nursing mothers to their puppies. Very few dogs are bothered by this mite, but when a dog's immune system doesn't work well, the mite runs rampant, and the affected area becomes inflamed and hairless. Symptoms first appear around the dog's eyes, elbows, and paws. Some dogs outgrow demodex, particularly if there are only a few spots affected. Most dogs require repeated dips to get well. Because a weak immune system, which allows demodex to spread, may be inherited, dogs that develop this type of disease should not be bred.

Ringworm   A misnamed ailment, ringworm is not a worm but a fungus. It is easily recognized by the distinctive red ring surrounding a circle of hair loss. The ring will form scabs and crusts that become painful sores. In other cases, though, no ring forms, only crusts and scabs appear. If your Yorkie develops

ringworm, he will be contagious to pets and people, especially to children. Avoid touching the area affected by ringworm.

Detecting ringworm isn't always easy, and to isolate this parasite, your veterinarian will have to use an ultraviolet light and obtain skin scrapings, which are placed under a microscope. Once ringworm is confirmed, the infected hair may be trimmed away and a special veterinarian-prescribed shampoo should be used to bathe and soothe the skin, as well as kill the fungus. Antifungal drugs are also successful in the treatment of ringworm. If the exam is inconclusive, a fungal culture will be performed.

> If your Yorkie develops ringworm, he will be contagious to pets and people, especially to children.

Left untreated, the signs of ringworm will usually disappear on their own within three months, but many times the infection remains, and infectious spores are shed into the environment and to people and other pets. Because this disease is so easily spread, it should always be treated as directed by your veterinarian.

Internal Parasites

Other parasites that depend upon your dog to survive live inside his body. Feeding upon your dog's blood, these foes can weaken the animal so severely that they can cause death.

A few different kinds of internal parasites can affect dogs. Most likely you've heard about worms that settle in specific areas of the body and siphon off the dog's supply of nutrients and fluids, which can harm the vital organs. These include roundworms, hookworms, tapeworms, and heartworm. Coccidia and giardia are not worms, but are tiny protozoan parasites that may make your dog sick as well.

Take a fecal sample to your veterinarian so she can check your dog for the presence of internal parasites. Heartworm medication can minimize the presence of worms, but does nothing against coccidia. If your dog is not on heartworm medication, he may be exposed to several internal parasites.

Roundworms   The most common internal parasites are roundworms. Resembling long strands of white spaghetti, they appear in the feces of young puppies. If roundworms are present in the womb, they will be transmitted from mother to puppy. They can also be picked up from a contaminated environment. Adult dogs often tolerate roundworms without any ill effects, but puppies can become very sick if they have a lot of them. Infection from roundworms can also be fatal for some puppies.

A puppy with roundworms has a dull coat with a heavy, swollen belly while his legs and chest look underweight. Symptoms of roundworm include diarrhea, vomiting, coughing, and possibly pneumonia. If you suspect your puppy has roundworms, contact your veterinarian immediately. She will ask you to bring in a fecal sample so that she can check it for the presence of roundworms.

Dogs rarely transmit roundworms to children and adults who handle them or play in grass-infected areas that may have eggs deposited on fecal material. In people, these worms don't live in the intestines, but the tiny larvae migrate through skin, causing problems if they travel to the brain, eye, or other internal organs. To avoid contact with round-worm infection in your own backyard, maintain sanitary conditions by promptly picking up feces and disposing of them in a sealed container. If your veterinarian detects the presence of roundworms, she can give you a deworming medication.

Hookworms   These internal parasites are dangerous if your dog comes in contact with them. Like the name suggests, these small worms are shaped like hooks and are about a quarter-inch to a half-inch long. Particularly found in warm, humid areas, they are most prevalent in the southern United States.

Originally these worms are transmitted to young puppies through their mother's milk, although grown dogs can get them by stepping on contaminated feces or soil. They can hook themselves into your dog through his feet and migrate to the intestines, or your dog can swallow them while licking. They remain in the intestine, feeding off the animal's blood supply and reproducing. The eggs are laid in the stool, and they hatch in the environment, where they wait, ready to infect other dogs who walk through the contaminated areas. Signs of hookworms in young puppies include anemia and bloody or black diarrhea. These symptoms are often fatal to puppies. Older dogs may show some of the same signs as puppies, with the addition of vomiting and an inability to maintain their body weight, but they rarely die. To detect hookworms, your veterinarian can check the dog's stool for the presence of eggs. Medication is available to rid the intestines of hookworm; however, a dog can develop another hookworm infestation if he comes in contact with contaminated environments.

Tapeworms   If you see small, white segments resembling rice clinging to the fur around your dog's anus, these are most likely dried-out tapeworms. These flat, ribbon-like worms are transmitted by fleas and can be shorter than an inch to as long as several feet. When a dog bites at an annoying flea, he can swallow the tapeworm egg, then when it is inside the dog's body, the cycle begins. If a dog is flea-infested, he likely has tapeworms too.

Tapeworms can also be found in some rodents and in dead animals, so never allow your Yorkie to eat these creatures if he encounters them.

Although tapeworms do not pose serious health problems for dogs, they will produce diarrhea, loss of appetite, and poor coat condition.

If you suspect that your dog has tapeworms, take a stool sample to your veterinarian and let her check for the presence of tapeworm eggs and make the diagnosis. If your dog does have tapeworms, your veterinarian can prescribe a deworming product.

Heartworms   Of all the internal parasites, heartworms are the deadliest. Found in areas of the United States where the mosquito population is the highest, heartworms are transmitted by common mosquitoes when they bite dogs. When a mosquito bites a dog, it injects tiny microfilaria—immature heartworms—into the dog's body. In a short time, they work their way into a vein and into the dog's bloodstream. Eventually they settle in the right side of the heart and in the pulmonary artery. Growing to adulthood takes almost six months, during which time they reproduce inside the heart, continuing the cycle. The microfilaria, or live offspring, live in the dog's bloodstream and are sucked up by mosquitoes as they drink a dog's blood. These mosquitoes then carry the microfilaria to other dogs that they bite.

> Adult heartworms can grow up to a foot long, blocking blood flow from a dog's heart to his lungs.

Adult heartworms can grow up to a foot long, blocking blood flow from a dog's heart to his lungs. The most common result of infestation is heart failure, but liver and kidney disease can also occur. Because a Yorkie heart is so small—about the size of a plump strawberry—and a heartworm is so large, Yorkies can develop serious disease with only one or two worms. The first signs are usually difficulty breathing, coughing, and lack of energy. In some dogs the first sign may be collapse or death. To confirm a diagnosis of heartworm disease, a veterinarian needs to take a blood test, possibly followed by X-rays.

Treatment for heartworm is difficult in part because dying heartworms may be carried into the lungs by the blood flow, especially if the dog exercises hard. This can make breathing difficult and death may occur.

Although over 90 percent of dogs with early heartworm disease are cured with treatment, preventing the disease is the easiest remedy. Even if you do not live in an area where heartworms are a problem, your Yorkie can come in contact with a stray mosquito even if he just goes outside for a brief period. Therefore, it's best to place your dog on a preventive heartworm medication that can be safely given once a month throughout the year. Puppies can begin taking preventive medicine at ten weeks of age, and as early as six months of age, your Yorkie can be checked for the presence of heartworm with a blood test. If he does not already have heartworm, your veterinarian can prescribe this medication. In chewable form, most Yorkies happily take it.

If for some reason you take your Yorkie off this medication, your vet will have to give him another blood test before prescribing it again.

Coccidia   A puppy raised in a clean, spacious environment will probably not have coccidia. A protozoan parasite, coccidia are normally found in the intestinal tract of puppies who are kept in filthy, overcrowded conditions. Puppies kept in pet shops, irresponsible breeders' kennels or shelters,

Collecting a Fecal Sample

When your veterinarian asks you to bring in a fecal sample, don't panic. You don't need to know how to perform sophisticated laboratory techniques. Collecting a fecal sample is easy and isn't messy. Follow your dog outside with a sandwich-sized plastic bag and a leftover food container that has a tight-fitting lid, such as an empty cottage cheese, sour cream, or margarine container. Use the plastic bag to pick up a piece of your dog's stool and place it inside the container. You do not need the entire elimination. Close the lid and take it to your veterinarian, making sure you label the container with your name, your dog's name, and the date the sample was taken. If you are unable to deliver it to your veterinarian within a few hours, refrigerate it.

or in puppy mills are most likely to be infested. Once infected, a puppy spreads coccidia to other puppies through its infested feces. Once contaminated with coccidia, kennels and yards are extremely difficult to clean.

Symptoms of this condition begin with mild diarrhea and progress to a bloody and mucus-type loose stool. Left untreated the dog can lose weight, feel weak, suffer dehydration, and become anemic; although most puppies show only minor illness, coccidia can be fatal if the infection is serious. Your veterinarian can check a stool sample for the presence of this parasite. If it is present, she can prescribe a medication for your dog. At the same time be sure to thoroughly clean your dog's outdoor environment by mixing a small amount of bleach into a spray bottle filled with water and spraying it on areas where infected feces were left before. You'll also want to recheck the stool several weeks after stopping medication to make sure the puppy has not been reinfected.

To prevent coccidia from beginning, pick up puppy waste as soon as possible. If you take your dog on outings to public places, be sure he stays away from other fecal matter left from other dogs. Before boarding your Yorkie at a kennel, ask the owner if you can inspect the premises. If it is unsanitary, find another place to leave your pet.

Giardia   Giardia is a protozoan parasite that can affect people as well as dogs. It is transmitted from animal to animal through stagnant, fecal-contaminated water that is left untreated. While giardia is rarely fatal, the parasite usually makes its host very uncomfortable. Drinking from a water supply that has been contaminated with the waste of other animals will cause mild stomach upset and diarrhea, which may be semi-formed, liquid, or explosive.

If you think your Yorkie doesn't have a chance of coming into contact with this parasite because you don't take him on hikes or camping into wildlife areas, guess again. Giardia can be contracted anywhere outdoors, or even from contaminated wells. If your dog finds a puddle in your neighborhood park and goes to it for a sniff or decides to take a sip of it, he can get giardia. Puppies are particularly susceptible and can get severely ill though adult dogs and humans can contract giardia as well. To control these protozoa, do not allow your Yorkie to drink anything other than water you provide while on an outing. If you do take him camping and want to use a local water source, boil the water first. You can also treat the water with a special chemical designed to kill this parasite. If you suspect your dog may have giardia, your veterinarian can check a stool sample for the presence of protozoa and can administer a medication that will kill these organisms.

How to Perform CPR on Your Yorkie

If you realize your dog is not breathing or has no heartbeat, transport him to the veterinarian immediately. On your way, try cardiopulmonary resuscitation (CPR). Although this is not a foolproof method to save your dog's life, the effort is worthwhile if your dog isn't breathing or is gasping for breath. The technique is difficult even for professionals but may be the only thing you can do for your dog in an extreme emergency.

First, check breathing, then look in your dog's throat and clear the airway of any objects. Next check if he is breathing at all. You can do this by watching his chest to see if it moves up or down. Holding a mirror to his nose may indicate a slight respiration if fog appears on the glass.

If your dog is not breathing, clear the airway and then grasp his muzzle closed and place your mouth over his nose and blow four or five quick breaths. Check for signs of breathing. If there is no response, repeat the procedure. Continue doing so until the dog is breathing on his own.

Feel your dog's inner thigh for a pulse. Check for a heartbeat on the chest at the spot where the elbow usually rests. If there is no heartbeat or pulse, lay him on his right side in front of you. Place your dog's left elbow back to his chest, simulating a normal standing position. This marks the heart. Slide the elbow out of the way, using two to three fingers to press his chest sharply where his left elbow lies. Repeat ten rapid compressions, one after another. Give your dog three breaths, then check for a pulse and breathing. Continue CPR until you have positive results and your dog has a strong heartbeat or pulse.

Illnesses and Emergencies

While it would be great if your dog never became ill or had an emergency, the reality is that someday he might. Like humans, dogs can get sick despite our best preventive measures. You should contact your veterinarian immediately if you suspect a serious problem, but it's helpful to know basic canine first aid so that you can assist your dog and make him comfortable until you can get him to the vet.

Insect Bites and Stings

Even if your Yorkie doesn't have too many opportunities to explore the great outdoors where bees, wasps, spiders, and mosquitoes are apt to be, a stray insect can always find its way indoors. Naturally, your dog will want to check out these creatures, and might get bitten in the process. You may not see the bug, but your Yorkie's body may react when he is bitten or stung. He may break out in hives, have severe itching, or have swelling in a localized area of his body.

Try to remain as calm as possible while examining the bite. Avoid touching this spot, as it is probably painful to your dog. However, if you see a stinger from a bee, use tweezers to carefully remove it. Avoid squeezing the sack attached to the stinger, as this will inject more toxin throughout your dog's body.

Giving your dog an antihistamine such as Benadryl will reduce the swelling in hives or injured areas. Before doing so, call your veterinarian to find out how much to give your Yorkie. If your dog has any trouble breathing or has facial swelling, rush him to the veterinarian right away. Swelling in the throat will impair breathing, which may lead to collapse and death.

Vomiting

It is not uncommon for dogs to vomit once or twice on occasion. This may be due to gulping too much water, chewing sharp blades of grass that irritate the lining of the throat, or eating something that didn't agree with them. If there are no other symp-

How to Take Your Yorkie's Temperature

This procedure sounds harder than it actually is. Once you get the hang of it, you'll be able to do it quickly and easily. Taking your dog's temperature will come in handy throughout his life, as diagnosis and treatment for many medical conditions depends on this information.

If you have someone who can assist you by holding the dog so he doesn't fuss, that helps. Start with a digital rectal thermometer that you have wiped with alcohol. Generously lubricate it with petroleum jelly and gently insert it into the rectum. It should remain there until it beeps. Remove it gently and ask your assistant to reward your Yorkie with a treat and tell him he's a good dog. If the temperature reads 103 degrees Fahrenheit or higher, there is infection or illness present. A 105-degree reading or above is an emergency.

toms, it's probably not too serious. Come mealtime, skip the regular food, letting the stomach rest for a full 24 hours. After that, a small meal of boiled rice and boiled chicken is best. If he keeps that down for one or two meals and he seems okay otherwise, add in his regular food by the third meal.

If your dog is vomiting and she is under a year old, is older than eight or nine, or has a serious medical condition such as diabetes, she should see the veterinarian right away. You should also take him to the veterinarian if she is running a fever (a temperature greater than 103°F). Unproductive vomiting demands a different course of action. This may be a symptom of bloat, and requires emergency veterinary attention.

However, if he repeatedly vomits or if he has stomach pains when touched or seems to feel sick, notify your veterinarian right away. This may be a sign of something more serious, such as poisoning, kidney failure, internal parasites, a foreign object lodged in the intestines, or cancer. Too much vomiting can cause dehydration so be sure your Yorkie has access to fresh water and drinks as much as he wants. Your veterinarian will determine what the problem is and prescribe treatment.

Diarrhea

Diarrhea is similar to vomiting in that it is either caused by something very inconsequential or is the result of a serious illness. It's a normal feeling for owners to experience panic when their dog has a loose stool, especially when it happens in the car or on the good rug. But if a dog has one or two loose stools, it does not necessarily mean the dog has a serious case of diarrhea. If the loose stools are followed by a normal bowel movement and he shows no other signs of illness, your dog is probably okay.

> Diarrhea can result from several different causes such as when a new food is introduced, he has had too much to eat, or he has eaten food that's too rich.

Keep an eye on your dog when he goes outside and watch to see if he is straining or if there is any blood present in his stool. Note the color and texture in case your veterinarian asks about it later. Diarrhea can result from several different causes such as when a new food is introduced, he has had too much to eat, or he has eaten food that's too rich. He can also lose bowel control if his water source has changed, he's feeling nervous due to an emotional upset, or has experienced too much excitement. A new travel experience can also send your dog's bowels into an uproar. If diarrhea is still present after a day or there is blood in the stool, your dog should probably see a veterinarian. If vomiting is also a symptom, most likely a problem exists. Call your veterinarian. Be sure to note the bowel changes in your dog and report them to your vet promptly. He may ask you to describe the color of the loose stool, and whether or not there has also been a bloody discharge, and may request a stool sample. If your veterinarian thinks that the diarrhea may be caused by a more serious disease, he may order some tests. Once the cause is known, treatment can include an over-the-counter human medication or one especially prescribed by your veterinarian. Many veterinarians recommend that you not feed your dog his regular kibble or canned food for a day or so and instead offer him cottage cheese and some rice to settle his stomach. Several smaller meals are recommended instead of one or two large ones. Make sure he continues to drink water so he doesn't become dehydrated.

Choking

Dogs love to snoop along and find interesting things to put into their mouths. Unfortunately, not everything they chew on is safe. If they swallow something that doesn't go all the way down, they can choke. Sounds of choking include coughing or gagging, although a foreign object can be lodged in their throats and you may not be able to hear anything. He may have other signs, such as struggling or thrashing on the ground while pawing at his mouth.

Your dog may panic during this time and may not want you to come close to his mouth. However, fast-thinking action on your part to clear his airway may save your dog. Usually you have no time to call a veterinarian for help so you have to act quickly. Remain calm. Try to open your dog's mouth by firmly placing one of your hands beneath your dog's jaw. With your other hand gently place your fingers around the top of your dog's jaw and gently try to pry his mouth

Choking—Performing the Modified Heimlich Maneuver

This life-saving technique is invaluable if you have a dog. If for any reason your dog is not getting enough air and appears to be gasping for breath, do the canine Heimlich.

Position your dog in front of you and place your hands behind and on his last ribs. Give them a quick, sharp squeeze that's not too hard but just enough to release air. Because your Yorkie is so small, you won't have to squeeze that hard. Just move his chest about one-quarter or one-half inch. Perform this procedure again until your dog has dislodged whatever is preventing him from breathing properly. Use caution—overdoing this maneuver can break ribs or rupture his spleen. Take him to the veterinarian so she can check for complications from the choking or maneuver.

open with his head down. Do not tilt his head backward or the object can become lodged even further.

If you can see the object, remove it with one of your fingers. If not, try the modified Heimlich maneuver on your dog (see sidebar). At that point, if your dog is still choking, rush him to the veterinarian. Remember that your dog cares for you but may bite when he is frightened.

Another reason a dog chokes is because he is having an allergic reaction to something and his throat is swollen. Take him to your veterinarian immediately if that is the case so that your vet can administer antihistamines.

Bleeding

When an owner sees his beloved Yorkie covered with blood, panic sets in. It's important that you remain as calm as you possibly can. If your dog has had a serious injury, you do not want him to become frightened, which might make him move suddenly and cause further damage.

Assess approximately how much blood is present and where it is coming from. A scratch or a scrape often looks worse than it really is. If the blood wipes off easily and doesn't reappear, it's probably nothing serious, but you do want to find the cause. Perhaps a bit of sharp wire is sticking out of your backyard fence, or maybe your dog has scraped his foot and snagged a nail. Wipe off the blood with a towel and, if the wound is superficial, clean it with 3 percent hydrogen peroxide. If you have an antibiotic ointment, apply it once the bleeding has stopped and you have cleansed the wound. If the wound appears deep or is a puncture, do not clean it. Instead, see your veterinarian immediately. Your dog's body will bleed more profusely in areas such as the ears, footpads, nails, mouth, and penis.

Because your Yorkie's coat is long, you may find it hard to locate the source of the bleeding right away. Part the hair, and the wound should be easier to find. If the bleeding continues, maintain pressure on the area by grabbing a sterile pad or a clean towel and holding it in place until the bleeding stops. Add another layer if the blood begins to soak through, and take your dog to the veterinarian. If you see blood spurting, continue adding direct pressure as well as applying pressure above the area. Because a Yorkie is so small, the loss of even a small amount of blood from more than a simple scrape can be serious. Do not hesitate to seek emergency veterinary treatment.

Shock

Shock is nature's way of shutting down the system when there has been a serious injury.

Shock

Different causes produce different symptoms of shock. When your dog is in shock, she may be weak and subdued. Her body temperature can range from below normal to normal or above normal (in cases of shock caused by a bacterial infection). Her pulse may be rapid and weak, and her gums may exhibit a delayed capillary refill time. (Test capillary refill time by pressing on your dog's gums, removing your finger, and counting the time it takes the gums to change from white back to pink. Normal is less than two seconds.) If your dog's gums seem to respond normally, but she is acting lethargic and confused, she may be in the early stages of shock.

In all cases of shock, immediate veterinary care is imperative. Control any bleeding, wrap your dog in a blanket, towel, or piece of clothing to keep her warm, and rush her to the veterinary clinic.

The supply of blood in the bloodstream and the flow of oxygen to the tissues cannot keep up with the needs of the vital organs during an emergency so they sometimes cease functioning. To see your beloved Yorkie in a state of shock can be alarming. Again, remain calm and remember this information. Emergency situations that trigger shock in dogs include poisoning, being hit by a car, severe loss of blood from an injury, or dehydration from an excessive amount of diarrhea or vomiting.

To determine whether your dog is undergoing shock, examine his gums to see if they are dry and pale pink or white. Other signs include a fast, weak pulse; rapid, shallow breathing; a very low body temperature; weak movement; and mental disorientation.

Terminal shock signals when the body can no longer sustain itself without oxygen and a blood supply. The dog may be unconscious and it will be difficult to feel a pulse. Heart and respiratory

rates are also slow. This is an extreme emergency situation requiring immediate veterinary assistance.

Fractures

A Yorkie is tough but can also be somewhat fragile at times. His bones can easily break if he misjudges the distance from the couch to the floor and jumps off, lands on, or falls into something hard. If he is chasing a ball and smashes into the wall or a fence, he can also break a bone. You might even hear a crack.

A complete break in the bone is known as a simple fracture, while a bone sticking through the skin is referred to as a compound fracture. While both conditions are reasons to see your vet, the compound fracture needs an immediate trip for treatment as your Yorkie may go into shock from the trauma and infection will quickly set in to an open bone.

If your Yorkie breaks a bone, either he may not want to move or may thrash around. If you try to touch the fractured area, he will probably scream in pain and may even attempt to bite you—not because he means to bite, but because he is protecting himself from further pain. Since moving him will be necessary and he might bite you in the process, criss-cross a long strip of gauze underneath and around his muzzle and tie it gently behind his head or beneath his jaw. Gently lift him beneath the neck and behind his rear and place him onto a couch cushion or a blanket before carrying him into your car. Keep a pair of scissors handy, however, and cut his muzzle immediately if he shows any difficulty breathing!

Try not to roll him onto the fractured limb. Your vet will take X-rays to determine the exact location of the break and will either put a cast on it or a splint. While he is recuperating, don't count on your Yorkie

feeling up to running after any vermin. If he doesn't exercise the injured limb for a few weeks, you can expect a full recovery in due time. Soon he'll be able to walk normally and be back to his normal energetic self.

Car Accidents

Many owners enjoy taking their Yorkies for car rides, which can be fun—or can be a nightmare to a small dog who is not either seat-belted like a small child or riding in a kennel. If you are involved in a car accident, your dog can easily be thrown through the window or knocked about in the car. He can also roll onto the floor where he may become trapped. The force of another car hitting yours can also propel your dog out of your car and into busy traffic, another solid object, or into an area where he could get lost. To further protect your Yorkie while he is riding in the car, be sure he wears a collar and an identification tag at all times. Should you be involved in an auto accident and he escapes, ID tags may be the only method of return.

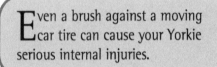

Even a brush against a moving car tire can cause your Yorkie serious internal injuries.

If you live on a busy street, your Yorkie on the loose is definitely at risk. He's much too small to be noticed by drivers until it's too late. Even a brush against a moving car tire can cause your Yorkie serious internal injuries. As harsh as it sounds, being hit by a car is likely to be fatal for a Yorkie.

Should an accident happen, approach your dog cautiously and as calmly as possible. His pain may be so great that he may try to bite you to protect himself. Shock is the main concern as well as broken bones. Use a stiff board, couch pillow, or something similar as a stretcher to carry your dog from the crash site. Use rolled-

Handling an Injured Yorkie

If your Yorkshire Terrier is injured, he may growl or snap when you attempt to touch or move him. Don't be offended by this unusual behavior. Your Yorkie is feeling pain, and this is the way he shows it. Remember this before handling your injured dog, and take a few steps to prevent injury to yourself.

First, talk to him quietly and calmly. He may be excited or anxious—aren't you when you're injured? Move slowly, and keep talking in a soothing voice.

Next, muzzle your hurt Yorkie. If you don't have a muzzle available, improvise with a man's necktie, a stocking, or a long strip of soft cloth. Loop the cloth over the Yorkie's muzzle and tie a half knot on top of the dog's muzzle, then tie another half knot under the chin. Wrap the material behind and below the ears and tie a full knot at the base of the dog's head. If your dog is having trouble breathing, avoid a muzzle if at all possible.

To transport your severely injured Yorkie to the emergency clinic, use a stretcher. A flat board—a sheet of plywood for example—works well. If something like that isn't available, use a towel or blanket. You don't want to injure your Yorkie more seriously, so be very careful moving him onto the makeshift stretcher. Slide one hand under your dog's rear and the other hand under his chest. Slowly inch the dog onto the stretcher and cover him with a towel.

Drive carefully but quickly to the veterinary clinic. Have someone ride with you and your Yorkie to keep the dog calm and still. Call ahead so that the staff expects you, and have them come out to help carry in the dog.

up blankets around the sides to keep his body still. Avoid moving his head or neck and try to keep his back from rolling.

Transport him to the veterinarian immediately.

Heatstroke and Heat Exhaustion

Prolonged exposure to the sun isn't good for your Yorkie, whose long coat can make him even hotter. Keep him inside during the heat of the day.

Dogs can get heatstroke and heat exhaustion very easily when the temperature climbs above their own natural body temperature of about 101 degrees Fahrenheit. In high humidity, even temperatures in the mid-80s can be dangerous. And never leave your dog in a parked car on a warm day, not even for a minute.

Dogs left outdoors without shade or those who exercise heavily in hot weather are susceptible to heatstroke. Dogs not accustomed to outings such as going on vacation or to an outdoor fair in warm temperatures can become stressed and more prone to heatstroke. Signs include panting and heavy breathing, vomiting, a high rectal temperature (104 degrees Fahrenheit or higher), a bright red tongue and mucous membranes, and drooling.

If you find your dog in this condition, cool him off as quickly as possible. Stand him on top of towels soaked in cool water or inside a pool of cool water and if the dog will take an ice chip, let him chew it, or rub the inside of his gums with ice chips. Place him in an air-conditioned car or direct a portable fan beneath his body and around his face, and get him to the veterinarian. These measures will cool your dog down and prevent further damage to his organs.

Seizures

If you have never seen a dog having a seizure, the experience can be frightening. The dog develops a strange look in his eyes and begins jerking his legs in an uncontrolled manner or shaking his head. He has no coordination and is unable to walk or respond to any verbal messages you might give him. You may see foaming at the mouth, loss of bladder or bowel control, and collapse. One seizure may last only a few seconds or take as long as several minutes. Seizures, which are the result of a momentary brain dysfunction, can occur once in a lifetime or reoccur frequently.

When a seizure ends, the dog appears slightly weakened but otherwise normal. He may stumble and fall in an effort to get up immediately after the seizure. Minutes later he may experience another seizure or he might live a long life without ever having another one.

There is little you can do to help your dog during a seizure except stay close by to comfort him and make sure he doesn't injure himself by falling into a solid object. If it has been a long time since a meal and you have a very young puppy, or one prone to hypoglycemia, carefully place a dab of honey or Karo syrup on his gums and go straight to the vet. Dogs will not swallow their tongues as some people believe, so you do not need to put anything in their mouths during this time to prevent this. In fact, touching the mouth of a convulsing dog is only likely to get you very seriously bitten. Note how long the seizure lasts and what you think might have triggered the reaction. When the seizure has ended, let him recuperate in quiet. If it is a first-time occurrence, call your veterinarian right away. It is likely he'll want you to come right in with the dog, as blood testing soon after a seizure may sometimes detect the cause.

> There is little you can do to help your dog during a seizure except stay close by to comfort him and make sure he doesn't injure himself by falling into a solid object.

Seizures are triggered for many reasons, including epilepsy, diseases, hypoglycemia, a reaction to a vaccine, very low thyroid, poisoning, and organ failure.

To determine the cause of a seizure, have your dog examined by your veterinarian. While one seizure is not life-threatening, repetitive seizures can be fatal. Medication is available for epilepsy and low thyroid, which will reduce the frequency of seizures.

Poisoning

Your curious Yorkshire Terrier is bound to investigate things that might not be good for him. Because of his small size, even a tiny amount of a toxic substance can be fatal. Therefore, make sure your home, garage, and yard are dog-proof and that all potential poisons are kept in a locked cabinet out of reach. You will include in your clean sweep many products not usually associated with causing danger to dogs. If flea and tick products and garden pesticides are ingested, they can attack the dog's neurological system and be fatal. Signs of flea-product poisoning vary, but may include vomiting, diarrhea, tremors, and excessive salivation. Ingesting common rat poisons will cause labored breathing, bloody diarrhea, and nosebleeds. Tobacco products are poisonous if swallowed and may cause immediate muscle weaknesses, drooling, and vomiting. They are fatal if a Yorkie eats large amounts of them.

> The National Animal Poison Control Center can answer any emergency questions you might have and advise you of antidotes 24 hours a day at (888) 426-4435.

Human medications, such as aspirin and other pain relievers, can cause anemia and hemorrhaging if swallowed in large amounts. Cold pills, allergy medication, antidepressants, and vitamins may be fatal. Cleaning and automotive products, such as toilet-bowl cleaner or antifreeze, are also deadly. These will cause symptoms ranging from mild stomach upsets to internal burns. While the sweet smell of antifreeze is alluring to your small dog, if he laps up just a teaspoon that you accidentally spilled on the driveway, it will threaten his life. If you suspect that your dog has walked in a contaminated area, rinse his feet in soap and water and visit your veterinarian right away.

Spoiled food rooted from the trashcan also be dangerous. It's best to keep tight lids on garbage cans and make sure any toxic products are stored up high. The best prevention is to not keep these things in your home at all and to use natural deterrents for garden pests. Even if poisons are used away from your yard, a rat can carry it back where your dog will surely find it. The National Animal Poison Control Center can answer any emergency questions you might have and advise you of antidotes 24 hours a day at (888) 426-4435.

Fishhooks

Your Yorkie will probably never encounter a fishhook if you always kept him indoors, but you may be like many owners who enjoy walking their Yorkies along the beach where fishermen are trying to hook the big one. Still other owners relish taking their Yorkie along for a boat ride, which may include walking on the dock to get to the boat. Your Yorkie will surely want to investigate the strong and appealing odor of nearby fishing equipment, but could get stuck in the process.

Should a fishhook become embedded in your dog's mouth or foot, or tangled in his coat, both of you are likely to be in panic mode. Remain as calm as you can, and do not yank the hook out, as it will savagely rip away at your dog's skin. Take your dog to a veterinarian, who will determine which way the hook is pointing and will decide whether to push it through and back into the top of your dog's skin or use wire cutters to slice off the barb and draw back the wire. Your veterinarian will give your dog an antibiotic to defend your dog's body against infection. If you are unable to take your dog for emergency treatment, you can try to follow the procedure just

described, being careful not to rush the process, then use a mild solution of saltwater to cleanse the wound, and visit a veterinarian as soon as possible to see if antibiotics are needed.

To prevent your Yorkie from encountering a fishhook in the first place, pick him up and carry him over hazardous-looking terrain and make sure all fishing equipment is out of his reach.

Burns

Most dogs can sense hot surfaces so are rarely burned. However, burns due to thermal or chemical causes can happen. Any type of burn is very painful to your Yorkie and burns that cover more than 15 percent of his body can be fatal. Coming too close to an open flame or being scalded by hot food or water is a thermal burn. If his coat catches fire, cover him immediately with a towel and attempt to smother the flames. If he goes into shock, treat that while arranging to get to your dog to the vet. Be sure to apply a towel soaked in ice water on the wound as you go to your veterinarian.

A caustic chemical dropped on a dog's skin can also cause burns. Most chemical burns are the result of the alkali contained in household chemicals. Shock may result and the burned skin may become discolored. First aid includes reading the label and following directions. In most cases, a fast bath is helpful, but in other cases it may cause more damage. A fast phone call to the

National Animal Poison Control Center may help you treat your pet quickly. Otherwise, go immediately to your veterinarian. If possible, bring the container so your vet can identify the chemical. Treat the shock and clean the wound immediately with lukewarm water. Read the chemical's container to learn whether an acid or an alkali product caused the burn, as your veterinarian will want to know when she treats the dog. Keep a cold compress on the burned area while en-route.

Electric Shock

Yorkshire Terrier puppies love to investigate loose wires hanging down from computers, appliances, and lamps or stretched along the floorboards. If your pup is prone to sniffing around electrical outlets and mouthing cords, beware! If he chews through an electrical cord, he may receive an electrical shock or receive electrical burns inside his mouth and along the tongue and palate. Symptoms include excessive drooling and possibly convulsions and loss of consciousness. He may also go into shock. If you see your dog receive an electrical shock, turn off the power in your home and then remove the cord before you touch him.

Take your dog to the veterinarian right away. If his heart stops or his airway is blocked and he stops breathing before you get to the veterinarian, perform CPR on your Yorkie immediately.

To prevent electrical shock, cover the cords along the floor with duct tape and pull the carpet over them. Place plastic covers over outlets that are not in use. You can also unplug appliances that are not being used and spray the cords with Bitter Apple. Also leave plenty of chew toys around the floor, and hopefully your Yorkie puppy will choose those instead. The best prevention is to never leave your Yorkie puppy unattended.

Allergic Reactions

Like people, dogs can suffer allergic reactions to some of the same substances that bother humans. Sometimes the

Did You Know?

Dogs see color less vividly than humans but are not actually color-blind.

allergic responses can range from itching and sneezing, to cough-ing and hair loss. Other reactions can be more serious, causing skin problems with rashes and hot spots, face rubbing, or foot licking. Household products or materials such as wool and carpet can be troublesome, as can dust and mold. Foods such as corn and wheat, soy, beef, or dairy products are likely culprits, as are drugs such as penicillin or vaccines. Pollens and bug bites are outdoor allergens you have to worry about.

> If your dog has persistent allergy problems, consult with your vet-erinarian.

All allergic reactions can be annoying and most can be soothed by over-the-counter products. Others are life-threatening, as your dog may react so violently that he goes into anaphylactic shock. This is an extreme, whole-body reac-tion that may result in trouble breathing, collapse, heart fail-ure, and death. If you expect an extreme allergic reaction, head immediately to your vet.

If your dog has persistent allergy problems, consult with your veterinarian. She may recommend trying new types of dog food that contain ingredients your dog has never had before. She can also perform skin testing and recommend treatment such as up-dating your air-cleaning system, or prescribe antihistamines and steroids. Changing the dog's bedding to a synthetic fabric is a simple solution but may be just the thing to help a dog with per-sistent face rubbing. In severe cases, your veterinarian may ad-minister allergy injections. Often, determining the cause of the allergy takes a dedicated system of trial-and-error testing and sometimes you never find the allergen. If you do discover what the offending agents are, a complete recovery could take months or years.

First-Aid Kit Essentials

○ Your veterinarian's phone number

○ An after-hours emergency clinic's phone number

○ The National Animal Poison Control Center's hotline number: (888) 426-4435

○ Digital thermometer

○ Tweezers

○ Scissors

○ Penlight flashlight

○ Rubbing alcohol

○ Sterile cotton balls

○ Hydrogen peroxide (3 percent)

○ Nonstick wound pads, gauze squares and roll cotton, elastic bandage

○ Syrup of ipecac and activated charcoal liquid or tablets (poison antidotes)

○ Eye dropper

○ Adhesive tape

○ Styptic powder for nails

○ Canine first-aid book

○ Ear-cleaning fluid

○ Benadryl

○ Imodium or other anti-diarrhea product prescribed by your veterinarian

○ A clean washcloth and a small towel

○ Antibiotic ointment

○ Betadyne

○ Sterile saline eyewash

○ Towel

Eye Injuries

Luckily, the Yorkshire Terrier does not have a lot of hair covering his eyes so you can tell immediately if he has an eye injury. If he has hurt his eye, his bright and shiny eyes may appear dull or he may blink a lot. It is normal for a Yorkie to have a watery discharge or even a mucus-type discharge that is clear or even light yellow. If you can wipe it away with a moistened tissue or damp washcloth soaked in warm water, it is not a problem. However, eye discharge that is thick and greenish is a sign of serious injury, infection, or disease.

When the eye is swollen or red, and if your dog continually paws at one or both of his eyes, he needs to be seen by a veterinarian. He may have a scratch on the cornea, a foreign body in the eye, or increased pressure in the eye from sudden onset glaucoma. If you suspect a foreign body, such as grass, seed, or sand, use sterile saline, such as contact-lens wearers use, to give a gentle flush. If you don't have this, drop a little clean tap water into the eye. Unless you get 100 percent relief within a half-hour, your Yorkie needs to visit the veterinarian.

Never use any products your veterinarian hasn't specifically prescribed. The wrong eye drops can cause permanent damage.

Obesity

Keeping your Yorkie in good shape is important to his overall health. Besides looking like a stuffed sausage, an overweight Yorkie is less healthy than dogs of normal weight. The extra weight he is carrying around puts a strain on his trachea, which can aggravate a weak trachea later in life. It also puts pressure on his entire body, increasing the pain of any arthritis or joint disease he may have. Dogs who are obese or overweight are ripe candidates to suffer heart problems, liver dysfunction, joint pains, and diabetes. If you want your dog to live a long, healthy life, keep him at a normal weight.

Maintaining a Healthy Weight

Even though it doesn't look like a Yorkie has room to store much fat, monitoring his weight throughout his life is important. Puppy food has a lot of calories, which your Yorkie needs when he is growing. However, as he grows into adulthood, his diet should change to an adult food recipe.

To determine whether your Yorkie is overweight, look at his ribs by standing above him and looking down. When viewed from the top, he should have a slight waist. Viewed from the side, does his abdomen tuck up from the ribs to the pelvis or does his belly sag? Place your hands over his sides and feel his ribs with gentle pressure. You should be able to feel two to three ribs, but he should not feel like a bony washboard. If you cannot easily feel the ribs, your Yorkie is overweight.

Overfeeding and giving too many snacks without enough exercise will cause obesity in dogs. If you think your dog will tell you when he's really hungry, guess again. Some dogs always act hungry. Limit snacks and only feed healthful tidbits. Use a measuring cup to give your dog the same amount at each meal. Ignore the recommended amount listed on the dog food bag. The correct amount to feed your dog is what will make him look fit and healthy.

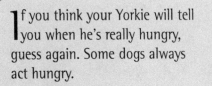

If you think your Yorkie will tell you when he's really hungry, guess again. Some dogs always act hungry.

If your dog is already overweight, try increasing his exercise a little each day and feeding a little less food once a day. If your dog still seems hungry, add a small amount of cooked vegetables (without butter or sauce) to his food.

Trimming Down a Chubby Puppy

If your puppy is overweight, don't add more food to his eating plan. As he continues to grow, he'll naturally take off a few ounces without your having to drastically reduce his food intake.

Cutting out extra table scraps and making sure you keep treats to a minimum helps as well. While a puppy who is too heavy may be healthier than one who is too thin, you don't want to continue this trend into adulthood.

Avoid putting your puppy on any kind of forced exercise program as this could prematurely damage his growing bones. Short walks are fine, as is retrieving a ball in the yard.

Health Concerns Specific to Yorkshire Terriers

No breed of dog is immune to health problems. Once you know what health problems Yorkies are prone to developing, you can take steps to guard against them or be on the lookout for their onset in your dog. Yorkies are more likely than most breeds to have a collapsed trachea, hypoglycemia, dental problems, Legg-Calvé-Perthes disease, luxating patellas, portosystemic shunt, hydrocephalus, hernias, congenital heart disease, acquired heart disease, and progressive retinal atrophy (PRA).

Collapsed Trachea

This common structural defect is found in many of the Toy breeds. The trachea, or windpipe, is lined with cartilage that is weaker than normal and can be easily damaged by the slightest pressure. As the dog ages, the windpipe weakens. The first sign of this condition is your Yorkie making a honking-cough noise, especially after exercise or a tug on the leash. If you rub his throat, he may gag or cough.

Symptoms may become constant as he ages and fluid builds up in the lungs, causing a blockage in the airway. Since he breathes against the obstruction, this results in chronic lung disease, which leads to other breathing complications.

Care must be taken to avoid applying too much pressure from the collar. Try to use a harness instead of a collar to prevent pressure on the neck. Also, try not to get your Yorkie too excited, which may bring on a sudden intake of air and trachea collapse. Instead of a collar, purchase a harness that puts pressure on the dog's chest and not his throat. Tracheal collapse is usually minor, but it may become serious and nearly constant. This can result in airway blockage, followed by a build-up of fluids in the lungs and an increase in blood pressure. Heart failure can result.

Your veterinarian can supply you with cough suppressants, which can control the coughing, or may recommend you use a cool-mist humidifier to ease breathing complications. In some cases, the trachea can be repaired with surgery. If a Yorkie is overweight, that will also aggravate trachea collapse. Your vet can also suggest supplements to build cartilage.

Hypoglycemia

When your Yorkie's blood sugar falls dangerously low, he is hypoglycemic. At that point his body and brain are not receiving the nutrients they need, and your dog can become weak and may even have seizures. Hypoglycemia is a common condition in Toy breeds and is usually brought on by illness, stress, or not receiving enough food.

Hypoglycemia is a common condition in Toy breeds and is usually brought on by illness, stress, or not receiving enough food.

Many times you will not be able to predict a hypoglycemic attack. Suddenly your dog has no energy or looks sleepy. He may wobble when walking or fall over.

The best defense is Karo syrup, honey, or Nutrical or Nutristat, which are veterinary products available from your veterinarian or at a pet-supply store. Liberally apply any of these products directly on the dog's gums if he is unconscious and the roof of his mouth. This pure sugar will be quickly absorbed into the bloodstream. Dogs usually like this and will lick and swallow it off the roof of their mouth, which stimulates the pulse rate.

Wrap your Yorkie in a blanket to maintain body heat. You may have to take your dog to the veterinarian if you are unable to revive him, but keep putting the sugar products directly on his gums en route, taking care not to obstruct his airway. If he is not licking, use only small amounts and place it only on the gums. Your vet will start him on a glucose intravenous solution right away.

A Yorkie's risk of hypoglycemia decreases significantly after six months of age. To prevent hypoglycemia, feed your Yorkie several small meals throughout the day. It's also a good idea to leave out some high-quality dry dog food for your dog to snack on throughout the day. It doesn't hurt to always give him a little honey just before bedtime.

Dental Problems

Yorkies frequently have retained puppy teeth. In other words, sometimes their puppy teeth need to be removed by a veterinarian. If your Yorkie has not shed her puppy teeth by 4 to 6 months of age, they will need to be removed to allow adult teeth to come into a healthy position.

Yorkies can have teeth that are crowded together and overlap one another, which allows food particles and bacteria to collect. Eventually this causes inflammation of the gums, loose teeth, and infected dental roots. Your veterinarian should evaluate your dog's mouth and remove teeth that are crowding other teeth. Frequent brushing can also prevent problems, especially in a crowded mouth. Ask your veterinarian to show you proper cleaning techniques that will work for your dog's unique dental needs.

Legg-Calvé-Perthes

Many Toy breeds have Legg-Calvé-Perthes disease (LCP), which is a disease of the hip joints. The head of the femur (thigh bone) begins to disintegrate over

> LCP is genetic; trauma may cause arthritis or a damaged joint, but not complete deterioration of the head of the femur as seen in this disease.

time. Yorkies usually experience this as youngsters, between the ages of six months and one year. It is very painful and will cause the dog to limp. Gradually arthritis sets in. Your veterinarian can take X-rays to confirm the condition. Unlike hip dysplasia, which causes arthritis in both the socket and thigh bone, LCP causes degeneration—total destruction of the femur, with the socket untouched. LCP usually affects only one side, but may affect both hips.

LCP is genetic; trauma may cause arthritis or a damaged joint, but not complete deterioration of the head of the femur as seen in this disease. Your Yorkie can have surgery and make him more comfortable, but affected dogs should not be bred.

Luxating Patellas

This too is a common structural problem in Toy breeds. Yorkie's afflicted with this disease have their kneecap pop in and out of the groove in the bones of the knee. It can happen to both knees or just one and is caused by weak ligaments and tendons or muscles. It can also happen to those Yorkies who were born with kneecap grooves that are too narrow or shallow. The knee can slip inward toward the body or toward the outside.

An exam will reveal dislocation, but your Yorkie will feel little pain unless secondary arthritis sets in. Almost all cases are genetic, but knee damage due to injury can also allow the kneecap to pop out of joint. An early warning that your Yorkie has luxating patellas is if he lifts one hindleg while running or walking.

> One way to treat this weakness is to limit activity and not allow your Yorkie to leap on the furniture.

The kneecaps can slip in and out or can slip and stay out. One way to treat this weakness is to limit activity and not allow your Yorkie to leap on the furniture. This only prevents the symptom, however, and does not cure the problem. When the problem is minor, your veterinarian can prescribe anti-inflammatory drugs in steroid and non-steroidal form if needed. The only true cure comes with surgery, and this is recommended if the kneecap tends to stay out of place or if your Yorkie has pain along with the condition.

Portosystemic Shunt

This is also known as a liver shunt, and in the Yorkie, it is most often found as a congenital condition (one that is present at birth). However, shunts can develop later in life from any serious liver disease, especially cirrhosis (hardening of the liver). In a portosystemic shunt, blood that is normally cleansed of toxic body chemicals by the liver is diverted around the liver by an abnormally placed blood vessel. This means that toxins accumulate in the blood, and can cause serious health problems. In particular, ammonia accumulates to dangerous levels, especially after a meal, and bile acids also increase.

There are many signs of liver shunt—including listlessness, walking or running in circles, excessive drinking, frequent urination, lack of muscular coordination, seizures, poor weight gain, sensitivity to drugs, drooling, weakness, vomiting, poor appetite, early bladder stones, coma, and pressing the head down on surfaces.

Your veterinarian will definitely need to diagnose your Yorkie. Diagnosis begins with blood and urine samples, and may involve x rays, ultrasound, or other special studies. Treatment may be medical or surgical. Medical treatment will reduce the amount of ammonia in the body. Feeding a low-protein diet will also help reduce production of amonia. Surgery to close the shunt carries some risk, but in most cases is completely successful, and returns the Yorkie to full health. If the shunt is untreated, the dog will get progressively worse and eventually die. Treatment success depends upon the location and severity of the shunt. Sadly, some cases are not treatable and lead to certain death. The heritability of congenital liver shunts is not known, but a genetic link is suspected. Affected dogs should not be bred, especially if they have siblings with the same problem.

Hydrocephalus

Hydrocephalus, also known as water on the brain, occurs in many Toy breeds of dogs. It is relatively common in the Yorkie, and is usually present at birth or soon after. Signs develop in most Yorkies within a few weeks to a year of age.

A puppy with hydrocephalus can have a variety of signs. These are caused by loss of brain tissue due to pressure from a buildup of fluids inside

the skull, and depend on which areas of the brain are affected. Some puppies show few signs, but most will have abnormal behaviors, such as trouble learning simple tasks (such as house-training), general sleepiness, blindness, trouble walking or unsteadiness, and seizures. Some dogs are hyperexcitable rather than sleepy.

Most Yorkies with hydrocephalus have a dome-shaped head and an open fontanel—a "soft spot" on the head—that does not close shortly after birth. A veterinarian can use ultrasound on this spot to visualize the brain and look for increased fluid or damage to confirm the diagnosis.

Treatment can be medical or surgical. Medical treatment attempts to reduce the pressure inside the brain. It may be effective in emergency situations, but in most dogs, medical treatment is unrewarding in the long run. Surgery to shunt the fluid from the brain into the abdomen, where it can be harmlessly reabsorbed into the body, is also available and is the definitive treatment. If surgery is anticipated, it should be done as early in life as possible in order to minimize brain damage.

Hydrocephalus can be inherited, but the mode of inheritance appears to be quite complex. Dogs with very mild hydrocephalus may lead normal, happy lives. In most cases, however, serious behavior problems and seizures are likely. When the pressure inside the brain rises to high levels, death is likely. It is wise to avoid breeding affected dogs.

Hernias

A hernia is a defect in the formation the body wall. Most hernias are small and found near the umbilical cord, in the body wall closest to the thighs (inguinal), or underneath the scrotum. They also can be found in the diaphragm, the muscle that separates the abdomen and the chest cavity.

Since the body wall holds the abdominal contents where they belong, the biggest risk of a hernia is that some of the contents will slip through the muscle wall. In most cases, this is only a tiny piece of fat and it will slip back inside quickly with no problems. However, if a piece of intestine slides out it may twist or swell, making it impossible for the intestine to return inside the body. This is considered an emergency, and must be resolved quickly with surgery.

If you see a smooth, soft, bulge that comes and goes with pressure at any of the three most common sites, your Yorkie has a hernia. If the site becomes swollen, hard, painful, or hot, your Yorkie may have trapped an intestine and you should go immediately to the veterinarian. Internal hernias are difficult to diagnose, but your Yorkie may have trouble breathing, a very skinny stomach area, or swelling of the abdomen. Your veterinarian will take x rays or perform an ultrasound to confirm a diaphragmatic hernia.

Because there is evidence that hernias are hereditary in the dog, it is wise to avoid breeding affected dogs or avoid repeat breedings from dogs that produce several pups with hernias.

Occasionally a very tiny hernia in a young puppy will close itself in the first few months of life. Most hernias, however, will need to be repaired surgically. Fortunately, this surgery is simple and quick, with a fast recovery time. Diaphragmatic hernias are much more complex, but they also have an excellent chance of cure when caught early. The three most common hernias (umbilical, inguinal, scrotal) are usually repaired at spay or neuter time. Hernias that are particularly large carry a risk of entrapment of intestines, so they should be repaired quickly.

In most species of animals, hernias are considered hereditary. In dogs there is certainly a hereditary component, but it is not as clearly expressed as in other species. In other words, a dog's hernia is most likely caused by inherited defects from one or both parents and he is likely to pass these genes on. However, his puppies may or may not actually be affected with the disorder. Because there is evidence that hernias are hereditary in dogs, it is wise to avoid breeding affected dogs or avoid repeat breedings from dogs that produce several pups with hernias. However, if the defect is very minor and the dog passes all other genetic tests, some breeders choose to continue to breed. Dogs born with diaphragmatic hernias or with ones that are very large should be spayed or neutered, as these defects are considered quite serious.

Congenital Heart Disease

Small dogs are at risk of developing several types of heart disease, and Yorkies are no different. Two types of congenital (present at birth) defects are relatively common: the atrial-septal defect (ASD) and patent ductus arteriosis (PDA). And as Yorkies age, the heart valves often weaken, causing valvular disease, particularly mitral valve insufficiency.

Both ASD and PDA are present at birth, and both are usually caused by inherited genetic defects, although not 100 percent of the time. In atrial-septal defect, there is a hole in the heart wall between the two upper chambers of the heart. Instead of blood flowing from the atrium to the ventricle with each beat, as it should, some blood will flow from atrium to atrium. This mix of blood causes several problems, and may ultimately result in heart failure.

PDA is similar in that there is a hole in the heart. This hole, however, is found between the pulmonary artery (the vessel that carries blood to the lungs) and the aorta, which pumps blood to the rest of the body. Before a pup is born, this hole is considered perfectly normal, as it shunts blood away from the unused fetal lungs. However, once the pup breathes a few times, the hole should close, redirecting half of the blood to flow to the lungs and half to the rest to the body. Puppies with PDA retain this hole, develop heart failure, and may die early in life. A few dogs with very tiny PDAs may live a nearly normal life span, but this is uncommon.

A Yorkie affected with either problem may show no signs at first, but your veterinarian should be able to hear a characteristic murmur early in life. Once heart failure begins, the puppy may tire easily on exercise, may cough, and may collapse. In some cases, the gums may look grayish or blue; in PDA it is more common, however, for the mucous membrane on the rear of the dog (around the rectum or vagina) to turn blue, while the gums stay pink.

These defects can be definitively diagnosed by echocardiography (ultrasound of the heart), or by using contrast studies of the arteries. The only cure for this problem is surgery. In skilled hands, the prognosis for dogs that undergo surgery for PDA is very good. In fact, 95 percent of puppies who undergo surgery in the first few months after birth survive to have a normal life. Surgery for an atrial septal defect is trickier, and should be performed only by a skilled cardiologist/surgeon. Because both ASD and PDA have a hereditary component, dogs born with these defects should not be bred.

Acquired Heart Disease

It is quite common for small dogs, such as Yorkies, to develop weakness in the valves of the heart as they age. Why this happens is not always known—it can be the result of infection of the valves, aging of the muscles of the heart, or an inherited weakness that becomes apparent later in life. The most common valve failure is the mitral valve, but any valve can be affected. Valve disease is considered serious, as it is likely to progress in time to heart failure.

The heart valves are thin membranes that lie between the chambers of the heart and between the vessels and the chambers. Their purpose is to allow blood to flow only one way—into the correct chamber—then to shut quickly and firmly to avoid back-flow. This assures that with each heartbeat the blood moves efficiently on its way throughout the body. When the valves become diseased, they lose efficiency. Blood will bubble back through the valve, causing turbulence and decreased blood flow. This disruption in flow makes the heart muscles work harder; eventually it will not be able to keep up with the extra work and will fail. Once the heart muscles fails, death will occur.

> The first sign of valve disease is usually picked up on an annual exam, and is only a murmur at the site of a valve.

The first sign of valve disease is usually picked up on an annual exam, and is only a murmur at the site of a valve. Your veterinarian is likely to hear this murmur long before your Yorkie shows any ill effects from the problem. When she does begin showing trouble signs, she's likely to get more tired on exercise and may begin to cough, especially when lying down. Later she may develop a more persistent cough, lose weight, and have a rounded, fluid-filled belly. Some dogs will die suddenly, shortly after the onset of signs. Others slowly decline in health over several years.

In humans, damaged or leaky valves are generally replaced by surgery. This is possible in dogs, but it is not often done due to expense and difficulty of getting a proper-sized valve, especially in a dog as tiny as a Yorkie. However, heart failure can be slowed down, although not cured, by a variety of medical interventions, such as diuretics to decrease blood volume and medicine to strengthen the beat of the heart.

It is probably wise to avoid breeding dogs with known valvular disease, especially if it has occurred in several siblings or the parents. Fact is, though, that signs develop as the dog ages, so many litters may be on the ground before any problems are suspected.

Progressive Retinal Atrophy (PRA)

PRA is an inherited eye degeneration that leads to blindness. If Yorkies are going to develop PRA, they usually do so by the age of five to seven years. You may first notice it if your dog is hesitant to go outdoors at night or to go into a darkened room, as night blindness is the first sign. Although this disease has no cure, a test that can predict which puppies may develop it is available. Yearly eye checks and vision exams can also spot developing problems.

If you are purchasing a puppy from a breeder, make sure that this test has been given.

Genetic Diseases and Disorders

The perfect dog hasn't been born yet, and every breed has its own genetic weaknesses. Today, many screening tests are available to detect genetic problems, and more are being developed every day in veterinary colleges and research programs across the country.

You can be as careful as possible with your Yorkie, yet sometimes diseases happen anyway. Make sure your veterinarian is up to date on the latest medical advances in Yorkshire Terrier health, and stay informed yourself. The purpose of learning about the diseases and techniques to diagnose or treat them will prepare you for emergencies. Hopefully, you will never need to use them.

Basic Training for Yorkshire Terriers

By Liz Palika

In This Chapter

○ When to Begin Training
○ The Teaching Process
○ What Every Good Yorkshire Terrier Needs to Know
○ Housetraining

Does your Yorkie bark? Does she try to escape from your yard? If she gets out of the yard, does she refuse to come when you call her? Does she raid the trashcan? Does she jump on your guests? These are not unusual behaviors for a young, untrained dog, but they are also unnecessary, potentially dangerous, and annoying behaviors that can be changed (or at least controlled) through training. All dogs, even tiny Yorkies, need training.

With training, your Yorkie can learn to control herself so that she's not reacting to every impulse. She can learn to sit while greeting people so that she's not covering them with muddy paw prints or ripping their pantyhose. She can learn to restrain some of her vocalizations and to ignore the trashcans. Training affects you, the owner, too. You will learn why your Yorkie does what she does. You will learn to prevent some of these actions, either by changing your routine or preventing the problems from occurring. Training your Yorkie is not something you do to her, but instead is something the two of you do together.

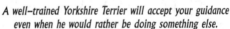

A well–trained Yorkshire Terrier will accept your guidance even when he would rather be doing something else.

Chester is a three-year-old male Yorkshire Terrier, owned by Clarence Sylvester of San Diego. Sylvester adopted Chester from the local animal shelter when Chester was about six months old. He had been given up by his previous owners because he was not house-trained, barked incessantly, and chewed up anything he could get his little jaws around. Sylvester said, "I couldn't believe that they gave up on a six-month-old puppy! They hadn't even really given Chester a chance." Sylvester enrolled Chester in a training class, started housetraining all over again, and within a few weeks began to see changes in Chester's behavior. Today, Chester is a very well-behaved dog who travels with Sylvester in his recreational vehicle. "I have never regretted adopting Chester," Sylvester says, "He's a good dog and great company."

Training is an ongoing process. As you learn how to teach your dog, you can apply the training to every aspect of your dog's life. She can learn how to behave at home, to ignore the trash-cans, to refrain from chasing the cat, and to chew on her own toys instead of your shoes. She can also learn how to behave while out

Basic Commands
Every Dog Should Know

Sit   Your dog's hips should move to the ground while her shoulders remain upright.

Down   Your dog should lie down on the ground or floor and be still.

Stay   Your dog should remain in position (sit or down) while you walk away from her. She should hold the stay until you give her permission to move.

Come   Your dog should come to you on the first call despite any distractions.

Walk on the leash   Your dog can walk ahead of you on the leash but should not pull the leash tight.

Heel   Your dog should walk by your left side with her shoulders by your left leg.

in public, including greeting people while sitting instead of jumping up. Your dog will learn, through practice and repetition, that training affects her behavior all the time—not just at home—and not just during training sessions.

When to Begin Training

Ideally, training should begin as soon as you bring home your new Yorkie. If you have an eight- to-ten-week-old puppy, she can begin learning that biting isn't allowed; that she should sit for treats, petting, and meals; and where she should go to relieve herself. By the time she is ten weeks of age, you can attach a small leash to her collar and let her drag it around for a few minutes at a time so she gets used to it. Always watch her closely, of course, so that she doesn't get the leash tangled up in something

What a Trained Dog Knows

A trained dog knows:

○ The appropriate behaviors allowed with people (no biting, no mouthing, no rough play, and no mounting)

○ Where to relieve herself and how to ask to go outside

○ How to greet people properly without jumping on them

○ To wait for permission to greet people, other dogs, and other pets

○ How to walk nicely on a leash so that walks are enjoyable

○ To leave trashcans alone

○ To leave food that is not hers alone (on the counters or coffee table)

○ Not to beg

○ To chew her toys and not things that belong to people

○ That destructive behavior is not acceptable

○ To wait for permission to go through doorways

A trained dog is a happy dog, secure in her place in the family.

and choke herself. Young puppies have a very short attention span but are capable of learning and are eager students.

Don't let your Yorkie pup do anything now that you don't want her to do later when she is full grown. For example, if you don't want her barking later, stop the puppy barking right away. Otherwise, you will find it much harder to change the habit later. Keep in mind as you begin your dog's training that, although Yorkies are small dogs, they are strong-willed and sturdy dogs with forceful personalities.

If you have adopted a Yorkie who is an older puppy or an adult, you can still begin training right away. Clarence Sylvester knew that beginning training with six-month-old Chester would help his new dog adjust to his new home and routine.

Kindergarten Puppy Class

The ideal time to begin group training is as soon as your Yorkie puppy has had at least two sets of vaccinations, usually between ten and twelve weeks of age. Many veterinarians recommend that you wait even longer. Ask your vet what he thinks. Kindergarten puppy classes introduce the basic obedience commands—sit, down, stay, and come—all geared for the puppy's short attention span. Puppy classes also spend time socializing the puppy with other people and other puppies.

Start teaching your Yorkie the rules you expect of her right away. If you don't want her on the furniture, never allow her on it, and don't make excuses. If you explain away her actions, "Oh, it's cold tonight so I'll let her come up and cuddle," you are doing neither your Yorkie nor yourself any good. Teach her right away what your rules are and enforce them. If you aren't consistent, your dog won't be either!

Is It Ever Too Late to Train?

Although training is most effective when started early in the dog's life and practiced consistently while she grows up, that doesn't mean it's too late to train an adult Yorkie. The downfall to starting training later in the dog's life is that you then have to break bad habits as well as teach new commands. With a puppy, you're starting with a blank slate and can teach the new behaviors

Start training early in your puppy's life so she learns good behavior instead of bad habits.

Basic Obedience Class

Most obedience instructors invite puppies to begin the basic obedience class after they have graduated from a puppy class or after a puppy has reached four months of age. Dogs (or older puppies) over four months of age who have not attended a puppy class would also attend a basic obedience class. This class teaches the traditional obedience commands—sit, down, stay, come, and heel. In addition, most instructors spend time discussing problem behaviors such as jumping on people, barking, digging, and chewing. A group class such as this helps your Yorkie learn to control herself around other dogs and people.

before she learns bad habits. If you've ever had to break a bad habit (smoking, for example), you know it can be difficult. However, with most Yorkies up to about eight years of age, you can, with consistent training and lots of patience, control most bad habits.

If your dog is older than eight years of age, your success at changing bad habits will be much more limited. You can teach new commands—sit, down, stay, and heel—and your dog will be able to learn these without much trouble. But trying to stop a problem barker will be much more difficult, and Yorkies who have not learned to come reliably on command by eight years of age will probably never be trustworthy.

Sometimes severe behavior problems are impossible to solve. A habit may be too deeply ingrained or the stimulus causing the behavior too strong. For example, if your dog has been raiding the trashcans, she has learned she'll find food there. If she is motivated by food (as most Yorkies are!), then each time she finds food, she is rewarded. You will have a hard time changing this be-

Private Training

Private training is normally recommended for Yorkies with severe behavior problems, such as biting, growling, dog aggression, or uncontrolled behavior. Private training is done one-on-one either at your home or at the trainer's facility. This training can usually be tailored to your dog's individual needs.

havior because the reward is too strong. Instead of fighting it, simply prevent it from happening and keep the trashcans out of her reach.

Basic Dog Psychology

Archeologists have found evidence showing that humans and the ancestors of today's dogs—wolves—share a history dating back thousands of years. At some point, for some reason that we don't yet understand, humans and some individual wolves decided to cooperate. Perhaps the wolves, being themselves efficient hunters, aided the human hunters. Perhaps the wolves took advantage of the human's garbage heap. For whatever reason, cooperation occurred and the result was domesticated dogs.

Families and Packs

In the wild, wolves live in packs. This pack has some important social rules that are seldom broken. If a youngster breaks a rule inadvertently or on purpose, she is corrected fairly but firmly. The correction may be a growl, posturing over the youngster (by the adult), or even a physical correction that consists of the adult pinning the youngster to the ground. Packs are usually fairly harmonious. Each member knows his or her place and keeps to it. However, if an adult dies, becomes disabled, or leaves the pack, there may be some posturing or fighting until the new pack order is established.

Dogs fit into our family life because of their pack history. Our family is a social organization similar to a pack, although our families have significant differences from a wolf pack and vary from each other depending on our culture. We do normally have an adult male and female, although today there may be just one adult. In addition, the rules of our family are often quite chaotic. In a wolf pack, the leaders always eat first; whereas in our families, people often eat any time and in no specific order. These family rules, or lack of rules, can be quite confusing to our dogs.

What Does it Mean to Be "Top Dog"?

"Top dog" is a slang term for the leader of the pack. In the wolf pack we discussed, the top dog is the dominant male or dominant female, often called the alpha male or alpha female. In your family, there should be no confusion: The top dog should be you, the dog's owner, and your dog should maintain a subordinate position to any additional human family members.

Often during adolescence, a Yorkie with a particularly bold

Don't let your dog use his body language to show dominance. Your dog should recognize you (and your children) as above him in the family pack.

You Are the Top Dog!

These rules will help you establish and maintain a leadership role with your dog.

○ Always eat first!

○ Go through doors and openings first; block your dog from charging through ahead of you.

○ Go up stairs first; don't let her charge ahead of you then look down on you.

○ Give your dog permission to do things, even if she was going to do it anyway. If she picks up her ball, tell her, "Get your ball! Good girl to get your ball!"

○ Practice your training regularly.

○ Have your dog roll over for a tummy rub daily.

○ Do not play rough games with your Yorkie.

○ Never let your dog stand above you or put her paws on your shoulders. These are dominant positions.

personality may make a bid for leadership of the family. Adolescence usually strikes at sexual maturity, usually between eight and twelve months of age. As bold, determined personalities, Yorkies making a quest for leadership of the pack can be quite tenacious. However, maintaining leadership of the pack is relatively easy. Because eating first is the leader's prerogative and is an action the dog readily understands, the owner should always eat before feeding the dog. You should also go through all doorways first and have your dog follow you. Make sure you can roll your Yorkie over to give him a tummy rub without any fussing on the dog's part.

Although it is very important that your dog regards you as the leader or top dog, don't look upon every action your dog makes as a dominance challenge. Most of the time your Yorkie won't care about her position in the family pack; she knows you're in charge.

However, during adolescence, and for more dominant personalities, training is very important.

The Teaching Process

Teaching your dog is not a difficult project although at times it may seem nearly impossible. Most dogs, especially most Yorkies, do want to be good—they just need to learn what you want them to do and what you don't. Therefore, most of the teaching process consists of communication. You need to reward the behaviors you want your dog to continue doing and to interrupt the behaviors you wish to stop. Let's again use barking as an example. When your dog begins to bark inappropriately, tell her, "Quiet!" in a firm, no-nonsense tone of voice. When she stops barking, praise her in a higher-than-normal tone of voice, "Good to be quiet!"

Did you notice I emphasized two different tones of voice? As verbal animals themselves, dogs are very aware of different tones of voice. When the leader of a wolf pack lets a subordinate know that he or she made a mistake, the leader uses a deep growl to convey that message. When things are fine, the pack has hunted, and all is well with the world, the leader may convey that with higher-pitched barks or even yelps. When you copy this technique—using a deep, growling voice when letting the dog know she's made a mistake and a higher-pitched tone of voice to reinforce good behavior—your dog doesn't have to stop and translate that information. She just understands.

Don't confuse high and low tones of voice with volume, though. Your dog can hear very well—much better than you can—and it's not necessary to yell at her. Instead, simply sound like you mean what you say.

As you begin teaching your dog, remember that human words have no meaning to your dog until she's taught that they do. For example, she's probably already learned some words. She may understand the words treat, cookie, ball, toy, walk, car, and bed. She may have already learned the meanings of leash, outside, go potty, inside, and no bite! But other words are just sounds, gobbledy-gook that has no meaning. As you teach her, she will learn that words like sit, down, come, and heel have meanings that are important to her.

So how can you teach your dog that these sounds have meanings? First, repeat the word as you help your dog perform the act. As you help your dog to sit, say the word, "Snickers, sit!" You can reinforce it by praising the dog after she has done as you asked by telling her, "Good girl to sit!" By using the word, your dog will learn that the word has meaning, that she should pay attention when she hears that word, and she should do whatever the word requires her to do.

Just as communication is a big part of the training process, so is your timing. You must use your voice to praise your dog as she is doing something right—*as* she is doing it—not

A treat can be a wonderful training tool to help teach your dog to pay attention to you. When he looks at you, praise him, give him the treat, and then follow through with other training.

later, not after the fact. The same thing applies to letting your dog know that she's making a mistake. Use your voice to let her know she's making a mistake as her nose goes into the trashcan. Don't wait until she's got the trash pulled out onto the floor. Instead, correct her with a firm, "No! Leave it alone!" *as* the nose goes to the trashcan. When your timing is correct, there is no

Corrections should be given as the dog is making the mistake, not after the fact.

misunderstanding; your dog knows exactly what message you are trying to convey.

Don't rely on corrections (verbal or otherwise) to train your dog. We all, dogs and people alike, learn just as much from our successes as we do from our mistakes and we are more likely to repeat our successes! Don't hesitate to set your dog up for success so that you can praise and reward her. If you want to keep your Yorkie off the furniture, have her lie down at your feet and hand her a toy to keep her busy *before* she jumps up on the furniture. You can then reward her for good behavior instead of correcting her for being bad.

A properly timed correction will let your dog know when she's making a mistake but doesn't tell her what to do instead. If your Yorkie is chewing on your leather shoes, by simply correcting her you convey that chewing on your shoes is wrong, but you won't teach her what she can chew on. Since chewing is important for dogs, that's an important message. So instead of *just* correcting her (to show her what is wrong), take her to her toys and hand her something of hers to chew on (to show her what is right); then praise her when she picks up one of her toys (to reinforce a good choice).

Teaching Your Dog to Be Handled

Although some Yorkies do have a very independent personality and might like to think they can care for themselves, they can't—that's your job. You must be able to brush her, comb her, bathe her, trim her toenails, and clean her ears. When she's sick or hurt, you must be able to take care of her, whether it's cleaning her

Training Vocabulary

Listed below are several methods you can use as you train your Yorkie.

Positive reinforcement: Anything your dog likes that you can use to reward good behavior including treats, praise, toys, tennis balls, and petting.

Praise: Words spoken in a higher-than-normal tone of voice to reward your dog for something she did right; part of positive reinforcement.

Lure: This is a food treat or a toy used to help position the dog as you want her, or to gain her cooperation as you teach her.

Interruption: The moment when you catch your dog in the act of doing something and you stop her. This can be verbal, in a deeper-than-normal tone of voice, or it could be a sharp sound like dropping your book to the floor. An interruption stops the behavior as it is happening.

Correction: Usually a deep, growly verbal sound or words to let your dog know that she has made a mistake, preferably as she is doing it. A correction can serve as an interruption, but you can also let your dog know that you dislike what she is doing. This can also be a snap and release of the leash. A correction should be firm enough to get your dog's attention and stop the behavior at that moment and that's all.

ears when she has an infection, caring for her stitches after spaying, or washing out her eyes if dirt gets in them.

It's important to teach your Yorkie to accept handling before there's an emergency. If you each her to accept handling of her body early (as a puppy or as soon as you bring her home), when she actually has a problem that requires special care, you will have already built that bond of trust and she will know to relax and let you care for her.

To introduce this exercise, sit on the floor and invite your Yorkie to lie down on the floor between your legs, on your lap, or in front of you. Start giving her a tummy rub to relax her. When

The Training Process

To teach a new command

○ Show the dog what to do with a lure, your hands, or your voice;

○ Praise him for doing it and reward him with the lure, if you used one;

○ Correct him for mistakes only when he knows and understands the command and chooses not to do it.

To correct problem behavior

○ Prevent the problem from happening when possible.

○ Set the dog up for success by teaching him to do something else and then rewarding it.

○ Interrupt the behavior when you catch the dog in the act. Let him know he made a mistake.

○ Show him the appropriate behavior.

she's relaxed, start giving her a massage. Begin massaging at her muzzle, rubbing your fingers gently over the skin, and at the same time, check her teeth. Then move up her head, touching the skin around her eyes, then move up to her ears. Handle each ear flap, look in each ear, and massage around the base of each ear. As you massage, look for any problems. Look for discharge from the eyes or nose. Look for dirt, excess wax, or redness in the ears. Let your fingers feel for lumps, bumps, or bruises on the skin.

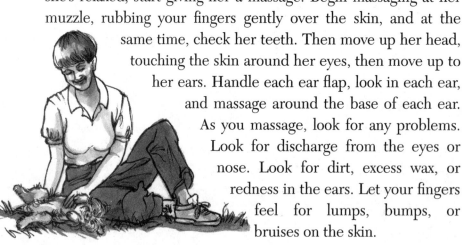

A tummy rub can help relax your dog if he's over-stimulated. You can also follow through with any needed grooming. In addition, this is a wonderful time for bonding with your dog.

Continue in this same manner all over your Yorkie's body. If she protests at any time, go back to

A Side Benefit of the Massage

There is a welcome side effect of the daily massage. When you're through massaging your Yorkie, he will be totally relaxed, like a limp noodle. So plan ahead and do it when you want your dog to be quiet and relaxed. If he's hyper and overstimulated in the evening when you would like to watch a favorite television show, sit on the floor, massage him, and then let him sleep while you watch your show!

the tummy rub for a moment, let her relax, and then continue. Do not let her turn this into a wrestling match; instead, keep it calm, relaxing, and gentle.

Do this exercise daily and incorporate your grooming regime into it. Daily combing and brushing is essential to keep a Yorkie's coat in top shape. It will reduce the chances of mats (tangles) developing and in addition, if you groom her daily, you can find other things (such as fleas or ticks) before they turn into major problems. If your dog needs medication or first-aid treatments, you can do that while massaging, too. Simply make it part of the massage and don't let it turn into a fight.

The Importance of Good Socialization

Socialization is a vital part of raising a healthy, mentally sound Yorkie. A young Yorkie who has been introduced to a variety of people of different ages and ethnic backgrounds will be a social dog, one who is happy to meet people and is unafraid. A Yorkie who has been kept in the backyard too much will be fearful. He may grow up afraid of children, or of senior citizens. A dog who has never met people of a different ethnic background than his owners may be afraid of different people. A Yorkie who is afraid can become aggressive out of fear, and these so-called "fear biters" are dangerous. A dog that bites out of fear often doesn't think before he acts, and most fear biters eventually have to be destroyed because of their danger to people.

Socialization also refers to meeting other dogs and pets. Your Yorkie should have opportunities to play with other well-behaved dogs so that he learns what it is to be a dog and how to behave around other dogs. Ideally, your Yorkie should also meet friendly cats, rabbits, ferrets, and other pets. Always protect your Yorkie by introducing him to pets that are known to be friendly to dogs, and in addition, protect those pets from your Yorkie. Don't let him chase the rabbit, for example, or the cat.

Socialization also includes the sights, sounds, and smells of the world around your Yorkie. Let him see and hear the trash truck that comes by each week. If he's afraid of it, have him on-leash when the truck comes by and give the driver a good dog treat to offer your Yorkie. Let your Yorkie watch the neighborhood kids go by on inline skates; just don't let him bark or chase them. Walk your Yorkie past the construction crew mending the pot-holes in the road. He can smell the hot asphalt as he watches the men work. Take your Yorkie to different places so that he can

Introduce your dog to other friendly, well-behaved, healthy dogs. Avoid rowdy, poorly behaved, aggressive dogs; they could scare your dog and ruin the socialization you've done so far.

smell new smells and see new sights. The more he sees, hears, and smells, the better his coping skills will become.

Don't overload your Yorkie, though, by trying to introduce him to everything all at once. You can start socialization when your puppy is nine to ten weeks of age by introducing him to calm, friendly family members and neighbors. Let these people pet him and cuddle him but don't allow rough games; keep the experiences very positive. Week by week, you can introduce your puppy to more people and different things.

Should your Yorkie puppy be frightened of something, don't hug him, pet him, and try to reassure him—your puppy will assume those comforting words are praise for being afraid. Instead, use a happy tone of voice, "What was that?" and walk up to

> You can start socialization when your puppy is nine to ten weeks of age by introducing him to calm, friendly family members and neighbors.

whatever scared him. Don't force him to walk up to it—just let him see you do it. For example, if your puppy sees a trashcan rolling in the street after the wind has blown it over, and he appears worried by it, hold on to your puppy's leash (to keep him from running away) and walk up to the trashcan. Ask your puppy (in an upbeat tone of voice) "What's this?" then touch the trashcan. Pat it several times so your puppy can see you touch it. If he walks up to it, praise him for his bravery!

A Crate Can Help Your Training

Originally designed as travel cages, crates have become very popular training tools for a variety of reasons.

Using a crate to confine your baby Yorkie during the night and for short periods during the day helps him learn and develop more bowel and bladder control since his instincts tell him to keep his bed clean. He is not going to want to relieve himself in his crate.

Using the crate to confine your Yorkie when you cannot supervise him will also help prevent problems from occurring. Your

A crate helps your puppy develop bowel and bladder control, prevents accidents from happening, and becomes your puppy's special place.

Yorkie can't chew up your shoes, raid the trashcan, or shred the sofa cushions if he's confined to the crate. By preventing problems from occurring, you are also preventing bad habits from developing. As he grows up you can gradually give him more freedom, but not until he's grown up and mentally mature—about two years old for most Yorkies.

Many first-time dog owners resist the idea of a crate, saying it's too much like a jail. But dogs like small, secure places—especially when sleeping. Most dogs quickly learn to like their crate and it becomes a very special place. My dogs continue to use their crates (voluntarily) on into old age because their individual crate is each dog's personal space where he can retreat to when tired, overwhelmed, or doesn't feel well.

Introduce the crate by opening the door and tossing a treat or toy inside. As the dog goes in, say the command phrase you wish to use, such as "Snickers, go to bed!" or "Snickers, kennel!" When he grabs the treat or toy, praise him, "Good boy to go to bed! Yeah!" Repeat this several times. When mealtime comes around, feed your dog his next meal inside the crate, placing the food toward the back. Leave the door open. Let him go in and come out on his own.

At night, put the crate in your bedroom next to your bed so that your Yorkie can smell you, hear you, and know that you are close by. He will be less apt to fuss during the night when he's close to you. You will also be able to hear him if he needs to go outside during the night. In addition, by being close to you, your

Choosing the Right Crate

Crates come in two basic types. There are plastic crates with solid sides that were originally designed for traveling with the dog and wire crates that look more like cages. Each style has its pros and cons. The plastic crates give the dog more security because of their solid sides. However, those solid sides make these crates bulky and they don't break down very much when you need to store them. The wire-sided cages usually fold down into a smaller, flat package, although they are still heavier than the plastic ones. The wire sides provide more ventilation for the dog but don't provide as much security. To choose the right one, look at your needs: Are you going to have to move the crate much? Are you short of storage space? What does your dog need: Does he need more air flow or more security? Choose a crate that will give your Yorkie room to stand up, move around, lie down, and stretch out.

dog gets to spend eight hours with you. In our busy lives, this is precious time!

Let your Yorkie spend the night in his crate and a few hours here and there during the day. Other than at night, your Yorkie shouldn't spend more than three to four hours at a time in the crate; he needs time to run and play during the day.

What Every Good Yorkshire Terrier Needs to Know

Dogs, including Yorkies, live by their own canine rules and those rules are not necessarily the same as yours. It's normal for dogs to sniff each other's rear end, for example, whereas people consider that extremely poor manners—even when a dog does it! Your

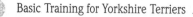

Yorkie needs to learn the social rules that you will require of him so that life with him is enjoyable rather than embarrassing.

Barking

All dogs bark; it's their way of communicating. Yorkies can, unfortunately, become problem barkers. Some bark for attention; some bark to protect their home from people walking by; others just bark for the fun of it. Your neighbors won't enjoy the fun, though, when your Yorkie starts barking nonstop! Therefore, teach your Yorkie that incessant barking isn't allowed.

> Some bark for attention; some bark to protect their home from people walking by; others just bark for the fun of it.

The first thing you need to do is teach your Yorkie a command that means "quiet" and enforce it while you're at home. Ask a neighbor to help you. Have her come over to your house and ring the doorbell. When your dog dashes to the door, making noise, tell him, "Snickers, quiet!" as you grab his collar. If he stops making noise, praise him, "Good boy to be quiet!" If he continues making noise, gently close his muzzle with your hand as you tell him to be quiet. When he stops, praise him.

Many Yorkies will learn this command with repeated training. However, some are a little more persistent about making noise. With these dogs, the correction needs to be a little stronger. Take a spray bottle and put one-eighths part vinegar to seven-eighths parts water. There should be just enough vinegar to smell. If it smells too strong (to your nose), dilute it a little more.

Then, when your Yorkie charges to the door barking or howling, follow him and quietly tell him, "Snickers, quiet!" If he stops, praise him. If he doesn't, spray the water/vinegar toward his nose.

He will be disgusted by the vinegar smell and will stop barking to think about the smell. As soon as he stops barking, praise him. The squirt bottle works as an interruption because your dog has a very sensitive sense of smell and he's going to dislike the smell of the vinegar. Therefore it can stop the bad behavior (the barking or howling) without giving an overly harsh correction.

Remember, though, that vinegar should never be sprayed in your Yorkie's eyes. Yorkies are small, with their eyes close together, so you must be extremely careful to not accidentally spray this solution into their eyes. Call your veterinarian if you do.

Use the same training techniques (verbal correction, collar, closing the muzzle, or the squirt bottle) to teach your Yorkie to be quiet around the house. When he is reliable in the house, move the training outside. If he barks at the gate when the kids are playing out in the front yard, go out front, outside of the gate, and correct him with a verbal command and a squirt from the bottle. Always, of course, praise him when he's quiet.

> If your Yorkie seems to make a lot of noise and doesn't understand your "quiet" corrections, he may not understand that he is making noise.

If your Yorkie seems to make a lot of noise and doesn't understand your "quiet" corrections, he may not understand that he is making noise. With some Yorkies, the noise just seems to come from somewhere inside them, and the dogs have no idea (consciously) that they are barking! For these dogs, teaching them to speak on command and praising them for speaking makes them more aware of the noise they're making. Set up a situation where your dog will make noise. For example, tease him with a favorite toy. When he barks, tell him, "Snickers, speak!" and praise him. Repeat this several times a day for a couple of weeks. Then tell him "Snickers, speak!" without the teaser and praise him when he

Anti-Bark Collars

Several different types of bark-control collars are available to dog owners. Some give the dog an electric shock or jolt when he barks, some make a high-pitched sound, and one gives off a squirt of citronella. The citronella works on the same principle as the vinegar/water squirt bottle: The smell disrupts the dog's concentration and is annoying enough that he stops barking. I recommend the citronella collar for most Yorkies, as it is very effective for most dogs and is a very humane training tool. However, make sure you order the smallest size collar available.

makes noise. Repeat this for a week or two. When the speak command is well understood, then you can start teaching "No speak!" in those situations where you want him to be quiet!

No Begging

Yorkies are very quick to pick up on a person who is an easy mark; and with that adorable face and brown eyes, who can resist a Yorkie? You should! There is no reason any Yorkie should beg for food from people who are eating. Begging is a bad habit and one that usually escalates to worse behavior. The dog may start by picking up food that has fallen to floor, then may start pawing at a hand or leg, trying to solicit a hand-out. Eventually the dog is actively begging and making a nuisance of himself. Sometimes it goes so far that the dog steals food from the kids' hands or off the table.

Fortunately, this is an easy habit to break, although it does require consistency from all family members. Later in this chapter we will teach the down/stay command. When your Yorkie has learned the down/stay, simply have him down/stay in a particular

Teach your dog to hold a down/stay while you're eating. He will learn that he gets to eat when you are finished so he must be patient.

spot away from the table (or where people are eating) and make him hold his position while people are eating. By teaching him to lie down and stay in a corner of the room, so that he's not underfoot, and so that he cannot beg under the table, you are breaking the bad habit. When everyone has finished eating, the dog can then be given his meal or a treat in his bowl away from the table.

When you begin teaching this new rule, use the leash and collar on the dog so that if he makes a mistake and tries to beg (and he will initially!), you can use the leash to take him back to the spot where you want him to lie down and stay. Correct him as many times as you must until he holds the position or, in a worst-case scenario, the meal is over.

No Biting

All it takes is one bite and your Yorkie could be taken from you and euthanized. All dogs owners must take this issue seriously because right now, the legal system works against dogs, not for them. There have been far too many bad dog-bite cases in which people, especially children, have been mauled or killed. Any dog bite is dangerous and should not be accepted.

A dog bite is legally defined as the dog's open mouth touching skin. Puncture wounds are not required to be considered a bite, nor must the skin be broken. Vicious intent is not necessary

No Exile

I don't like to exile dogs to the backyard while people are eating. Although putting the dog outside and closing the door is much easier than training the dog, it tends to build up more frustration in your dog. He knows you're eating and knows he's been exiled, which is enough right there to cause frustration. When you let your dog in the house later, he's likely to be wild!

However, if the dog is allowed to remain in the house, and is required to behave himself, he learns self-control. He knows he will get something to eat after the people are done so he learns to wait.

either. If your Yorkie is in the backyard and decides to grab the neighbor's son (who has the dog's toy), that is considered a bite, even if the skin is not broken.

It's important to teach all dogs that teeth are not allowed to touch skin—ever! That means the dog is not to grab your hands when he wants you to do something. Nor should he use his mouth to protest when you're taking a toy away from him. To keep your dog safe, never allow him to use his mouth so that teeth (or the mouth itself) touch skin.

It's easy to teach young puppies that they should not use their mouth. Take your hand away as you correct the puppy verbally. A consistent, "No bite!" in a deep, growly tone of voice is usually all that is needed. If your Yorkie puppy tries to use his mouth during playtime, tell him "No bite!" and get up and walk away, ending the game. If he bites hard, say "Ouch!" in a high-pitched, hurt tone of voice, followed by a deep, growly "No bite!" If the puppy is persistent about using his mouth, grab his collar with one hand while you close his mouth with the other hand as you tell him, "No bite!"

No Rough Games!

Yorkies are not large dogs, but they are sturdy little dogs who like to play and love to play rough. Unfortunately, some rough games, like wrestling and tug-of-war, give the dog the wrong message about how he should regard or treat people. Wrestling teaches the dog to use his strength against you, to fight you, and to protest when you hold him tight. Tug-of-war teaches him to use the strength of his jaws and his body against you. Neither game teaches him to respect you or to be gentle with you.

After too many of these rough-and-tumble games, every time you try to trim his toenails, a wrestling match will ensue. Or when you try to have him hold still, he will fight you. When you take something out of his mouth, he may decide to play tug-of-war with it instead! Bad behavior!

Instead of playing these detrimental games, play hide-and-seek instead, or play retrieving games.

If you have trouble teaching your Yorkie to stop using his mouth, if he seems intent on mouthing you, or you have a gut feeling that he may bite someday, call a professional trainer or behaviorist to help you. Don't wait until a bite has already happened.

Digging

Dogs dig for a number of reasons, all of which are very natural to the dog. Some Yorkies like a tight, close, snug place to cuddle up in, and a hole in the ground is just right. As hunting animals, Yorkies also like to follow scents, and that might be a beetle digging in your grass or a mouse under the pile of firewood.

Because digging is so natural, you should offer your Yorkie a spot where he can dig to his heart's content—maybe out behind the garage where it won't be too obvious to you. Dig up this area

Time Out!

Sometimes when puppies are corrected for what is natural behavior to them (such as mouthing), they will throw a temper tantrum. If your puppy should throw himself around, flail, and act like a cornered wild animal, don't correct him or try to stop it. Simply put him in his kennel crate and give him a time out. Don't yell at him, don't scold him, and don't try to reassure him. Just put him in his crate, close the door, and walk away. In 15 or 20 minutes, if he's quiet and calm, simply open the door and let him out, but don't make a big fuss over him.

Most puppies—just like most human children—will throw one or two tantrums sometime during puppyhood. If you give in to it, your puppy will learn that this horrible behavior works. However, if you give him a time out and put him away, he'll learn that this behavior doesn't work and is not rewarding.

and make the dirt soft. Bury a few dog toys and treats and invite your dog to dig here.

In the rest of the yard, fill in the holes and spread some grass seed. If he is going back to one or two holes and re-digging them, crumple up some hardware cloth (wire mesh) and put that in the hole. Then fill it in with dirt. When he tries to re-dig that hole, the wire mesh will prevent him from doing so because it will not feel at all comfortable on his paws.

Destructive Chewing

As with many other undesirable activities, destructive chewing is a natural behavior for puppies. Most Yorkie puppies begin to chew when they're teething—losing the baby teeth and getting in their adult teeth. The gums are sore and chewing seems to help

Too Many Toys?

If your dog is a chewer, don't try to change his behavior by giving him lots of toys. Too many toys will give him the idea that he can chew on anything and everything because virtually everything is his! Instead, give him just two or three toys at a time. If he likes toys, you can buy him new ones, but rotate the toys so he has only two or three at a time. On Monday, you could give him a rawhide, a squeaky toy, and a Kong toy. On Tuesday, substitute a new rawhide, a rope tug toy, and a tennis ball. By rotating the toys, you can keep him interested in them without overwhelming him.

When your dog picks up one of his toys, rather than something of yours, praise him! Tell him what a smart dog he is and how proud you are of him! Really go overboard. When he learns this is a good choice, he'll be more likely to repeat the behavior later.

Remember that if you find he's chewed something up earlier, don't punish him. After-the-fact corrections don't work.

relieve the discomfort. Unfortunately, at this point many puppies learn that chewing is fun. Besides being fun for the puppy, chewing can be incredibly destructive and costly. In addition, because the puppy who chews will inevitably swallow something he shouldn't, chewing is also dangerous. Therefore this bad habit needs to be controlled.

You can prevent a lot of bad behavior by keeping your puppy close to you when he's in the house. Close doors or put up baby gates; don't let him have free run of the house. Under your supervision, you can teach him what is right to chew on and what is wrong. When he picks up one of his toys, praise him: "Good boy to have a toy! Good toy!" When he picks up something he shouldn't, correct him, take it away, and walk him to one of his toys, saying, "Here. This is yours." When he picks up his toy, praise him.

As with many other problem behaviors, prevention is very important. Keep your Yorkie close to you, close closet doors, keep the dirty clothes picked up, and empty the trashcans. If you can prevent him from getting into trouble as a puppy, when he grows up he won't have any bad habits and won't be tempted to try them.

Other Bad Habits

Yorkies are usually pretty good dogs, but if your Yorkie has some other behavior problems, you can approach them in the same manner as we did these. What is your dog doing? Why is he doing it? When does he do it? Can you use your training to teach him? Can you prevent it from happening?

If you are unable to solve this problem yourself, don't hesitate to call a professional trainer or behaviorist for help. Ask your veterinarian whom he recommends.

Housetraining

Housetraining your Yorkie is primarily a matter of taking him outside when he needs to go, making sure he does relieve himself while out there, teaching him a phrase that tells him to try to go, and then restricting his freedom until he is reliably trained.

Using a Crate to Housetrain

When we introduced the crate a few pages ago, I said that a crate is a wonderful tool to help you housetrain your Yorkie. Because dogs are born with an instinct to keep their bed clean and will toddle away from their bed as soon as their legs will support them, the crate helps the puppy develop bowel and bladder control. You, of course, must never leave the dog in the crate too long. If you do, he will have to relieve himself and will be upset at doing so in such a confined space.

Housetraining Guidelines

Using a crate is not all that needs to be done to housetrain a baby puppy, older puppy, or adult Yorkie. He needs to be taught when to go outside, where you want him to relieve himself outside, and what the phrase you wish to use means.

> Because dogs are born with an instinct to keep their bed clean and will toddle away from their bed as soon as their legs will support them, the crate helps the puppy develop bowel and bladder control.

Just sending the dog outside won't work. If he's alone, how will you know whether or not he has relieved himself when you let him back in? He may have spent the time sniffing for rabbits rather than relieving himself and once you let him in, he may remember his bladder is full and then—woosh! It's all over your floor!

You need to go outside with him. When he's sniffing and circling, tell him quietly, "Go potty!" (Use whatever word or phrase works for you.) When he does what he needs to do, praise him, "Good boy to go potty!" Once he's done what he needs to do, bring him inside with you but restrict his freedom. Close doors or put up baby gates to keep him close. Do not consider him reliably housetrained until he's eight or nine months of age and hasn't had an accident in months! If he's younger and hasn't had any accidents, it just means you're doing everything right!

Keep in mind, too, that your Yorkie is a very small dog. What is two steps for you is ten steps for him. When his bladder is full and he needs to relieve himself, he needs to get outside quickly.

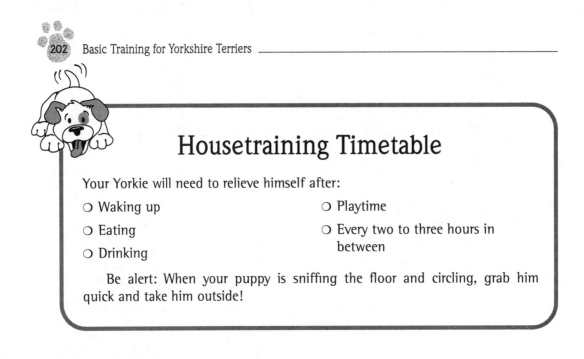

Housetraining Timetable

Your Yorkie will need to relieve himself after:

○ Waking up

○ Eating

○ Drinking

○ Playtime

○ Every two to three hours in between

Be alert: When your puppy is sniffing the floor and circling, grab him quick and take him outside!

Don't give him so much freedom in the house that he can't get to the door fast!

When Accidents Happen

If you catch your puppy in the act of relieving himself inside, you can let him know he's making a mistake, "Oh, no! Bad boy!" and take him outside. However, if you find a puddle and he's already moved away, don't correct him. It's too late.

Keep in mind that your Yorkie must relieve himself so the act of urination or defecation is not wrong. Instead, when an accident occurs, it is the place he did it rather than the act that is wrong. If you correct him after the fact, he could easily misunderstand you and think that you're angry about the act or urination or defecation. Then you'll have a dog that sneaks off behind the furniture to relieve himself.

Go outside with him, praise him when he does it outside, and supervise him in the house. Correct only those accidents that you catch happening.

Asking to Go Outside

Because so many Yorkies have a hard time controlling their barking, I do not like to teach Yorkies to bark to go outside. Why emphasize a behavior that could already be a problem? However, your dog does need a way to let you know he has to go outside so let's teach him to ring some bells instead.

Go to a craft store and get two or three bells (each one to two inches across). Hang them from the doorknob or handle of the door where the dog goes in and out. Make sure they hang at your dog's nose level. Cut up a hot dog into tiny pieces and rub one piece on the bells. Invite your dog to sniff it. When the bell rings, praise him, take him outside, and give him a tiny piece of hot dog outside.

Repeat this three or four times per session for a few days. When he starts ringing the bells on his own, praise him enthusiastically and let him outside!

Five Basic Obedience Commands

Every dog should know these five basic obedience commands. These are the foundation for good behavior, and with these commands, your Yorkie will learn self-control and be well behaved at home and when out in public.

Sit

The sit exercise teaches your Yorkie to hold still, a hard concept for many young Yorkies! When he sits, he isn't jumping on people and you can get his attention so he can do other things. This is an important lesson in self-control. There are several different ways to teach any dog to sit, and as long as the method is humane and works, that's fine. One of the easiest methods uses a treat as a lure. Tell your Yorkie, "Snickers, sit!" as you take a treat and hold it above his nose. Move the hand back toward his tail, over his head. As his head goes up to follow the treat, his hips will go down. As he sits, praise him, "Good boy to sit!"

Another easy method involves shaping the dog into position. With your Yorkie close to you, tell him, "Snickers, sit!" as you place one hand on his chest under his neck and

Hold a treat in your hand and let your dog sniff it. Then take the treat up and back over his head. As his head comes up, his hips will go down.

push gently up and back as the other hand slides down his hips and tucks them under. Think of a teeter-totter—up

When your dog sits and his hips are on the ground, praise him.

and back at the front and down and under at the rear. As you position your Yorkie in the sit, praise him, "Good boy to sit!"

With one hand on the front of the dog's chest under his neck, push gently up and back as you slide the other hand down his hips. At the same time, tell your dog to sit. Praise him when he does.

Down

When combined with the stay command (which will be taught next), the down teaches your Yorkie to be still for gradually increased periods of time. You will be able to have him lie down and stay while people are eating so he isn't begging under the table. You can have him lie at your feet while you're watching television in the evening; or you can have him stay down quietly while guests are visiting. The down/stay is a very useful command.

Start by having your Yorkie sit. Once he's sitting, show him a treat in your right hand. As you tell him, "Snickers, down!" take the treat from his nose to the floor right in front of his front paws. Lead his nose to the floor. As

Have your dog sit and then show him a treat. Tell him to lie down as you take the treat from his nose down to the ground in front of his paws.

his head follows the treat, your left hand can be resting on his shoulders to help him lie down. If

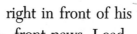

As your dog lies down, praise him.

he tries to pop back up, the left hand can keep him down. Once he's down, praise him and give him the treat. If he doesn't follow the treat down, gently pull his front legs forward and shape his body into the down position. Try to help him do the command himself rather than physically positioning him.

Stay

If your dog doesn't lie down for the treat, just scoop his front legs out from under him and gently lay him down. Praise him even though you're helping him do it.

You want your Yorkie to understand that stay means hold still. He will do this both in the sit and in the down although he will never be asked to sit/stay nearly as long as he will be able to hold a down/stay—simply because the down/stay is an easier position to hold for longer periods of time. He should hold either position until you give him permission to move.

Start by having your Yorkie sit. With an open palm toward his nose, tell him, "Snickers, stay!" At the same time, put a little pressure backwards (towards his tail) with the leash so he won't be as apt to follow you when you take a step away from him. When he seems to be holding still, release the pressure of the leash. After a few seconds, go back to your dog and praise him.

As he learns the command (in both the sit and down positions), you can gradually increase the time and distance away from him. For example, for the first few days, take one step away and have him hold the stay for ten seconds. Later that week, have him hold the stay while you take three steps

The signal for stay is an open-palmed gesture right in front of the dog's face.

away and be still for 20 seconds. Increase it gradually, though. If your Yorkie makes a few mistakes, you're moving too fast.

Walking Nicely on the Leash

It's no fun to take a dog for a walk who chokes himself on the leash. That's torture, not fun! However, when your dog learns to walk nicely, without pulling, and pays attention to you when you talk to him, then walks are fun!

Hook the leash up to your Yorkie's collar and hold the leash in one hand. Have some good dog treats in your other hand. Bend over, show your dog the treats, then back away from him so that it appears you're leading him by his nose. When he follows you, praise him. When he's following you nicely, turn so that he ends up on your left side and you're both walking forward together. You are going to have to bend over a little (Yorkies are not tall dogs!) as you use the treat to encourage him to pay attention to you. Stop, have him sit, and praise him! Practice this often and keep the walking distances very short, with lots of sits and praise. If, while you're walking, your dog gets distracted, simply back away from him again and start all over.

If your dog is too distracted to pay attention to the treats or is fighting the leash, use the leash to give him a snap-and-release correction. Back away from him, let him hit the end of the leash, and give him a snap-and-release correction at the same time you give him a verbal correction, "No pull!" When he reacts to the correction by looking at you, praise him for looking at you, "Hey, What happened? Good boy!"

Use a treat and your happy verbal praise to encourage the dog to follow you on the leash as you back away from him. Praise him when he follows you.

Show your Yorkie that when he walks with you nicely without pulling, good things happen (praise and treats); but if he pulls on the leash or ignores you, he will get a leash and verbal correction. Don't be in a hurry to stop using the treats; it will take time for this to become a new habit.

When your dog is following you nicely, turn so that the both of you are walking forward together. Keep a treat handy to pop in front of his nose should he get distracted. Praise him.

Come

It is very important that your Yorkie understands that "come" means he should come directly to you, on the first call, every time you call him. He isn't to come just when he wants to, or when nothing else is very interesting, but instead he is to come at once, every time.

Have your Yorkie on the leash and hold the leash in one hand. In the other hand have a box of dog treats. Shake the dog treats and, as you back away from your dog (so he can chase you), call him to come, "Snickers, come!" Let him catch up to you, have him sit, and then give him a treat as you praise him, "Good boy to come!"

The box of dog treats is a sound stimulus that makes your verbal command much more exciting. Since this command is so important, use the sound

Make sure your dog will come to you reliably all the time before you try it off-leash.

stimulus (the box of treats) often during your training.

When your dog is responding well on the leash, make up a long leash (20 to 30 feet in length) and repeat the training with the long leash. Continue using the box of treats, too. Don't be in a hurry to take the leash off your Yorkie. Most Yorkies aren't mentally mature and ready for off-leash training until they are at least two years old. Some aren't ready for off-leash training even then. Your training on-leash must be very, very good with few mistakes before you should ever try it off-leash and then do so only in a fenced, secure area.

Training: An Ongoing Process

Training your Yorkie can be a lot of work, as these little dogs can be stubborn, opinionated, and distracted. You need to pay attention to your dog, respond to him, and teach him right from wrong. You may also need to make some changes around the house and other family members will have to cooperate. But the reward is a well-trained dog—a friend and companion who is a pleasure instead of a pain!

A well-behaved dog is a joy to own and a pleasure to spend time with.

7

Grooming

In This Chapter

○ Home Grooming Versus Professional Grooming
○ Routine Care Every Yorkshire Terrier Needs

If you choose a Yorkshire Terrier because you admire her long, silky coat, you'll soon learn that she doesn't look that way naturally. Your Yorkie must be bathed once a week and her tresses need to be combed every day. In addition to coat care, you will also be responsible for your dog's general grooming tasks such as cleaning her teeth, cleaning her ears, and trimming the hair around her toes, face, eyes, and ears. You will also have to continually wipe her eyes clean and keep her toenails short.

While this may seem like a lot of maintenance, think of it as another way you can spend quality time with your Yorkshire Terrier. Some people even find it therapeutic and relaxing to brush and fuss with their dog. No doubt your Yorkie will treasure the attention you lavish on her.

Combing your dog every day will give you opportunity to learn much about her overall health. You will be alert to any problems, such as tumors, ear infections, skin problems, and flea or tick infestations before they become full-blown emergencies. You will also observe hair loss, lumps, redness, or tenderness on your Yorkshire Terrier. Report these signs to your veterinarian immediately.

Even if you decide to take your dog to a professional groomer, introduce your puppy to grooming and be familiar with the basics.

Home Grooming Versus Professional Grooming

While the Yorkshire Terrier looks like she would require constant upkeep and a resident professional groomer to do the job properly, any owner can groom a Yorkie. Even if you have never groomed a dog before, you can learn to do the job yourself.

> The earlier you establish a regular grooming session with your Yorkie puppy, the better.

The earlier you establish a regular grooming session with your Yorkie puppy, the better. She will begin to look forward to the experience if you introduce it in a positive, fun way.

You can begin the minute you bring her home. Pet her entire body from head to tail. To reassure her, talk to her in a soothing, upbeat voice. Handle her feet, including her toes and nails, feel her head and ears, and look into her mouth. Lightly place one of your fingers along her gum line. At first she may not let you do any of this, but if you repeat this exercise once a day for at least five minutes, she will gradually relax and eventually enjoy the massage. Choose a time when you are not rushed and can enjoy the brief encounter yourself.

Place your Yorkie on your lap or up on a raised surface such as your dining table or the bathroom or kitchen countertop. Use a rubber-backed mat or plastic tablecloth so she doesn't slip. Never leave her unattended on a high surface for any reason. This includes if the phone rings or you need to leave and get something.

If your puppy was not handled much in her previous home, this may be challenging. If so, try rewarding her with a food treat or a toy if she lets you handle her body for only a brief moment.

Even if you decide to take your Yorkie to a groomer, you will need to comb her every day. Although you may take a while to get your routine down pat, you'll enjoy the advantages of grooming your Yorkshire Terrier yourself. You won't have to transport her anywhere or pay someone to do the job. You'll also know where your dog is at all times and won't have to worry about her.

On the other hand, if you are physically unable to groom a dog or have a busy schedule, arranging professional grooming for your Yorkie may be far more convenient.

Selecting a good groomer is almost as important as finding a competent veterinarian. Groomers are experienced, trained professionals who should enjoy working with dogs. To locate the right person to pamper your pooch, ask other dog owners or your veterinarian—the voice of experience—to recommend reputable groomers in your area. Visit these locations personally and ask the grooming shop owners a few questions about their grooming experience, especially with Toy breeds and Yorkshire Terriers. They should take the time to answer your questions politely and accurately.

What to Look for in a Groomer

The groomer you select for your Yorkshire Terrier should:

○ Have certifiable knowledge and hands-on experience with Toy breeds.

○ Treat clients with courtesy and listen to their concerns.

○ Have a good rapport with dogs and handle each dog firmly but gently.

○ Require experienced personnel to handle dogs.

○ Show a genuine love of dogs.

○ Never allow puppies that are not fully vaccinated to be around older dogs.

○ Know how a Yorkshire Terrier should look when finished.

○ Never allow dogs with communicable diseases in the shop.

The grooming facility should:

○ Be sterile and clean.

○ Supply an adequate number of crates in all sizes to house clients' dogs.

○ Be large enough to space multiple grooming tables well apart from one another.

○ Provide a special outside area for potty breaks that is safe and clean.

Inquire about the type of brushes or combs used, shampoos, and cream rinses or detanglers.

Ask if they require proof of vaccinations and whether a current bordetella vaccine is required. Find out what services they offer and how long they have been in business. If you found the groomer on your own, ask for a list of references.

Also observe how other employees in the shop relate to the dogs and the kind of care they give them. Do they leave the dogs unattended on the tables? Are the groomers rough-handed or kind with the dogs? They should be firm but gentle and confident. Do they work on more than one dog at a time? The atmosphere should be relaxed, with groomers not showing signs of stress or exhaustion.

Look at the shop itself. Other than a few clipped hairs on the floor, is it generally neat and clean? The wash area should also be clean. Is the room temperature fairly warm but comfortable? Is the groomer someone with whom you feel you can talk? If you feel comfortable leaving your Yorkie in the care of this person, your dog will no doubt enjoy the experience. There's a lot to be said for dropping your dog off and returning to pick up a healthy, happy, perfectly well-groomed dog in just a few hours.

Routine Care Every Yorkshire Terrier Needs

Yorkshire Terriers should be combed once a day for a few minutes and bathed once every week or two. This keeps his beautiful long and silky coat in good, healthy condition. With puppies between the ages of four and eight months, bathing them once a month is enough.

Dogs have sebaceous glands that mildly cover their coats with oil. Some breeds of dogs have an undercoat, which protects them against the cold, but a Yorkie does not. While the oil in his skin is enough to keep him from getting soaked to the skin when it rains, not having an undercoat won't give him extra warmth when it's very cold. If you bathe your Yorkie too much, his body cannot produce enough oil to keep him protected, and his hair and skin will become dry and chapped.

Essential Grooming Tools

Pin brush

Slicker brush

Metal comb with fine spacing at one end and wide spacing at the other

Flea comb

Several bath towels

Sponge or wash cloth

Mat rake

Grooming glove

Ear lotion

Round-tipped scissors

Nail clippers

Nail file

Styptic powder

Doggie tooth brush and paste

Shampoo (either made for a dog's show coat or a regular human shampoo)

Conditioner (for most Yorkies a cream rinse is best. For oily coats use a rinse made with vinegar and water or a small amount of baking soda mixed with water)

Fine-mist sprayer bottle filled with a mixture of one teaspoon hair conditioner and water

Hair-dryer

Clippers

Tiny latex rubber bands

If a Yorkie has dandruff, it means he has dry skin. Frequent bathing, the wrong shampoos and grooming products, or low humidity in your home can cause this.

While you wouldn't bathe many breeds of dogs with human hair-care products, you can use many mild formulas safely on a Yorkie because of their unique coat.

Because the Yorkie's coat is a lot like human hair, the cleaner you keep it, the healthier it will be. Luckily this breed is small enough to be bathed in your kitchen sink. Other grooming tasks—nail clipping, ear cleaning, dental care, and checking anal glands—are just as important.

Bathing

A pet Yorkie with a full, unclipped coat can stay beautiful if she has a bath once a week or once every two weeks. This takes less than an hour. If your Yorkie goes outdoors a lot, she will surely need this bath because her long, silky tresses will pick up a lot of dirt. Even going out on a dewy morning will attract dust like a magnet. You shouldn't have to give her a bath more frequently than once a week if you also brush her for only a few minutes each day. A coat without any tangles is less likely to pick up bits and pieces of dirt and grime.

Because she is so tiny, you can probably bathe your Yorkie in your own kitchen sink, although you may find the bathroom, where you can store and lay out all of your dog's grooming items, more convenient. For owners who don't want to bathe their dog in their own tub or in their kitchen, you can always find another alternative. Some people prefer to use a raised portable bathtub made specifically for dogs. You can set it up wherever you have the most room or even outdoors on a warm day. The advantage to this tub is you won't clog your bathroom drain with dog hair. The disadvantage is that your Yorkie will not have warm water outdoors unless you carry buckets of heated water yourself from the house or have an nozzle to put on your indoor sink and run a hose outside.

Whatever bathtub you choose to use, a spray nozzle attachment is helpful. Set up a small table to hold essential bathing tools. If you are indoors, a raised counter area will come in handy to stand your dog on where you can also dry her with towels and a hair-dryer.

Before beginning the washing ritual, assemble all items you will need and

Did You Know?

Nose prints can be used to identify dogs just as fingerprints are used to identify humans.

place them near the wash area. Once your Yorkie gets wet, you won't want to leave her to get something you've forgotten.

Be sure you place a few towels nearby and have the hair-dryer plugged in. You can also use a small fan heater but keep it at least one foot away from your dog.

> Before beginning the washing ritual, assemble all items you will need and place them near the wash area.

Do not attempt to brush your dry dog before bathing her, especially if her coat is dirty. This process will break the hair. Instead, use your fingers to loosen whatever tangles she might have accumulated. Mist her coat with the spray bottle filled with conditioner and water and let it sit for about ten minutes. Use a comb to untangle any mats.

○ Place your Yorkie on a nonskid mat in the tub.
○ Place a cotton ball in each of your Yorkie's ears to prevent water from penetrating.
○ Using lukewarm water, rinse your dog's head and body.
○ Apply shampoo on your Yorkie's body. Do not use any around her eyes.
○ Gently rub the shampoo through her coat and underneath her body, including her rear end.
○ Rinse well.
○ Apply a grooming rinse and leave it on for one to two minutes.
○ Rinse well again.

Avoid bathing sick or injured Yorkies.

Drying your Yorkie is very important. Do not let her run soaking wet around the house, thinking she will air-dry, because she may catch a cold. Use a big, thick towel to wrap her up and soak up as much excess water as possible. Avoid rubbing the coat as it may tangle. When she is damp, begin blow-drying her with a hair-dryer. Use the lowest setting and do not bring the dryer any closer than eight inches from your dog's body.

While holding the dryer in one hand, use a wire brush to help move the warm air through your dog's coat. Lay your Yorkie in your lap on her back or on a table and begin brushing her belly and legs first. Then rotate her and begin drying the outermost layers of the top coat while extending the brush outward toward the ends of the strands at the same time. Use your fingertips to separate tangles before brushing them. Place your fingers between the snarl and your dog's body so you don't inadvertently hurt her.

To dry the rest of your Yorkie's body, especially her tail, paws, and head, use a comb. Once the entire dog is dry, apply a few mists of grooming spray on the brush.

Brushing

You would think that all this fussing would annoy a Yorkshire Terrier, but quite the opposite is true. Once she becomes accustomed to the grooming rituals, she will actually love to be pampered and will begin to look forward to the time you lavish on her.

While it sounds like a time-consuming and complicated process, brushing an adult Yorkie coat takes only ten minutes a day. With a puppy, brushing takes just a few minutes. When your Yorkie is six to eight months of age, she will be ready for longer grooming sessions.

While many dogs shed twice a year, Yorkies do not. The only hairs they lose are the ones that adhere to the comb and brush or the ones that must be cut

Conquering Grooming Disasters

Here are some common grooming problems and the best ways to handle them:

Burrs   Although romps through fields or wooded areas offer wonderful exercise for your dog, you may pay the price of burrs, seeds, twigs, or other things sticking to your dog. A Yorkie's long hair is especially attractive to these hangers-on. Try to remove them immediately with a fine-toothed comb. Mink oil conditioners, available at grooming shops or supply stores, can make the coat sleek, which makes it easier to remove burrs.

Skunk Spray   You may have heard that tomato juice takes out the smell of skunk. This is not true. Not only does tomato juice not take the smell out, it also leaves you with a pinkish, sticky dog! Instead, use a high-quality skunk shampoo; your pet-supply store or groomer should be able to recommend one. Remember to brush your dog thoroughly before bathing him (plugging your nose if need be) since any dead, loose fur just retains the smell and prevents the shampoo from penetrating all the way down to the skin.

Another option that comes highly recommended is a special "recipe" you can easily prepare at home. Include in your dog's bath one quart bottle of 3% hydrogen peroxide, $\frac{1}{4}$ cup of baking soda (sodium bicarbonate), and one teaspoon of liquid soap. Follow the bath with a tap-water rinse.

No matter what you use, though, your dog may continue to smell slightly skunky every time he gets wet for several weeks or even months.

Paint   Before it hardens, immediately wash out any latex paint your dog brushes against or rolls in. This paint, which is toxic, thankfully is water soluble. If your dog gets into oil paint, you'll have to cut away the fur with paint on it. Never use varsol or turpentine, and never let your dog chew at the paint.

Gum   You discover a bright pink wad of bubble gum stuck to your Yorkie's fur! Don't rush for the scissors yet. First, try rubbing the gum with ice cubes to make it brittle. If the gum is stuck only to the ends of the hairs, you should be able to break or lift it off. If it's down in the coat, however, try using peanut butter as a solvent. If your dog steps in gum, try rubbing it with ice and then peeling it off the pads. If the gum is attached to the hair on the paw, cut it away.

Tar   Hot tar can scald your dog. If your pet has come in contact with hot tar, apply cold water immediately and see your veterinarian. If your Yorkshire Terrier has a too-close encounter with cooled, sticky tar, apply ice cubes to harden the tar and then cut it away with scissors.

out in extreme cases of matting or tangling. To help safeguard the coat from mats, check it after an outing and promptly remove anything foreign such as leaf fragments or bits of grass. If such debris is allowed to remain in the hair, it will also collect dirt, which will lead to matting.

When you are beginning a brushing session, first get rid of minor tangles by using a wire brush to loosen the hair. Use your fingertips to separate the remaining knots of hair. Then comb it until the hair is smooth, starting with the tips of the hair. With one hand, hold a strand of hair close to the skin and with the other hand comb through the outermost hair until there is no resistance. Repeat sections of the coat until the comb moves smoothly from the roots to the tips. Just because you can't see your dog's abdomen and chest hair doesn't mean those areas shouldn't also be brushed. They will mat easily so be sure to comb them every day.

When you are through combing, use the wire brush to brush the entire coat. It's almost like a massage that your Yorkie will love. This technique loosens hairs and stimulates growth. When you are done, spray some finishing spray onto the brush and run it through the coat with swift quick strokes. Finally, use a natural-bristle brush to put on the finishing touches. Your Yorkie's coat will shine and glisten and be completely straight.

There is also some styling involved. The hair on the Yorkie's body should be parted down the middle of the back and hang down smoothly on both sides. Start when your dog is young and use the comb to part the hair from the bridge of the nose to the tip of the tail. Comb down evenly on both sides.

Creating that stylish topknot is easy. Aside from his glistening coat, the Yorkie's trademark is his tuft of hair held together with a red or an orange bow. Called the topknot, it keeps the hair from hanging in your dog's face and eyes.

To achieve this look, comb the hair from the corner of the eye up toward the ear as if to part it. Gather it together on each side, being sure to include the hair on the back of the head, which is known as a fall. Use a latex rubber band to gather it into a ponytail. Don't pull the hair too tight and do not catch skin in the topknot. This might cause baldness or skin fungus. On top of the band, fasten a plastic barrette. You may use a bow on top of the barrette if you wish. While you adjust the barrette and bow, be careful not to poke your Yorkie in the eye with the comb.

> Aside from his glistening coat, the Yorkie's trademark is his tuft of hair held together with a red or an orange bow.

The Yorkie's beard also has to be groomed every day. As neat an eater as she is, food bits will still accumulate in her beard. When combined with water droplets from drinking, the beard will mat in no time. Therefore after every meal, take a damp cloth and remove the food bits from the beard and muzzle. Comb the beard and the hair beneath the muzzle. Work downward to pull the comb through the hair. If you groom correctly, the beard may practically reach the ground.

You may need to clean your dog's hindquarters. Check the rear end as stray bits of fecal matter sometimes stick to the long hair in the back, forming crusts that should be removed. Use a wet washrag to keep the anal area clean so it does not become infected.

Nail Clipping

Yorkie paws are no different than those of other dogs. Toenails grow all the time and must be trimmed on a regular basis, preferably once a week. If allowed to grow, they will become overgrown quickly and will cause problems for your dog. Nails that hang too far over the pads of the feet will start to curl back toward the bottom of the toes and can cut into the dog's pads. These nails impair the dog's movement and make it nearly impossible for her to have any traction on a floor and she can easily slip and fall. Neglected toenails will also make the toes spread out and cause the foot to flatten. Not only is this unattractive, it slows down the dog's movement as well. Long nails can also give you deep scratches when you pick up your Yorkie and can easily snag on your clothing, carpets, and upholstery, as well as tall grasses or outdoor plants.

To help you remember before they grow too long, choose the same day every week when you have a few extra minutes. The day you bathe your Yorkie and are already thinking about grooming is convenient, but toenails can be done at any time.

Start trimming her puppy toenails the first week you bring her home. Hopefully her breeder or previous owner already trimmed her nails several times so she is accustomed to the process. If not, or you have an older dog, it's never too late to train her to accept and even like it.

If you have never trimmed a dog's toenails before, it is natural to feel nervous. Most owners assume they will cut the nail back too far and the dog will bleed to death! Since most Yorkie toenails are black instead of pink or white, it may be hard at first to find the quick, which is where a blood vessel joins the nail. To help you locate the quick on your Yorkie's black toenail, use a flashlight. It also helps to have the container of styptic powder close at hand in case you do cut into the quick.

Before beginning any clipping, examine one of your dog's nails and look for the point at which the nail starts to curve down toward the tip. That's the end you're going to take off.

You'll find several different types of nail trimmers in pet-supply stores. You'll want to select the smallest size for your Yorkie. When shopping for a nail clipper, hold it in your hand to see whether it is a comfortable fit. One model, a guillotine type, has handles like pliers with a small circle at the other end. When you squeeze the handles together, a blade comes out through the circle and quickly cuts the nail you have placed inside the circle. Another style is a scissors design.

When you decide to begin trimming your dog's nails, start slowly and just handle your Yorkie's feet and touch the toes. Depending upon how often her feet have been handled in the past, you may not be able to do any more than this. Repeat this a few times over the next several days until your Yorkie is more comfortable with you touching her toes.

When you are ready to proceed, enlist a friend to help you. You may want to put your Yorkie up on a table, but be sure to put a nonskid pad underneath her. Or, one of you can hold the dog against your chest, letting the feet dangle, while the other person can clip the nails.

Another position is to turn the dog upside down either on the floor or between your legs on your lap. If you do the nail-trimming after Yorkie's bath, her nails will be softer and easier to cut.

Dogs who squirm when you start to trim their nails really want to be in charge of the situation. Unless the quick has been a cut once or twice before or they had some other bad experience with nail trimming, they are rebelling against their feet being held tightly by you or someone else—not about the actual trimming, which is painless when done correctly.

Send a firm but nonviolent message to your dog that you are in charge. The more you perform these maneuvers, the more your dog will relax.

Make sure you have plenty of light. Some Yorkie owners actually prefer to do their dogs' nails outdoors in natural light when it is brightest.

Gently but firmly start with one or two toenails. If your Yorkie is very relaxed and doesn't fuss too much, trim as many nails as you can. If she has a temper tantrum, be firm and at least hold one toe without clipping it. Do not quit until you are ready—not when your Yorkie decides she doesn't want to stand still. While you don't want to be too harsh about making your Yorkie stay, encourage her firmly with a verbal command to "Stop!" When she pauses for even the briefest moment and allows you to trim the first nail, immediately offer a tiny food treat. This teaches your Yorkie that nail trimming is a positive experience.

Once your dog settles down a bit and you are ready to trim, ask your assistant to gently hold your Yorkie's head and body while you lift the foot. Using your index finger, press slightly on the pad of the foot. At the same time, use your thumb to press down on the first joint of your dog's toe nearest the nail. This extends the nail as far as it will go and doesn't allow the nail to retract. If your dog is behaving, verbally praise her.

Trim off the tip of the nail that is pointing downward. If by accident you should cut into the quick, pour a little styptic powder into the cap of the container and gently dip the bleeding nail into the powder. The blood will clot immediately and your dog will not "bleed to death."

Did You Know?

The bloodhound is the only animal whose evidence is admissible in an American court.

When you are just learning how to cut nails, take off just a little bit rather than the whole growth. Once you have trimmed all the nails, you can use an emery board (the kind people use to file their nails) to remove any sharp edges.

If nail trimming becomes a stressful experience for you and your dog, you can always take him to a professional groomer to do the job.

Trimming the Paws

Besides trimming the toenails, the hair that grows between the pads of the feet and between the toenails should also be trimmed. These areas can attract dirt and small mats, which can be painful for your Yorkie. Use small scissors to trim these areas. Separate the pads with your fingers while trimming. The hair covering the back of the toenail should also be trimmed off. This is not difficult unless your Yorkie won't hold still!

Ear Care

Yorkie ears also need attention once or twice a week. Because most Yorkie ears are alert and open, they are prone to dirt, mites, and infections. Ears that flop over or down instead of standing up are particularly susceptible to yeast infections. The moisture that is trapped inside the ear fold becomes a breeding ground for mites.

Using a Q-tip is the easiest way to keep ears clean.

Using a Q-tip is the easiest way to keep ears clean. Be sure you use a separate Q-tip for each ear. Dip the Q-tip in an ear-cleaning solution available from your veterinarian. This veterinary ear rinse will break up any wax that may have accumulated inside the ear. Or you can dribble a few drops of the solution directly into the ear. Cover the ear with a cotton ball or two, as your Yorkie will probably shake her head. Grasping the sides of the ear gently, squeeze the folds together up and down. You will hear the liquid make a squishing sound. This loosens the debris. Use a Q-tip or a small piece of cotton to clean the area. If you notice dark brown or black debris on the cotton, a bacterial or yeast infection or ear mites is a possibility. Repeat this procedure the next day and continue until the cotton comes out clean. Be sure to dry the ear thoroughly each time you use the ear rinse.

If you are afraid you will puncture your dog's eardrum by using a Q-tip, don't worry. While the ear canal is at the base of the actual ear, the eardrum is actually located much farther down and out of reach.

If your Yorkie yelps a bit when you clean her ears, that means the solution feels cold and she isn't accustomed to the sensation. If an infection is present, the area is probably sensitive and the cleaner may sting a bit.

If you see your Yorkie shaking her head or scratching at her ears several times, she may have ear mites. Mites thrive on ear wax and debris in the ear canal and can irritate or cause an allergic reaction in your Yorkie that results in severe itching.

Several products on the market are designed to rid your dog of ear mites. Ask your veterinarian for a recommendation. Because ear mites are highly contagious, if one dog has ear mites, any other dogs you have will get them, too.

Ear-Hair Trimming

The hair around the edges of the ears should also be trimmed once every two or three weeks. The ears should only be trimmed down one-third of the ear

from the tip. Be sure to leave the hair on the back of the ear leather so that your Yorkie will retain some body heat.

Tooth Care

Teeth cleaning is another aspect of good grooming for many breeds, but is especially important for Yorkies and other Toy breeds. Yorkies have weaker gums, which leads to tooth problems and premature tooth loss. Tartar builds up quickly and plays host for bacteria and the resulting odors of bad breath. Gums become swollen and red, or bleed, often causing pus between the teeth and the gum line. A Yorkie who is hesitant to eat or drink and loses interest in favorite chew toys may be showing signs of gum disease. If teeth are neglected, periodontal disease will set in, and teeth may have to be pulled because they have decayed. Your dog can also develop heart or kidney infections from tooth decay.

> A Yorkie who is hesitant to eat or drink and loses interest in favorite chew toys may be showing signs of gum disease.

You can prevent problems from starting by brushing your dog's teeth several times a week. This procedure will break down tartar and keep the teeth clean. Some toothpastes for dogs have an enzyme that breaks down and eliminates plaque inside the mouth. Caring for your dog's teeth on a regular basis will help you avoid having to take your Yorkie for veterinary cleanings and anesthesia, which can be risky for a small dog.

Like nail trimming, begin cleaning your dog's teeth during the first days you have her. At first, use your finger to gently lift her upper lip to examine the teeth, then quickly massage the teeth and gum line. Do this many times a day for several days. This is an easy way to let your Yorkie know it's okay to allow something foreign in her mouth. When your puppy is a few months old, she will be teething and even more reluctant to allow you to touch her mouth. Do so gently, and don't give up. Once she allows you to put your fingers in her mouth, choose a convenient time when you're not rushed to clean her mouth.

Place a small amount of the canine toothpaste on your finger and gently rub it over a few teeth. Do not use human toothpaste because it is not formulated for a canine stomach!

You can also purchase a finger-sized toothbrush made for this purpose. Place the paste between the bristles instead of on top where it may fall off and simply land in your dog's mouth. Begin brushing in a circular motion just like you would brush your own teeth. For the first few times, your Yorkie may not let you do her whole mouth. If that happens, just brush a few teeth each time. Remember to make this a positive experience for your dog.

Soon you will be able to concentrate on your dog's rear teeth, where most of the plaque and tartar tends to accumulate. When you brush the front teeth, angle the brush 45 degrees. Eventually you will want to brush the whole mouth for almost a minute.

If your dog's mouth has been neglected for a long time, you may want to have the teeth cleaned by your veterinarian and then start cleaning them yourself after that.

Anal Glands

Another and more unpleasant aspect of grooming is checking your Yorkshire Terrier's anal glands. These two small scent glands, which lie on either side of the anus, normally are emptied when the dog defecates. Occasionally, though, the glands fill up and the dog is uncomfortable. She

will scoot her bottom along the floor in an effort to bring some relief and bite or lick at her rear. If the glands do not empty on their own, they can become infected or impacted.

Your veterinarian will have to clean them out by expressing them and might prescribe an antibiotic to clear the infection. Once they've had an anal gland problem, some Yorkies may become fixated on the area and will frequently chew or bite at it.

To continually check the glands yourself, ask your veterinarian or groomer to show you how to express them. The glands have quite an odor so, if you choose to do this task yourself, you might want to do the expressing in the bathtub, but before giving your dog her bath.

Some Yorkie owners have discovered that feeding their dogs small bits of raw carrot once a day helps to naturally empty the sacs without any manual intervention.

8

Family Life

In This Chapter

❍ Playtime
❍ Playing Nicely with Children
❍ Yorkshire Terriers and Other Animals
❍ Traveling with and Boarding Your Yorkshire Terrier

I f you want a dog to shadow your every move, a Yorkshire Terrier is the canine for you. This small but energetic Toy enjoys being with his people. To him, family life
means keeping up with all the activities in which the family is involved, including outdoor exercise, canine sports,
visiting folks in the hospital, or just playing nicely with
the children. Because he is so intelligent, your Yorkie is a
good listener and can learn new games quickly. Provide
early socialization and teach proper behavior and your
Yorkie will be a real member of the family for many years
to come.

Playtime

All puppies love to play. The world is brand-new to them and everything is a potential toy. They will chase a butterfly, bark at the sound of the piano, and take great delight in stealing tissues out of the bathroom trash. It's a good thing Yorkie pups are always ready for fun because playtime is a necessary activity for healthy growth and development. Productive play helps release any aggression and satisfies your Yorkie's need to be active. Hopefully he will develop a positive sense about his environment and learn to play with items of which you approve.

Your Yorkie will want you to play with him and will bring you a toy and look at you, hoping you will get the message. With his ears pricked up and his tail wagging back and forth, he'll likely give a few sharp barks to encourage you. His front legs will be flat on the ground and his rear end will be raised in the air. This canine sign for "Come play with me" will definitely catch your attention.

When you build a bond with your dog through playtime, you'll have so much fun that you'll want to schedule extra time for playing with your Yorkie!

To help your Yorkie keep this joy about life, you can provide many opportunities for acceptable activities—taking a walk in the neighborhood, visiting patients in the hospital, and competing in canine sports such as obedience, flyball, and agility. Not only are such activities good for your Yorkie, but you may benefit as well!

As long as he is healthy, a 15-minute walk each day will give your Yorkie a chance to get out and see the world plus get some exercise. The important thing is to let your dog have a good time and keep his playful attitude.

Common-Sense Rules
for Kids and Yorkshire Terriers

○ Parents must supervise all interactions.

○ Never leave a baby or small child alone with any breed of dog.

○ Crate-train your Yorkie, but children should be taught to never go into the dog's crate. Teach the child that the crate is the Yorkie's special, private room.

○ Never bother a dog when he's eating or sleeping.

○ Never tease and always be gentle. No yelling, feet stomping or arm swinging. Never let children rough-house with a Yorkie.

○ Don't poke or pull eyes, ears, nose, tail.

○ Don't permit snack stealing from kids. Place the Yorkie in his crate or another room with his own doggie snack during little people snack time.

○ Don't allow kids to supervise your Yorkie. Parents must be in charge of doggie discipline.

Exercise

The normally active Yorkie is always ready to go. Once the leash is out and your dog knows it's time to take a walk, be prepared for lots of darting, scampering, bouncing, and hopping. The exercise is good for him, and unless he is trained to walk on a leash, don't expect him to stroll leisurely. He will want to forge ahead, so walking out in public can be a challenge.

Avoid taking him on a flexi-leash—one that allows your Yorkie to walk up to 12 feet away from you—because he will get too far ahead and you'll be unable to protect him if a big dog without a leash approaches. Some big dogs think Toy dogs are fair game and treat them like prey. Many Yorkies have been injured when

their owners weren't prepared to pick them up immediately in a dangerous situation.

To protect your Yorkie on outings, walk him on a short non-retractable leash. Using a harness is also a good idea so he does not strain his neck and injure himself if he pulls.

Obedience

Teaching your dog not to pull on the leash is the safest alternative. Here is where obedience training using positive reinforcement methods comes in handy. A necessity for many dogs, obedience training can also become a wonderful outlet for an active Yorkie and perhaps become a competitive hobby for you and your Yorkie. It's also a good way to meet other people who share your interest in dogs.

> A necessity for many dogs, obedience training can also become a wonderful outlet for an active Yorkie and perhaps become a competitive hobby for you and your Yorkie.

The American Kennel Club began holding obedience competitions in 1936, and although the exercises are basically the same, the competition level has risen considerably. Every dog who enters can qualify for a title if he is properly trained (and the handler doesn't make too many errors!). Three qualifying scores are needed to earn a companion dog (CD) title.

To earn a CD title, a Yorkie must pass a series of basic exercises, including sit, down, stay, heel, and come. Once that title is won a dog can build on those commands to enter more advanced competitions and compete for companion dog excellent (CDX) title and a utility dog (UD) title. These exercises build confidence in any dog, but Yorkies particularly assume an air of importance when they can accomplish these tasks.

Further competition and a lot more work lets you achieve the utility dog excellent (UDX) title and/or the obedience trial champion (OTCH). To attain these levels, you (or your trainer) and your dog should attend obedience practice matches and many sets of classes.

Although Yorkshire Terriers don't always get the same high scores that Golden Retrievers, Shetland Sheepdogs, Labradors, and Border Collies receive, several Yorkies have earned UD and UDX titles. According to American Kennel Club records, two Yorkies—Jo-San's Golden Lexus owned by Leann Golden and Howard's Being Good owned by Cathy Parker—earned UD titles in 1999. There have been two Yorkies in the history of the breed—Thomas and Chance—who have earned OTCH titles.

Yorkies are capable of earning all of these titles. Many have earned remarkably high scores. If for some reason your dog does not reach the top-level competition after you have done the training, you at least reap the benefits of having a trained dog who looks forward to pleasing you.

To earn a CD title, your dog must enthusiastically heel by your side on- and off-leash as you walk in a slow, medium, and brisk pace. He'll also have to sit next to you when you stop, stand still while a judge examines him, sit and stay off-leash, followed by a lie down and stay while you are at the opposite end of the competition ring.

In CDX and UD competitions, the Yorkie must perform more advanced exercises, including retrieving a dumbbell you have thrown and jumping over an obstacle. Every dog is given 200 points at the beginning, and points are deducted for missed exercises. Any dog who passes with a score of at least 170 and does not fail any exercise qualifies for a title. After three qualifying scores, the title is awarded.

Although every trainer has her own methods of training, most use a nylon collar instead of a choke chain and all avoid putting much pressure on the neck.

To prepare for the obedience ring, or even if you do not plan to do any formal obedience training, train your Yorkie for the Canine Good Citizen (CGC) test. Sponsored by the American Kennel Club, the CGC test evaluates the dog's reactions to ten situations he may encounter in real life. Dogs either pass or fail the test, and you need to complete it only once to earn the title CGC. Owners are given a CGC certificate, which is good evidence that you have a well-behaved dog.

Canine Good Citizens must accept a friendly stranger, sit politely for petting, be well-groomed, walk on a loose lead, and move assuredly through a crowd. He must also sit and lie down on command, stay in place, come when called, and behave politely around other dogs. Two more challenging tests include the Yorkie remaining confident when there is a distraction, and being comfortable when his owner leaves for a few seconds.

Canine Sports

Just because a Yorkie is small doesn't mean he can't participate in the same canine sports the big dogs do—agility, Frisbee competition, canine freestyle, tracking, flyball, and backpacking are a few.

Agility was first introduced in England at the Crufts Dog Show in February 1978, and the AKC acknowledged it in the United States in August 1994. Agility is a fun sport for participants and spectators because it's fast, lively, and very exciting.

Working without a leash, the handler either runs alongside his dog or positions himself on a course and guides his dog through a sequence of obstacles. A timed event also based on accuracy, the dog goes through a tunnel, balances on a teeter-totter, goes over an A-frame, climbs across a catwalk, and sits on a table. Additional variations require hand and verbal signals to direct the dog.

Max, a six-pound Yorkie bundle of energy, was taken to agility classes by his owner to gain some confidence and to have some fun. "It took him a few times not to run away from the tunnel, but once he realized it wasn't going to hurt him, he began zooming through it in a flash," Max's owner says.

Until your dog is totally trained on each piece of agility equipment, it's a good idea to keep his leash on and closely supervise his movements. One slip off the catwalk, and your Yorkie could suffer injury. Be wary also of bigger or more aggressive dogs who are competing in the same class. They can view your dog as prey or may injure him by stepping on him.

Frisbee

Trying to catch a disc that is flying through the air will delight any Yorkie. Although Frisbee competitions were once held with larger dogs in mind, Chigger, a Yorkie owned by Sharon and John Thompson, not only competed in Frisbee competitions but won two regional Frisbee Championships. Chigger was also responsible for adding a new rule to the sport, which allows smaller dogs to use a smaller Frisbee.

Canine Freestyle

A fairly new canine sport is freestyle, which pairs a dog and a human partner. Incorporating obedience sits and stays, ca-

Did You Know?

The Beatles song "Martha My Dear" was written by Paul McCartney about his Sheepdog, Martha.

nine freestyle is a synchronized dance competition set to music. The dog and owner can perform together or as part of a group. Although Misha only weighs two and a half pounds, her spins are spectacular. As part of her routine, she runs through her owner's arms and legs. She gives demonstrations in the sport all over the country.

Backpacking

When you think about going out in the wilderness and hiking with your canine companion, you probably picture a medium- to large-size dog. Not Pam Wengorovius. Pam hikes five miles at a time with her seven-pound Yorkie, Meg, and that's with Meg carrying her own food and water! Beginning with hankies tied to her back, Meg now has her own backpack. Training started slowly but lengthened over several sessions.

Tracking

The American Kennel Club offers another organized sport for which Yorkies are naturals: tracking. In tracking tests, a dog has to sniff out a certain trail. While many Hound breeds excel at this, most dogs, including Yorkies, can follow a trail by scent. What Yorkie doesn't love to sniff out treats dropped along the ground?

You do have to practice and teach your Yorkie the elements of tracking, and you can get help preparing your Yorkie for this sport through some performance clubs.

This sport involves some training but is not a timed or a competitive event against other dogs. You do have to practice and teach your Yorkie the elements of tracking, and you can get help preparing your Yorkie for this sport through some performance clubs.

To earn a tracking dog (TD) title, your Yorkie wears a special tracking harness to sniff out a track that is one to two hours old and not longer than 500 yards with two right-angle turns. The dog must locate a scented article that has been placed at the end of the track. Once that title is earned, he can progress to working on a tracking dog (TDX) title. The track for this test is three to five hours old and is longer—up to 1,000 yards long. It may incorporate tall grass, slight ditches, and false-scent articles.

Six Yorkies have earned Tracking Dog titles. Arlene King and her Yorkie, Illusion's Sarah Ferguson ("Fergie") completed the first TDX title in the history of the breed. Arlene began training Fergie in the prairies of Illinois when Fergie was slightly less than four months old and weighed only two pounds. She was so small that the only harness that would fit her was a hot-pink cat harness. Shortly before her second birthday, Fergie earned her TDX title.

Flyball

Another canine sport that appeals to many small-dog owners is flyball. In this event two dog teams compete against each other in a timed relay race. Each dog runs a short distance to a box containing tennis balls. The dog must jump on a lever that releases the ball. After catching the ball the dog runs back and gives the ball to his owner, thus enabling another dog on his team to start his relay to the flyball box. The dogs wait in excitement for their turn to run and get the ball.

Yorkie backpacker Meg also does flyball and is on a flyball team. Although she uses smaller tennis balls, she still manages to keep up with the big dogs.

Service Dog

While many large breeds of dogs are trained to be guide dogs for the blind and to assist their owners confined to wheelchairs, Yorkies can also be trained to help their owners. Many organizations train dogs for service work.

Timmy, bred by Cathy Sullivan, is learning to be a service dog for his owner who has post-polio syndrome and hearing loss. Timmy helps around the house and alerts his owner to noises of which she wouldn't normally be aware. When he's not working, he's also a great lap warmer.

Earthdog Trials

Dachshunds and several Terrier breeds—Australian, Bedlington, Border, Cairn, Dandie Dinmont, Jack Russell, Smooth and Wire-Haired Fox, Lakeland, Norfolk, Norwich, Scottish, Sealyham, Skye, Welsh, and West Highland White—participate in Earthdog Trials with much enthusiasm. In Earthdog Trials, dogs must dig into the ground and choose the correct underground tunnel that leads to a small rat in a cage. Once they have located the rodent, they have completed the trial.

> In Earthdog Trials, dogs must dig into the ground and choose the correct underground tunnel that leads to a small rat in a cage.

While Yorkies are not currently permitted to enter these trials in the American Kennel Club, the rules may one day be changed to include them. Historically, the breed was used to kill rats and other varmints that tunneled underground. For that reason, some Yorkie owners feel they are qualified to participate.

The dogs do not need any prior training, as tunneling for rodents is based on instinct alone.

Other Jobs—Therapy Work

If you are looking to do something with your Yorkie that is less active but just as challenging, consider taking your dog to visit patients in hospitals and nursing homes. Only therapy dogs are usually allowed in these residence facilities, and you and your Yorkie can bring much joy to people confined there. Imagine the smiles you will see on patients' faces when they see your small but confident Yorkie coming to greet them. Studies have shown that petting a dog can lower one's blood pressure and provide a calming effect. Letting your Yorkie interact with children, adults, or elderly patients is a wonderful way to share your dog's cheery disposition.

Many therapy dog organizations around the country welcome dogs in all sizes and shapes. These provide training leading to a certificate your dog can earn before any visits are made. Once your Yorkie passes the test and becomes a therapy dog, he can start making the hospital rounds with the rest of the dogs in his group.

Two Yorkies, Maggie and Pixie, owned by Mary Riordan, are part of a team of therapy dogs that includes Golden Retrievers, a Cocker Spaniel, a Rottweiler, and a Collie. The dogs visit the Iowa Methodist Medical Center/Blank Children's Hospital in Des Moines, Iowa.

Being able to rest on the bed up close and personal with patients is an advantage Yorkies have over bigger dogs. Debbie Oliver enjoys taking Little Princess Annie, a certified therapy dog with Pet Pals of Texas, to visit patients because Annie likes nothing better than snuggling up in bed with her admirers.

Ten Great Games Kids Can Play with a Yorkshire Terrier

Once children are prepared for life with a Yorkie, they can have a wonderful playmate. Yorkies' intelligence enables them to distinguish between different objects, which delights young and old alike. Adequate parental supervision will enhance the fun and is vital to keep both the dog and child safe. Here are several popular games you might suggest for kids who want to play with your Yorkie.

Balloon Toss: The object of this game is to keep the balloon airborne without letting it touch the floor. This game is a favorite of Catherine and John Forewell of Toronto.

They begin by clearing away some of the furniture in a room. The children sit on the floor at either end of the room. Their Yorkies, Tetley and Pekow, sit in the middle. The children bat the balloon back and forth while the Yorkies try to catch it. Occasionally Tetley or Pekoe manages to steal it by grabbing the tie portion and giving it a shake or two, but they return it when offered a treat.

Hide and Seek: The Forewell children give Tetley and Pekow a "wait" command while they go and hide. Once the kids are out of sight they yell, "Okay, come!" and the dogs seek them out. When the Yorkies locate them, the kids hand out treats and praise them.

Retrieve: Although Mary Wilson didn't have children in her home at the time, when she walked her Yorkie "Lacey" down the street, Lacey found a playmate in a little boy playing ball.

"He would throw the ball for her and she would bring it back," says Wilson. "After a while he started telling her to wait until he threw it and to bring it back without nipping at his hand. They became great friends and he would often come over to ask if Lacey could come out and play."

Roll the Ball: Lacey's playmate has since moved away, but whenever Mary Wilson has small children in her home, they are allowed to play this game.

"The children sit down and roll the ball to one another while my female Yorkie brings it back to them," says Wilson.

Beauty Parlor and Dress Up: Once children understand how to safely handle a Yorkie and have demonstrated they can behave around them, E. Susan Brown recommends allowing children to play this game first adopted by her six-year-old niece.

"She puts pretty bows in my Yorkie's hair and the dog loves it," Brown says.

Both children and good-natured Yorkies love to play dress up. Doll clothes make a great fit for many Yorkies, and as long as your Yorkie enjoys the attention and fussing, it's a game that doesn't require much energy.

Grooming: With supervision, children can help brush the dog and handle his feet. Not only is this good for your Yorkie, but children get the experience of handling the dog in a positive way.

Frisbee Toss: Keep the Frisbee low so both children and Yorkies can catch it easily. Playing outdoors gives your dog some good exercise.

Bring Your Leash: Whenever you are planning an outing, leave the dog leash in a location your dog can easily find and reach. The first time you play this, you may have to walk your dog over to where the leash is and put it in his mouth. Reward him when he picks it up on his own, and he'll gladly retrieve it whenever you ask.

Get Your Green, Red, Blue Ball: Because Yorkies are so smart, they can distinguish between different objects. Ask your dog to retrieve one toy. When he brings it back to you, praise him heavily. Then ask him to go fetch a different toy with a different color. Be sure to tell him how wonderful he is when he returns the correct item.

Scent Discrimination: Your Yorkie must locate a specific object you have handled. Handle one object and put it into a box with three other objects you have not touched. Ask your dog to find the one that you handled. Be sure to reward him when you are finished.

To keep your therapy Yorkie a welcome hospital visitor, make sure he is comfortable around people as well as around unusual equipment such as wheelchairs and walkers. Strange smells should not bother him either. Don't neglect his grooming for these occasions because he should be clean and free from fleas.

Playing Nicely with Children

Yorkie owners are always cautious when young children approach their dogs. Sometimes children are too rough or uncoordinated, or haven't learned how to behave around little dogs, and can inadvertently hurt a Yorkie. Once children are shown how to act around a Yorkie they can become good companions, but the combination must always have an adult present to supervise. Parents should be prepared to establish some rules and be willing to teach the child how to act with a dog.

Before introducing a child to a Yorkie, talk to the youngster about how fragile a small dog can be. To enable the child to picture the size difference, ask the child to think about a time when she was in the company of grownups and felt small herself. Explain that she should let the dog smell her hand first and that gentle touches beneath the dog's chin are good. Once the Yorkie is comfortable with those gestures, small pets along the body are permissible.

> Before introducing a child to a Yorkie, talk to the youngster about how fragile a small dog can be.

It doesn't take long to get the message of caution across. Ideally, a child should be at least three or four years old when a Yorkie comes to live in the same household, although older children need to be watched and given rules as well.

When the time actually comes for the youngster to meet the dog, ask her to sit down on the floor first. If the dog will allow the child to hold him, remind the child not to squeeze or grab the dog's coat or head. Instead, support his body underneath and keep all movements quiet and still without any sudden jerks. Hopefully they will become fast friends on the spot. However, if you notice any hesitation on your dog's part, avoid placing your dog in your child's lap right away; instead, let him study your child from a short distance.

If the child is afraid when she sees the Yorkie, it might take days and even months to reassure her that the dog will not hurt her. During that time it's best to act as naturally as possible until the child overcomes her fear. Don't remove the dog from the room every time the child cries out, as that simply reinforces the child's fear. To avoid injury to your Yorkie, or to prevent your dog from attacking a child, it's wise to take these precautions.

Even if you have no children in your home, your Yorkie may encounter them when you travel. Always be on guard when you take your dog on an outing, as toddlers often run right up to a dog and try to pet or hug him without asking first. Prevent the stranger from doing that and explain the importance of gentle petting without any fast movements.

Yorkshire Terriers and Other Animals

Having a Yorkshire Terrier live in harmony with another dog, cat, or bird in the same household is fine, though it may take your watchful eyes and initial training in the beginning. Yorkies will get along very well with other dogs and even cats, especially if they grow up together.

If an older cat lives in your home when your Yorkie comes to stay, evaluate the cat's personality. Some cats are predators and may consider a Yorkie pup a conquest. If your cat likes to kill squirrels, mice, or birds and bring them back to you as a trophy, your new little Yorkie may be in danger. Watch all interactions until you are sure the play is friendly.

If an older dog lives in the home before your Yorkie makes his appearance, introduce them slowly and cautiously and on neutral territory, such as down the street from your house. Your first dog may be very territorial and may not want another dog to intrude. If you have a big dog, always watch them to make sure he does not injure your small Yorkie. Another smaller dog will also require supervision while around the new Yorkie, but at least the threat isn't as great from a dog about the same size.

How can you help your other dog accept your Yorkie? If they are different sexes and spayed and neutered, they are less likely to feel too competitive with one another. Females in most breeds are sometimes maternal and may want to mother a new member of the opposite sex. While males may not be as maternal as females, a well-socialized male often defers to an older female.

As with people, there are always personality conflicts that need to be settled. Only one will become top dog between them, while the other must learn to accept the dog in charge. Some tips that might help support the top dog is to feed the first or top dog before the newer member and to take the first dog out for a walk before the second. Most of the time the new dogs will work out their own ground rules, but their interaction should be monitored until they reach a happy rapport.

Many people have multiple Yorkies that get along just fine, but it may not have started out that way. If your dogs don't get along well, ask your veterinarian and/or a professional trainer for tips to bring harmony back into your home. Do it right away, before the dogs have the chance to develop battle lines and bad habits that may become permanent.

Making Your Yorkshire Terrier a Good Neighbor

Teaching your dog how to interact with other family pets and children in or out of the home is important, but he has to get along with the rest of the neighborhood, too. No one appreciates a barking dog at odd hours so don't let your Yorkie bark at inappropriate times. If you plan to be gone during the evening, make sure your Yorkie is left indoors in a confined room or inside his crate so he doesn't disturb the neighborhood.

When you take your dog for a walk down the block, cleaning up after him is important. No one appreciates a dog who leaves a mess behind. Hopefully you have also taught your dog some manners so when he greets strangers or friends on the street, he is eager to see them without barking or jumping all over them.

You'll want your Yorkie to be a good neighbor and, with just a little foresight on your part, you can have the most popular dog on the block.

Traveling with and Boarding Your Yorkshire Terrier

One fun thing about owning a small dog is being able to take him along with you wherever you go. On an airplane a Yorkie fits nicely inside an airline-approved carrier or tote bag stowed beneath your seat and certainly doesn't take up much room inside a car on a road trip. Many hotels accept well-behaved dogs, which makes getting out to see the world easy.

> If for some reason you do not want to take your Yorkie along, you can always board him with a friend or boarding kennel facility.

Kathy and Joe Garciga enjoyed traveling all over the West Coast with their six-pound Yorkie in tow. She never barked and always stayed on Kathy's lap if they went into a restaurant.

If for some reason you do not want to take your Yorkie along, you can always board him with a friend or boarding kennel facility. If he has been well-socialized to strange and new surroundings since puppyhood, he should enjoy staying at a reputable kennel for a few nights.

Making the Decision—Pros and Cons

Deciding whether or not to bring your dog along on your trip can be gut-wrenching. Leaving your "baby" behind is an awful concept for many dog owners for whom the separation issue is strong. If you feel reluctant to leave your dog, chances are he will react that way as well.

Some places are not suited to dogs so leaving them behind is the only alternative. Or your Yorkie may have had a bad experience on his last trip or does not enjoy short trips around town.

Try to put yourself in your dog's position. If you are accustomed to going on outings around town and love to go, then a vacation is right up your alley. If, on the other hand, you are terrified to get in the car and leave the house, it's probably wise to stay home.

A business trip is probably not conducive to spending quality time with your dog. Chances are you will be too busy to really enjoy your dog and the locale, and you may have to leave him alone in the hotel for long periods of time.

The weather forecast should play another role in deciding whether or not to take your dog with you away from home. If you're going to hot climate, keeping your dog cool and comfortable can be difficult. Freezing temperatures will likewise make your dog uncomfortable.

Traveling with Your Dog

Once you decide to take your dog along, you'll need to make some preparations. If he has a lot of experience traveling by car or in an airplane, there's little for him to do. If he's inexperienced with travel, you should expose him to as many short auto trips as possible.

Taking a ride over to the airport and carrying your dog in a bag as you walk through the passenger ticketing area will accustom him to the noise. The American Humane Society does not recommend giving tranquilizers to pets who are traveling. Dogs need to maintain their balance in case they are tumbled around in their airline kennel or in your car. So if you think your Yorkie needs medication because he is too nervous to travel, he should probably be left at home.

It's also a good idea to prepare a bag containing items just for your dog to use. Include his own dog food, grooming supplies, and medications such as anti-diarrhea, antihistamines, an antibiotic ointment, ear-cleaning products, and heartworm preventive. New favorite toys are also a must. If you are driving and have room in your car, by all means, take his favorite bedding.

Before You Leave

If you are traveling by air, your dog will need a health certificate signed by your veterinarian within a few days of your departure for domestic flights. International travel can be difficult and filled with paperwork. Begin planning at least 30 days before the planned departure date. Contact the U.S. Department of Agriculture, Animal Plant Health and Inspection Service, Veterinary Services, to find out travel requirements for your destination, then make sure to meet these requirements to the letter. Otherwise, your Yorkie will be refused entry—and stranded at an airport.

Make sure your dog has two snug-fitting collars and has an ID tag with current information. It's also a good idea to have another contact name and phone number of a friend who knows your whereabouts engraved on the tag's reverse side. This will come in handy if you and your dog become separated for any reason during your trip. Having your dog micro-chipped or tattooed is another identification safeguard (see Chapter 2).

Having an extra collar and leash on hand is always a good idea in case something happens to the other one.

When vacationing with your dog, bring along some bottled water and allow your dog to drink only that, as different water sources can upset your dog's system.

Traveling by Car

Make sure your dog wears his collar and leash inside the car and insist that he wears his canine safety harness or rides in his kennel the whole time you are traveling on the road. Your Yorkie can ride in any of many different kennel types, depending on the space in your vehicle and what your dog likes. A kennel will come in handy if you have to leave your dog unattended in a hotel room and provides a safe place in case thunder or fireworks scare him.

When choosing canine seat belts, you can choose from several different safety models, depending on what your dog will use with confidence and enjoy. Above all, you do not want your dog jumping up and down from the floor onto your lap while you're driving. Without protection in the car, he could become seriously or fatally injured if the car is involved in an accident.

While your Yorkie may appreciate having fresh air, letting him ride with his head out the window is not a good idea. Fragments such as sand, rocks, and salt can fly into his eye and seriously injure him.

As you travel, stop every few hours for your dog to exercise and relieve himself. While rest stops often have "pet only" areas, they are usually frequented by a variety of dogs, some of whom may not be vaccinated. Instead, select clean roadside areas that do not have a lot of other dog traffic. Be sure to carry plastic bags with you and clean up any messes your dog leaves behind. Do not allow your Yorkie to drink from stagnant water sources, as they can transmit giardia and other diseases. Also be on the lookout for any bits of food left lying on the ground. You certainly don't want your dog eating anything unhealthful.

Traveling by Air

When making your reservation, let the airline know you are bringing a dog. They will ask you about the dog's size and remind you about keeping him in an

Did You Know?

According to the American Animal Hospital Association, more than 40% of pet owners talk to their pets on the phone or through the answering machine.

airline-approved kennel or bag once you are inside the plane. Keep a copy of your dog's health certificate with your own airline tickets so you always know where it is.

When choosing an airline-approved canine tote bag, look for one that has mesh panels with roll-up flaps with top and front zippers. An adjustable shoulder strap is also convenient. The bag should have a plastic bottom on which you can put a piece of fleece to cushion your dog's trip.

Do not feed your dog in the hours preceding travel, although the airlines may require a water container be affixed to the front door of the kennel. You can freeze some water in that container the night before so it stays cool during your flight.

Hotels and Campgrounds

When traveling with a dog to a hotel, motel, or campground, make sure you make a reservation first and ask if the establishment accepts well-behaved dogs. Many overnight accommodations will ask you to pay a security cleaning deposit in addition to the regular nightly rate. Usually this charge is $25 to $50 and compensates the establishment owners for any mess your dog leaves behind.

> Motels usually designate some areas—such as the pool, landscaped areas, or the lobby—off limits to dogs. Respect the hotel owner's wishes.

Once you check in to a hotel or motel, treat the place as if it were your own home. Clean up the messes your dog leaves behind and do not let him bark. Either keep him off the bedspread entirely or bring along a sheet to protect it from hair or paw prints your dog might leave.

Hotels often insist that you not leave your dog unattended in your room. You can put him securely in his crate if you go out for dinner or take a shower. Leave the television on to keep him company. Motels usually designate some areas—such as the pool, landscaped areas, or the lobby—off limits to dogs. Respect the hotel owner's wishes. Many places no longer accept dog guests because of bad (or messy) experiences with previous canine visitors. Don't be the dog owner who is responsible for adding your chosen hotel's name to the "We will not take dogs" list.

At campgrounds, follow the same manners with your dog. Just because you are out in the wilderness doesn't give you license to let your dog run wild. Keep him on his leash for outings and do not allow him to bark incessantly. Avoid contact with wildlife by keeping your Yorkie on his leash at all times.

Boarding Your Dog

Deciding to leave your dog behind in a boarding kennel is often the best choice for you and your dog. Choosing the best boarding facility is another challenge.

Because the best kennels seem to fill up far in advance, once you've made the boarding decision, choose a kennel and make a reservation as soon as possible. For Thanksgiving and Christmas holidays and peak summer weeks, it is not unusual for kennels to fill four months in advance.

To locate reputable, clean kennels, ask for referrals from friends or your veterinarian. Word of mouth always spreads quickly about good or bad facilities. Plan a trip to the best places on your list before you actually have to make a reservation. Investigate each location to check for cleanliness and safety. Talk to kennel employees to get an idea about their level of canine experience and devotion to the dogs left in their care.

Kennel runs should be large. Even a Yorkshire Terrier needs room to play and move about since he will have to spend a few days or longer in the same facility.

No doubt the dogs will probably bark at you when you come to look at their environment. This is natural. What isn't normal is for the runs to be dirty, with feces littering most pens. There shouldn't be too strong an odor, although many dogs left together will smell pretty "doggy."

Water buckets filled with clean, fresh water should be inside every kennel.

Key Questions to Ask

Make sure you understand what hours the kennel is open and when your dog can be dropped off or picked up. Many boarding facilities operate like regular businesses; workers do not want to be disturbed in the middle of the night. They may restrict the hours when clients can drop off or pick up their dogs.

Even if you cannot pick up your dog at just any time, you should choose a kennel that has supervision 24 hours a day, seven days a week. In case of fire or other emergency, someone needs to be responsible for your dog's welfare.

Inquire if employees are knowledgeable about the special needs of small dogs. They should know, for example, that housing a large dog next door to a small one can be too intimidating, and that locating two males next to one another is often not a good idea.

Find out whether you can bring in your dog's bedding. Most kennels have easy-to-clean concrete floors, with little or no soft places for dogs to lie down. Because the runs are usually washed out each day, any bedding not picked up will get wet. If you have an airline-approved kennel that un-screws, you can sometimes bring in the lower half of the kennel and include some soft crate pads and bedding on the bottom. This arrangement will keep the bedding from getting wet and will protect your Yorkie from the cold, wet cement floor.

Also ask if you can bring your own food. This guarantees that your dog will have the same diet he is accustomed to at home and eliminates the chance for your dog to develop an upset stomach and diarrhea. If your dog is taking any medication, make sure you notify the kennel staff so it can be continued. Some kennels charge extra for this responsibility.

Inquire whether the kennel has a separate area to which your dog can be taken for exercise or whether someone can walk your dog a few times each day. This will brighten up your dog's day considerably and almost make him forget he is away from home. Again, there may be an extra charge for this service.

> If your dog is taking any medication, make sure you notify the kennel staff so it can be continued.

Most kennels will require you to provide up-to-date vaccination records to prove that your Yorkie has been inoculated for rabies, distemper, and parvo within the last year. Other kennels insist that all dogs have a bordetella vaccine within the last six months. If your veterinarian's vaccination schedule is different from what the kennel requires, ask him to write a letter giving permission for the dog to be boarded without these vaccines.

Find out whether the kennel can give your dog a flea bath before he leaves to come home. Although there is usually an extra charge for this service, you won't want to bring fleas into your home when you return.

The kennel owner should take as much time as you need to answer your questions about his facility. If he is curt or evasive, choose another location to leave your dog. You'll find many options available if you do your homework in advance.

Hiring a Pet Sitter

If you know someone reliable who is able to stay with your dog while you are gone, this is a better alternative than taking your dog to a boarding kennel. He'll get to stay home with all his favorite toys and bedding, plus will have someone to keep him company in your absence. No doubt the pet sitter will fuss over him and he will get plenty of attention. By staying home, your Yorkie won't be exposed to kennel cough, can't get fleas, and won't feel isolated in a strange place.

> By staying home, your Yorkie won't be exposed to kennel cough, can't get fleas, and won't feel isolated in a strange place.

To find a reputable pet sitter, ask friends and your veterinarian if they know anyone. Word of mouth is generally a good reference. Schedule appointments with the people you have found and arrange to have them come to your home to meet you and your Yorkie before you hire one of them. As each one walks in the door, you'll be able to tell right away what your dog thinks of the candidate. A good pet sitter will establish a rapport right away with your dog and will enjoy his company. Many times pet sitters are veterinary technicians and like being around animals.

Ask your potential pet sitters these key questions:

○ *Do you belong to any professional pet sitting organizations, such as the National Association of Professional Pet Sitters?* A member of this group has met basic standards set by the organization.

○ *Do you have references?* A list of happy customers will help you feel comfortable that your dog is in this person's care.

○ *Are you bonded and do you have commercial liability insurance?* Ask to see proof of insurance and ask exactly what coverage it provides.

○ *How long have you been working as a pet sitter?* Ask about any unusual experiences that the candidate might have encountered while on the job.

○ *What experience do you have with emergency medical care?* If your dog has an emergency, be sure this person will be able to provide or obtain emergency medical treatment.

○ *What hours will you be staying in my home?* Does the candidate expect to just come in and feed the dog and leave, or will the person spend the whole evening or overnight?

○ *What experience do you have taking care of small dogs?* Find out whether this person knows how to meet your Yorkie's special needs and can perform basic responsibilities such as combing, brushing, and bathing if necessary.

Once you select a pet sitter, arrange a meeting to explain the dog's routine and any medical problems he or she may need to be aware of. It is also a good idea to show the pet sitter where the main controls are for water, electricity, and gas in case there is an emergency while you are gone. The pet sitter should also present you with a contract that lists all the services he will be providing for you and the fee he will be charging.

Leaving a List for the Dog Sitter or Boarding Kennel

Despite the level of experience either your pet sitter or the boarding kennel has with dogs, they don't know about your dog. Leaving a detailed list of instructions will help organize your thoughts about how to care for your dog in your absence. It will also give someone else a guide to feeding, exercising, and administering any medication. If there is anything special a caretaker needs to know about, put it in writing so the caretaker can refer to it if necessary.

This will give you some ideas about what kind of information to leave. You may think of adding your own advice.

❍ Phone number, address, and location where you can be reached

❍ Feeding amounts

❍ Time and number of times to feed your dog

❍ Any medication your dog needs, as well as times and amounts of medication to be given

❍ Your veterinarian's name, address, and phone number

❍ The name of another contact who will take responsibility for your pet if needed in an emergency

❍ The name of another person who can care for your dog if something permanent should happen to you

❍ Permission for the pet sitter or boarding kennel to obtain treatment for your dog in your absence

❍ Your dog's favorite toys or games

❍ Words or commands your dog knows or doesn't know

❍ Short history of your dog's medical problems

❍ List of any foods or toy items your dog should not be given

❍ List of fabrics or substances to which your dog may be allergic

❍ Your dog's age and birth date

❍ Whether your dog is micro-chipped

❍ A list of your dog's inoculations

Properly preparing for your separation from your Yorkie will help both you and your dog better deal with your time away.

When you leave on vacation, make sure you have plenty of dog food, biscuits, and any medication your dog will need. Don't expect your pet sitter to run errands unrelated to pet care. On the other hand, your pet sitter should not be opening your home to friends or abusing the right to stay in your home. It is also a good idea to give the sitter a call a day after you've left to see if everything is going well and to find out whether she has any questions.

Holiday Hazards

Your Yorkies are members of the family and are usually at the forefront of any holiday celebrations. They wouldn't think of letting you exclude them. Be aware that the holidays bring joy to everyone in the household, but they can also bring a few hazards you might not expect. Because you are busy with holiday plans and festivities, you may forget to be vigilant in keeping an eye on your Yorkie and what he does around the house.

At holiday times your dog may encounter some unusual decorations, noises, and food treats to which he may not be accustomed. Take some time to look over your environment and try to anticipate any potential problems these things might cause your dog. Once you are aware of them and take steps to watch for danger, your festivities will be happy ones.

Beginning with New Year's Eve and the next day, your Yorkie might not understand the loud celebrations in your neighborhood. Fireworks, loud parties, and rude-sounding noisemakers may disturb your Yorkie if he has never heard them before. If the party is in your home, make sure your dog is supervised or placed in his crate so if he becomes startled, he cannot bolt away from the house. On the other hand, if your Yorkie enjoys a crowd, make sure all the party food is placed up high out of his reach. If possible, eliminate toothpicks completely for finger foods you might serve; otherwise, keep an eye on your Yorkie, who might try to eat one.

Chocolate candy can be a major hazard for your Yorkie. Hide those Valentine's Day treats! Keep in mind chocolate is toxic to dogs, so make sure chocolate is out of reach to prevent your Yorkie from sampling it.

> Fireworks, loud parties, and rude-sounding noisemakers may disturb your Yorkie if he has never heard them before.

St. Patrick's Day, Memorial Day, and the Fourth of July may bring another barrage of odd sounds and fireworks. Be ready to keep your Yorkie as far as possible from any offensive noise if he is bothered by it. You might want to confine him to his crate or have him restrained on his leash in case he suddenly becomes afraid of them. If you're going to a picnic on one of these holidays and insist on taking your dog, make sure he has adequate shade and plenty of fresh, cool water. Resist the temptation of offering your dog bits of leftovers. Offer him dog treats instead, like a healthful dog biscuit or pieces of cheese or fruit.

Halloween can scare even the most secure Yorkie. Strange costumes and masks and unsure movements can startle him. Every time the doorbell rings with trick-or-treaters, your Yorkie will feel the need to protect his household and will probably bark. The stress can also trigger trembling. On the other hand, some Yorkies love to play dress-up and may even enjoy having their own costume for the holiday.

When Thanksgiving comes, it's a good guess that food has taken over your home. Keep people food and leftovers out of your Yorkie's reach so it can't take over his life. If you want to offer your Yorkie a few leftovers, choose wisely, give no more than a tablespoon or two, and skip the gravy and dressing, which are high in fat.

Most greenery used to decorate the house for Christmas, such as mistletoe, holly, and poinsettia, can be dangerous if your dog chews and swallows these plants. Mistletoe is poisonous, holly has sharp edges that can irritate a Yorkie stomach or cause damage to his mouth, and poinsettia will cause vomiting at the least. If you have a Christmas tree and hang ornaments within a Yorkie's reach, they can become dangerous play toys for your dog. Other tree decorations—such as lights and electrical cords—are deadly if bitten. Tinsel is hazardous if swallowed. Consider putting a small barrier fence around your tree to keep your dog away from it.

Remember, you want your holidays to be happy for one and all, including your Yorkie.

9

A Lifetime of Love and Good Health

In This Chapter

○ Your Aging Yorkshire Terrier—What to Expect
○ Age-Related Disorders
○ How to Keep Your Older Yorkshire Terrier Comfortable
○ Saying Goodbye

Your Yorkshire Terrier has enjoyed a long, full and happy life with you. She anticipates your every move and seems to understand what you're thinking about almost before you do. At times it seems as if she has been with you forever and yet at other times it seems like only yesterday when you brought your tiny Yorkie puppy home, cute as a button. You learned how to brush and bathe her and how to anticipate her every need. You have kept her in excellent physical condition and have safeguarded her health to the best of your ability.

Then one day you look at her and you realize she's not a young dog anymore. She's more content to sleep longer hours and doesn't rush for the doorbell the minute it rings. Shuffling from room to room, your Yorkie has lost the spring in her step and her eagerness to take on the world.

The hardest part of owning a dog is watching them age. You can do a few things to make their last years comfortable, but you can't reverse the aging process. The best you can do is to fill their remaining days with love and caring and know when the time is right to say goodbye.

Your Aging Yorkshire Terrier— What to Expect

Generally small dogs live longer than big dogs do. Your Yorkshire Terrier is no exception. Unless she encounters a fatal accident or disease, you should expect to have your Yorkie at least 12 years. Many Yorkies live as long as 15 years.

When dogs reach their seventh birthday, some people consider them senior canines. For every human calendar year, dogs age roughly five to seven years, though this depends on a variety of factors. By seven years, they start to lose some of the elasticity in their joints and will begin to take life at a little slower pace. It's

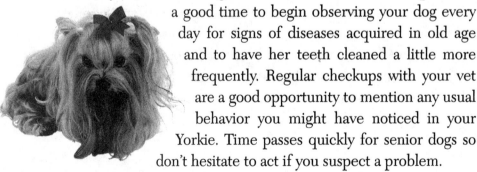

a good time to begin observing your dog every day for signs of diseases acquired in old age and to have her teeth cleaned a little more frequently. Regular checkups with your vet are a good opportunity to mention any usual behavior you might have noticed in your Yorkie. Time passes quickly for senior dogs so don't hesitate to act if you suspect a problem.

Senior Health Care

Many veterinarians recommend a geriatric screening for your dog at the appropriate age. A geriatric screening usually includes a physical exam, blood tests, and an electrocardiogram or specialized tests for your dog's specific health conditions. Diseases of older dogs that are not usually seen in young dogs include arthritis, diabetes, Cushing's disease (obesity and muscular weakness caused by malfunction of the adrenal or pituitary glands), cancer, and kidney, heart, and liver disease. Your veterinarian will perform blood tests during a geriatric visit to screen for many of these diseases.

Since dogs of different size age at different rates, screening begins at different ages:

Up to 15 pounds

Begin geriatric screening at age nine to 11

16 to 50 pounds

Begin geriatric screening at age seven to nine

51 to 80 pounds

Begin geriatric screening at age six to eight

Over 80 pounds

Begin geriatric screening at age four to six

Your veterinarian may recommend semiannual visits once your dog becomes a senior. Between visits, be alert to changes in your Yorkie that could indicate serious illness and require immediate veterinary attention, such as:

○ Sudden loss of weight

○ Serious loss of appetite

○ Increase in appetite without increase in weight

○ Diarrhea or vomiting

○ Increased thirst without a change in activity level and increased urination

○ Excessive fatigue

○ Extreme limited mobility

○ Coughing and excessive panting

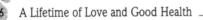

Age-Related Disorders

Every living being ages. While some dogs age gracefully, others are not so lucky. With advanced years comes the likelihood of life-threatening disease. If these serious health problems can be caught at first onset, you might be able to give your dog a few extra years to enjoy life with you.

Arthritis

Arthritis can affect people as well as dogs. This degenerative joint disease causes stiffness in the joints, which can be quite painful. You may notice that your dog suffers from it if she struggles to get up from a nap, moves stiffly, or seems hesitant when she moves. Always have your suspicions checked out by your veterinarian.

Fortunately, many advances have been made in medical technology for the treatment of arthritis. Today more relief for pain is available and dogs can live comfortably for longer periods of time. Your veterinarian will be able to suggest medication and new treatment alternatives, such as acupuncture and chiropractic procedures.

> If your dog has the beginning stages of arthritis, be sure and continue her exercise program once or twice a day while continuing to feed him a good quality well-balanced diet.

Changing your dog's environment to make him more comfortable will also help ease the pain of arthritis. Keeping your dog's bed warm and out of drafts will keep his joints elastic. To prevent slips and possible falls and broken bones in the house, cover any slick flooring you might have in your home with rubber-backed rugs or plastic runners.

Be aware that your Yorkie may be very sore when you go to pick him up. If he yelps in pain, note the area of his body that is bothering him and select a different area next time you lift him. And, of course, make sure your vet is aware of any yelping—it may signal more serious problems, rather than simple aches, pains, or arthritis. If he insists on jumping up on the couch, consider setting up a ramp made from firm pillows to make climbing up much easier.

If your dog has the beginning stages of arthritis, be sure and continue his exercise program once or twice a day while continuing to feed him a good quality well-balanced diet.

Obesity

As dogs age, they become less active and generally require a lot fewer calories than they did as youngsters. If they continue to eat the same amount, they will gain weight.

Dogs who border on obesity tend to develop diabetes and will have more health problems, especially with arthritis. The weight adds more pressure on vital organs and joints and causes the dog to feel even less energetic.

Prevent obesity by cutting back on the amount of food you give your dog or switch to a senior recipe, which has slightly fewer calories. Cut out any snacks and instead feed her a few pieces of fruit or tiny vegetables. You can also cut her portion size down and allocate it toward another meal sometime during the day.

Be sure to maintain your dog's regular exercise program or increase it slightly. This will help your dog to lose weight as well.

Diabetes

Diabetes mellitus an abnormal increase in blood sugar level usually caused by a deficiency of insulin. Although treatable, diabetes can be responsible for long-term complications for your dog. The cause of insulin-dependent diabetes mellitus is unknown, but many factors contribute to its appearance in your dog—genes, obesity, infection, and inflammation of the pancreas may all play a role in the development of diabetes in an older dog.

For signs of diabetes, watch how much food and water your dog takes in. An increased appetite and more water consumption increases his urination, but there may also be weight loss. As diabetes advances, your Yorkie may lose weight, even with an increased appetite. In the last stages a dog will become depressed, discontented, and refuse to eat.

If you suspect that your dog has diabetes, take her to your vet for laboratory tests and an evaluation. If left untreated, diabetes may cause blindness, infections, weight loss, pancreatitis, and death. For dogs with diabetes, you can control the disease with insulin injections once or twice a day. Preventing obesity may prevent diabetes.

Cancer

Years ago people who were told they had cancer knew it meant the end of their lives. Nowadays better treatments are available and more lives are saved if the disease is diagnosed and treated in time. The same is true for dogs. Unfortunately, many of the cancer treatments for dogs, such as radiation, chemotherapy, surgery, and gene therapy, are expensive. Still, these options are always there for you to consider.

Cancer is one of the most common health problems senior dogs may have. It occurs when abnormal cells grow out of control, damaging normal body function. Types of cancer found in dogs include bone, breast, mouth, uterine, and testicular. Early spaying or neutering can prevent uterine, and testicular cancers.

As certain types of cancers run in animal families, ask your breeder whether your dog's ancestors had cancer. Because cancer appears in many different types, be sure to ask what kind your dog's canine relatives might have had.

Continually check your dog's body for lumps or sores that do not seem to be healing. If you do find something, notify your vet right away. Growths can be removed and a biopsy taken to determine whether or not they are benign or malignant.

> Types of cancer found in dogs include bone, breast, mouth, uterine, and testicular. Early spaying or neutering can prevent uterine and testicular cancers.

Many older dogs develop soft lumps beneath the skin. These are often fatty tumors, which are not cancerous and do not cause any problems. Even if you suspect the lump is harmless, it's always safest to have it checked by your veterinarian. Early detection of cancer can improve your dog's chances of surviving the disease and reduce the cost of treatment.

Kidney and Liver Failure

The kidneys can become injured by infection, toxins, drugs trauma, shock, or immunologic attack at any age. Senior Yorkies can also develop kidney failure simply because the kidneys wear out in old age.

The kidneys' job is to eliminate waste products from the blood and to control body fluids, electrolytes, and regulate the water content of the body. They also produce hormones and chemicals the body needs. When kidneys fail to function, the entire body shuts down, leading to serious illness and death.

If a dog has unusually bad breath, becomes dehydrated, drinks a lot of water and is constantly urinating, he may have kidney disease. Blood tests can be done that will indicate whether the kidneys are functioning properly.

It's a good idea to give your older dog a blood test every year or so. This will catch problems before they become serious.

To keep the kidneys functioning at their optimum, your veterinarian can suggest special prescription diet foods to give your dog. Good management of kidney disease includes controlling the amount of protein in your dog's diet. This can improve the quality and length of your dog's life.

Liver shunt, which was discussed in Chapter 5, also occurs more frequently in older dogs.

Heart Disease

Although heart disease is rarely curable, it can be managed with drugs and diet, often giving dogs years of extra life. As with most problems, the earlier it is discovered, the more effective treatment will be.

Some dogs also develop cardiomyopathy, or a weakness of a heart muscle. This condition limits blood flow to the body. Symptoms include coughing, weakness, and swelling of the belly.

Dogs who may be experiencing heart problems seem weak and may not have as much energy as they once did. It's not their fault. As they age, the heart valves may become worn and won't close as completely with each beat of the heart as they once did. Some blood flows backward through partially closed valves, which creates a heart murmur.

Many small dogs develop heart murmurs in old age. Your veterinarian should regularly monitor your dog's heart.

Deafness

Partial or complete deafness in older dogs is common. While chronic ear infections can be responsible for deafness, hearing loss can occur for any reason. Hearing loss happens gradually, and you might not even notice how often your dog does not respond to you right away. A younger, healthy Yorkie might choose to ignore you from time to time. Then one day it occurs to you that your dog cannot hear you come in the door or misses the dinner bell completely.

Your veterinarian should check your dog's ears to make sure there isn't an ear infection or other treatable condition present. If one isn't found, be aware that your dog may startle easily and he may, depending upon his temperament, respond aggressively to being surprised. Additionally, dogs with hearing loss need special care. They can no longer hear cars, or approaching dogs or people. Never let a deaf dog wander alone. You can teach her hand signals to replace verbal commands. In time, you will both adjust.

Eye Disorders

Cataracts can be a problem for all older dogs. The lens of the eye becomes milky white, blocking light and interfering with vision. Cataracts often grow slowly, but in some dogs the vision loss may be complete and sudden. In addition, very mature cataracts can cause painful inflammation of the eye. Veterinary ophthalmologists (eye specialists) can evaluate each dog's particular case and possibly perform surgery to cure the cataract and restore vision.

Older dogs also develop nuclear sclerosis, another age-related problem in the structure of the eye lens. Nuclear sclerosis looks like a very early cataract, but it does not interfere with vision. The lens of the eye will turn slightly cloudy or grayish in color. Your veterinarian should evaluate any cloudy eye to make sure your dog doesn't have a cataract. Nuclear sclerosis needs no treatment.

Glaucoma, a build-up of pressure inside the eye, is another problem that comes with older age. An eye with glaucoma is usually reddened and weepy. It may also appear swollen, enlarged, and be either painful or hard when you touch it through the eyelid.

Glaucoma is not only painful, but it can cause rapid, permanent blindness. In neglected cases, the eye may even rupture.

There are several medical treatments available for glaucoma— and the earlier it's detected the better the chance of curing it.

If your dog's field of vision is narrowing, and she has trouble getting around the house, try to picture your home from her viewpoint (close to the floor with limited vision) and make accommodations. For example, try not to move any furniture around and keep new objects out of the paths she regularly takes. Be extra careful to keep sharp objects out of her way. Certain areas of your home may be dangerous, such as the doorway to outdoors and the top of a stairway, so take precautions to guide your dog through these areas.

Urinary Incontinence

One of the least appealing problems of older dogs is loss of bladder control. You have just taken your dog out for a walk and she walks back in the house and leaves a puddle on the floor. It's exasperating. Older female dogs in all breeds are often prone to urinary incontinence, and it seems you can do little to prevent this. You'll find little puddles in their beds or urine will drip from the dog's vulva without the dog even realizing it. In her younger days, she would sooner hide from you than mess in her own bed.

Be sure to have your veterinarian evaluate the problem. Sometimes incontinence can be treated with oral medication that will clear it up almost immediately.

How to Keep Your Older Yorkshire Terrier Comfortable

Your Yorkshire Terrier has no doubt led a pampered and well-cared-for existence, but at this special time in his life, you can do a few more things to make him as comfortable as possible.

Exercise

Exercise will maintain your dog's muscle tone and cardiac conditioning. It is also healthy for him to maintain his circulation and will help his digestion and keep his weight at a reasonable level. It will remind him that he is just as important to you in his old age as he once was when the two of you could walk for blocks.

> You don't have to go as far or as fast as you once did, but go! Exercise gives your Yorkie mental and physical stimulation.

You don't have to go as far or as fast as you once did, but go! Exercise gives your Yorkie mental and physical stimulation. Because an older dog may feel a little down sometimes, this activity will keep his spirits up and remind him of his routine, which he once treasured.

Bedding and Sleeping Area

A soft cushy bed will help your dog's creaky bones. Your Yorkshire Terrier will also enjoy having one of those heated beds to keep the drafts away. They can be found in most pet-supply stores, pet-supply catalogs, or through pet Web sites on the Internet. Do not substitute with a standard heating pad. These are prone to having hot spots, and can leave serious burns on your Yorkie.

Yorkies are very fond of fleece bedding. This can be purchased through fabric outlets and cut into sheets into a size manageable for your dog's bed area.

Grooming

It is more important to maintain your dog's regular grooming schedule when he is a senior than ever before. Above all, he will enjoy your fussing over him and the calming effect grooming can have on both of you. Talk to him while you are grooming him, just as you always have, and remind him how special and handsome he is!

Continue looking for any lumps over your dog's body while you are grooming him. Combing him every day and bathing him once a week or every other week is just as important now as it was in his younger days. Chances are he will not have as much natural oil in his coat as he once did, but the continued grooming will keep the skin healthy by stimulating the natural oils.

Don't neglect clipping his nails either, as they grow quicker in old age. As your dog ages and walking becomes more difficult for him, long nails can further hamper his mobility. If you place him on a grooming table, be sure to supervise him. If you leave him alone up there even for a minute, he can easily lose his balance and fall off in the blink of an eye.

Maintain a regular dental-cleaning schedule too. You will want to keep his teeth in good condition so that he can continue eating his kibble without a problem.

Veterinary Visits

As with elderly people, canine senior years mean more trips to visit the doctor. New health issues crop up more frequently, and often it's better to have your veterinarian check things out so he can diagnose problems earlier and possibly prevent their becoming serious.

If your elder Yorkie has arthritis or vision loss, be sure to lift him dog into the car and don't let him jump in or out. Once at the vet, remember your Yorkie's vision and hearing may not be as good as they once were. Be on the lookout for the sudden appearance of big dogs who could easily frighten him.

Somewhere between seven and ten years of age, your veterinarian will probably want to perform some screening exams to check your Yorkie's body function, both to look for early signs of disease and to establish a baseline to measure against as your dog gets older.

Did You Know?

The old rule of multiplying a dog's age by seven to find the equivalent human age is inaccurate. A better measure is to count the first year as 15, the second year as 10, and each year after that as 5.

These tests might include a urinalysis, blood work, and chest X-rays. Some veterinarians also like to administer an electrocardiogram and thyroid tests.

Nutrition

Ask your veterinarian what type of diet is recommended for your senior Yorkie (generally veterinarians recommend a senior dog food recipe once your dog reaches the age of seven).

If your Yorkie is a picky eater, don't offer table scraps, as the situation will only get worse. Do offer food that's fresh and try to monitor how much your dog is getting in case there's a problem later.

> Sometimes older dogs are fussy about their food and water as they age so it's best to keep the water dish clean and to have fresh and cold water available at all times.

Make sure your dog drinks plenty of water. If you notice that he seldom drinks water, try adding water to his food. Sometimes older dogs are fussy about their food and water as they age so it's best to keep the water dish clean and to have fresh and cold water available at all times. Decreased water intake can indicate many problems, from painful teeth to kidney failure. If you notice decreased food or water consumption, contact your veterinarian.

Communication

It's easy to lose patience with a senior dog, but you must not. No doubt you are feeling frustrated because time has simply passed and your once glorious Yorkie is now an old dog who may not be able to hear or see you. He can still sense your presence, though, and can find you at a moment's notice if necessary.

To keep both of your spirits up, try to offer new treats or toys fairly often. Mostly he will enjoy being around you as often as will allow him. If he has never wanted to snuggle in bed with you before, that may be all he wants to do now. If you leave the room for too long, he may bark to find where you are.

He will feel your hands on his coat, and your reassuring pets and snuggles are a great way to make him as comfortable as you can.

Saying Goodbye

When your Yorkie was a puppy and you were housetraining him and cleaning up one mess after another, you could never imagine the time would come to say goodbye to him. Suddenly here it is. If only you could relive all those years when your Yorkie was young and full of life.

You have shared a dozen or so years with your Yorkie day in and day out and you know each other's moods and movements. The worst part of the life cycle is having to make the decision when your dog's time has come to leave this world. The thought of losing a pet is very painful.

How to Know It's Time

Choosing the right time to say goodbye and end your pet's life is different for each person. Some people cannot stand to see their dog lose their eyesight, while others can tolerate many more old-age symptoms. A terminal illness can often make the decision for you since you don't want to see your pet suffer in pain. Sometimes in the end, dogs do not make the decision an easy one. As in life, they will look to you to make the best choice for them. Here is where you may face the hardest test of being a good owner. You must decide what is best for him, not what's best for you.

If your Yorkie has trouble walking, is refusing food, has lost control of most of his bowel and urinary functions, and seems totally disinterested in you or his surroundings, it's time to think about putting him to rest. To prolong your dog's life when he is struggling every day to do the most basic tasks is purely for your own benefit, not for his.

Consult with your veterinarian who will be able to evaluate your dog's health status and offer any medical advice. She should spend as much time with you as you need and will help discuss the situation. No doubt she has euthanized many dogs in her experience and has some empathy for what you are going through. Usually, however, owners will know when the time is right.

What to Expect

The decision to end your dog's life, which your veterinarian refers to as euthanization, can take weeks or months; but the actual act of putting your dog to sleep takes mere minutes. Once you understand how euthanization works and what your pet may feel at the end of his life, you may feel some measure of comfort.

When your vet euthanizes your dog, she will be injecting a large dose of barbiturates into the dog's bloodstream. Your dog's brain will cease functioning, which will cause the dog to lose consciousness seconds after the injection. His heart will stop beating and respiration ceases. Some veterinarians will administer a sedative prior to the barbiturates to calm the dog and reassure the owner that the dog will not suffer or feel afraid.

Rainbow Bridge

Just this side of Heaven is a place called Rainbow Bridge. When an animal dies that has been especially close to someone here, that pet goes to Rainbow Bridge. There are meadows and hills for all our special friends so they can run and play together. There is plenty of food, water, and sunshine, and our friends are warm and comfortable. All the animals who had been ill or old are restored to health and vigor; those who were hurt or maimed are made whole and strong again, just as we remember them in our dreams of days gone by. The animals are happy and content, except for one small thing; they each miss someone very special to them who had to be left behind.

They all run and play together, but the day comes when one suddenly stops and looks into the distance. His bright eyes are intent; his eager body quivers. Suddenly he begins to run from the group, flying over the green grass, his legs carrying him faster and faster. You have been spotted, and when you and your special friend finally meet, you cling to each other in joyous reunion, never to be parted again. The happy kisses rain upon your face, your hands again caress the beloved head, and you look once more into the trusting eyes of your pet, so long gone from your life but never absent from your heart.

Then you cross Rainbow Bridge together.

—Author unknown

The Rainbow Bridge Web site (www.rainbowbridge.tierranet.com/bridge.htm) includes this story, written by an unknown animal lover. The site includes tributes to and photos of deceased pets, a message board, and grief support. For owners who are sad after the loss of a pet, from dogs to guinea pigs, "the Bridge" is the place to go for understanding, sympathy, and help. If you've recently lost a beloved pet friend, be sure to check out this very popular web site, run by Kathie Maffit and a host of volunteers.

But don't forget a hankie!

Euthanasia is a completely painless method. Your dog will relax so much that he drifts into a peaceful sleep prior to the cessation of any bodily functions. One minute the dog is looking up at you or the veterinarian, and the next minute he is not. There is no fear and the experience is a calm one.

There are many wonderful and dedicated veterinarians who will come to your home when the time comes to euthanize your dog. There, in the comfort of your own home, you can say your final goodbye. Other veterinarians will show extreme sympathy and usher you and your dog immediately into an exam room instead of insisting you remain in the waiting room until the time comes for the last vet visit. Help your veterinarian out by letting him know with a phone call that you may need to euthanize your pet so they can prepare and make the process as easy as possible on everyone.

> If you feel you cannot stay with your Yorkie when his final moments arrive, don't feel guilty. Every person has to do what is best for him or her.

Feel free to talk to your Yorkie and reassure him. Pet him, and if you feel comfortable remaining in the room during the procedure, by all means do so. No doubt he will be comforted by the sound of your voice. If you feel you cannot stay with your Yorkie when his final moments arrive, don't feel guilty. Every person has to do what is best for him or her.

We are the ones who suffer by having to make the decision, but our dogs are relieved of any suffering they had due to illness or old age. Sometimes euthanization is the only thing you can do for a dog who has undergone painful medical procedures that have not brought any relief. If your veterinarian's prognosis is that your dog will only go downhill, you have little choice.

If you face this situation, give some thought to the quality of your Yorkie's life. What pleasure could you have seeing him suffer for days on end? If your pet could take on the responsibility of making the decision of how you would spend your last days, no doubt he would want you to be happy.

Leaving Your Pet in Your Will

Who will care for your pet if you die before she does? Many people neglect to think this could happen, with the result of their beloved pet being placed in an animal shelter after their death. Talk with family and friends and find someone who is truly willing and able to take care of your Yorkie if you should pass. Then speak with your lawyer and include your pet in your will. You may also want to specify a certain amount of money to go to the person caring for your dog to offset the costs of food, veterinary care, and other pet-related expenses.

Remembering Your Pet

If you have taken lots of photographs of your dog during his life-time, take them out and look at them. It will help spark memories of long-forgotten great times you shared with one another. Your pet would want you to cherish his memory because after all, he spent so much time trying to please you.

Feel free to talk about your pet as much as you want to, and don't feel embarrassed if tears fall easily. People who have not loved or become attached to dogs do not understand how devastating it can be to lose a dog.

Many owners say they spent weeks, even months or longer, trying to avoid crying at the mention of their dog's name. These people say they never imagined the pain that loss would bring. You need not apologize for grieving for a dog you loved and cared for so intently for such a long period of time.

Ignore people who say, "It's just a dog" or "Why don't you just get another one?" They will never understand how devastating your loss is.

Veterinary Teaching Hospital Grief Hotlines

○ University of California, Davis, California, (530) 752-4200, 6:30–9:30 P.M. PST, Monday through Friday

○ Colorado State University, Fort Collins, Colorado, (970) 491-1242

○ University of Florida, Gainesville, Florida, (352) 392-4700 (ext. 4080), takes messages 24 hours a day; someone will call back between 7:00 and 9:00 P.M. EST

○ Michigan State University, East Lansing, Michigan, (517) 432-2696, 6:30–9:30 P.M. EST, Tuesday, Wednesday, and Thursday

○ Ohio State University, Columbus, Ohio, (614) 292-1823, takes messages 6:30–9:30 P.M. EST, Monday, Wednesday, and Friday

○ University of Pennsylvania, Philadelphia, Pennsylvania, (215) 898-4529

○ Tufts University, North Grafton, Massachusetts, (508) 839-7966, 6:00–9:00 P.M. EST, Monday through Friday

○ Virginia-Maryland Regional College of Veterinary Medicine, Blacksburg, Virginia, (540) 231-8038, 6:00–9:00 P.M. EST, Tuesday and Thursday

○ Washington State University, Pullman, Washington, (509) 335-4569

Grieving

Grief is a normal human emotion that consists of several stages that you may or may not feel. Once your pet has died, you will probably feel very sad and numb. It's as if part of you is not connected. Shock and denial are other emotions in the first stage. You find it hard to believe your dog could possibly be gone.

Depression and anger follow. When you try to go back to your normal routine, it's common to feel emotional when you realize your dog is no longer there. Or you may sense it's time to stop what you're doing to feed the dog then you remember you don't have to perform that task any longer,

You may experience some anger at the veterinarian or a family member who might have had some responsibility for your dog's death. It may be hard to concentrate on your work during this period of time or enjoy your regular hobbies or spare time.

Eventually you will accept the death of your pet. The pain will subside enough that you can again perform your daily tasks, but you'll always hold a special spot in your heart for your dear Yorkie. If this final stage of acceptance takes a while to arrive, do not hesitate to contact a grief counselor. Many understanding counselors are available who can help you get to this last stage. They will not expect you to forget your dog, but will encourage you to remember him in a healthy way.

While some people advocate rushing out and getting a new dog to replace your old one, that may not be the best decision for you. You may need time to process all that has happened. Because each dog is unique, a new dog will never fully replace your lost Yorkie. No matter how many dogs you will have in your lifetime, each will occupy a special place in your heart that no other dog can fill.

Appendix A: Resources

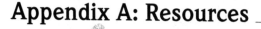

Boarding, Pet Sitting, Traveling

books

Dog Lover's Companion series
Guides on traveling with dogs for
several states and cities
Foghorn Press
P.O. Box 2036
Santa Rosa, CA 95405-0036
(800) FOGHORN

*Take Your Pet Too!: Fun Things
to Do!,* Heather MacLean
Walters
M.C.E. Publishing
P.O. Box 84
Chester, NJ 07930-0084

Take Your Pet USA, Arthur Frank
Artco Publishing
12 Channel St.
Boston, MA 02210

*Traveling with Your Pet 1999:
The AAA Petbook,* Greg
Weeks, Editor
Guide to pet-friendly lodging in
the U.S. and Canada

Vacationing with Your Pet!,
Eileen Barish
Pet-Friendly Publications
P.O. Box 8459
Scottsdale, AZ 85252
(800) 496-2665

...other resources

The American Boarding Kennels
Association
4575 Galley Road, Suite 400-A
Colorado Springs, CO 80915
(719) 591-1113
www.abka.com

Independent Pet and Animal Transportation Association
5521 Greenville Ave., Ste 104-310
Dallas, TX 75206
(903) 769-2267
www.ipata.com

National Association of Professional Pet Sitters
1200 G St. N.W., Suite 760
Washington, DC 20005
(800) 286-PETS
www.petsitters.org

Pet Sitters International
418 East King Street
King, NC 27021-9163
(336) 983-9222
www.petsit.com

U.S. Department of Agriculture
Animal and Plant Health Inspection Service
Import/Export rules, forms, and news

Breed Information, Clubs, Registries

American Kennel Club
5580 Centerview Drive
Raleigh, NC 27606-3390
(919) 233-9769
www.akc.org/

Canadian Kennel Club
Commerce Park
89 Skyway Ave., Suite 100
Etobicoke, Ontario, Canada M9W 6R4
(416) 675-5511
www.ckc.ca

InfoPet
P.O. Box 716
Agoura Hills, CA 91376
(800) 858-0248

Jo-An's Yorkshire Terriers
Comprehensive Yorkie Web site
www.members.home.net/jrogan/

The Kennel Club
(British equivalent to the American Kennel Club)
1–5 Clarges Street
Piccadilly
London W1Y 8AB
ENGLAND
www.the-kennel-club.org.uk/

National Dog Registry
Box 116
Woodstock, NY 12498
(800) 637-3647
www.natldogregistry.com/

Tatoo-A-Pet
6571 S.W. 20th Court
Ft. Lauderdale, FL 33317
(800) 828-8667
www.tattoo-a-pet.com

Toy Dogs
Lee and Bob Baker
Plympton MA 02367
(781) 582-2304
www.toydogs.com

United Kennel Club
100 East Kilgore Rd.
Kalamazoo, MI 49001-5598
(616) 343-9020
www.ukccdogs.com

Yorkshire Terrier Club of America
www.ytca.org

The Yorkie House
262 Fairway Lane
Raeford, NC 28376
(910) 875-7880
www.yorkiehouse.com/

Dog Publications

AKC Gazette and AKC Events Calendar
51 Madison Avenue
New York, NY 10010
Subscriptions: (919) 233-9767
www.akc.org/gazet.htm
www.akc.org/event.htm

Direct Book Service
(800) 776-2665
www.dogandcatbooks.com/directbook

Dog Fancy
P.O. Box 6050
Mission Viejo, CA 92690
(949) 855-8822
www.dogfancy.com

DogGone
P.O. Box 651155
Vero Beach, FL 32965-1155
(561) 569-8424
www.doggonefun.com

Dog World
500 N. Dearborn, Suite 1100
Chicago, IL 60610
(312) 396-0600
www.dogworldmag.com/

Fun, Grooming, Obedience, Training

books

The Complete Idiot's Guide to Fun and Tricks with Your Dog,
Sarah Hodgson
Alpha Books

Dogs on the Web, Audrey Pavia and Betsy Siino
MIS: Press

Dogs and Kids, Parenting Tips, Bardi McLennan
Howell Book House

Pet Care on a Budget, Virginia Parker
   Guidry
Howell Book House

Surviving Your Dog's Adolescence, Carol
   Lea Benjamin
Howell Book House

...other resources
American Dog Trainers Network
161 W. 4th Street
New York, NY 10014
(212) 727-7257
www.inch.com/~dogs/index.html

American Grooming Shop Association
4575 Galley Road
Ste. 400A
Colorado Springs, CO 80915
(719) 570-7788

American Herding Breed Association
1548 Victoria Way
Pacifica, CA 94044
www.primenet.com/~joell/abba/main.htm

American Kennel Club (tracking, agility,
   obedience, herding)
Performance Events Dept.
5580 Centerview Drive
Raleigh, NC 27606
(919) 854-0199
www.akc.org/

American Pet Dog Trainers
P.O. Box 385
Davis, CA 95617
(800) PET-DOGS

Animal Behavior Society
Susan Foster
Department of Biology
Clark University
950 Main Street
Worcester, MA 01610-1477

Association of Pet Dog Trainers
P.O. Box 385
Davis, CA 95617
(800) PET-DOGS
www.apdt.com/

The Dog Agility Page
www.dogpatch.org/agility/

Grooming supplies
Pet Warehouse
P.O. Box 752138
Dayton, OH 45475-2138
(800) 443-1160

Intergroom
76 Carol Drive
Dedham, MA 02026
www.intergroom.com

National Association of Dog Obedience
    Instructors
PMB #369
729 Grapevine Highway
Hurst, TX 76054-2085
www.nadoi.org/

National Dog Groomers Association of
    America
P.O. Box 101
Clark, PA 16113
(724) 962-2711

North American Dog Agility Council
HCR 2 Box 277
St. Maries, ID 83861
www.nadac.com

North American Flyball Association
1400 W. Devon Ave, #512
Chicago, IL 60660
(309) 688-9840
www.muskie.fishnet.com/~flyball/

PETsMart
www.petsmart.com

United States Dog Agility Association,
    Inc.
P.O. Box 850955
Richardson, Texas 75085-0955
(972) 231-9700
www.usdaa.com/

United States Canine Combined Train-
    ing Association
2755 Old Thompson Mill Road
Buford, GA 30519
(770) 932-8604
www.siriusweb.com/USCCTA/

Grief Hotlines

Chicago Veterinary Medical Association
(630) 603-3994

Cornell University
(607) 253-3932

Michigan State University
College of Veterinary Medicine
(517) 432-2696

Pet Loss Grief Support
www.petloss.com/

Tufts University (Massachusetts)
School of Veterinary Medicine
(508) 839-7966

University of California, Davis
(530) 752-4200

University of Florida at Gainesville
College of Veterinary Medicine
(352) 392-4700

Virginia-Maryland Regional College of
   Veterinary Medicine
(540) 231-8038

Washington State University
College of Veterinary Medicine
(509) 335-5704

Humane Organizations and Rescue Groups

American Humane Association
63 Inverness Drive E
Englewood, CO 80112-5117
(800) 227-4645
www.americanhumane.org

American Society for the Prevention of
   Cruelty to Animals (ASPCA)
424 East 92nd Street
New York, NY 10128-6804
(212) 876-7700
www.aspca.org

Animal Protection Institute
   of America
P.O. Box 22505
Sacramento, CA 95822
(916) 731-5521

Friends of Animals
P.O. Box 30054
Hartford, CT 06150-0054
(800) 321-PETS

Humane Society of the United States
2100 L St. NW
Washington, DC 20037
(301) 258-3072, (202) 452-1100
www.hsus.org/

Massachusetts Society for the
   Prevention of Cruelty to Animals
350 South Huntington Avenue
Boston, MA 02130
(617) 522-7400
www.mspca.org/

SPAY/USA
14 Vanderventer Avenue
Port Washington, NY 11050
(516) 944-5025, (203) 377-1116 in Con-
   necticut
(800) 248-SPAY
www.spayusa.org/

Yorkshire Terrier National Rescue, Inc.
www.yorkshireterrierrescue.com/

Medical and Emergency Information

books

The Allergy Solution for Dogs, Shawn
  Messonnier, D.V.M.
Prima Publishing
3000 Lava Ridge Court
Roseville, CA 95661
(800) 632-8676
www.primalifestyles.com

The Arthritis Solution for Dogs,
Shawn Messonnier, D.V.M.
Prima Publishing

*Dr. Pitcairn's Complete Guide to Nat-
  ural Health for Dogs and Cats,*
Richard H. Pitcairn, D.V.M., PhD, and
  Susan Hubble Pitcairn
Rodale Press, Inc.

*Dog Owner's Home Veterinary
  Handbook,*
Dr. Delbert Carlson and James Giffin
Howell Book House

*Old Dogs, Old Friends: Enjoying Your
  Older Dog,*
Bonnie Wilcox, Chris Walkowitz
IDG Books Worldwide

Pet First Aid: Cats and Dogs, Bobbi
  Mammato, D.V.M.
Mosby Year Book

*Skin Diseases of Dogs and Cats:
  A Guide for Pet Owners and
  Professionals,*
Dr. Steven A. Melman
Dermapet, Inc.
P.O. Box 59713
Potomac, MD 20859

...other resources

American Academy on Veterinary
  Disaster Medicine
4304 Tenthouse Court
West River, MD 20778
(301) 261-9940

American Animal Hospital Association
P.O. Box 150899
Denver, CO 80215-0899
(800) 252-2242
www.healthypet.com

American Holistic Veterinary Medicine
  Association
2214 Old Emmorton Road
Bel Air, MD 21015
(410) 569-2346
www.altvetmed.com

American Kennel Club Canine Health
  Foundation
251 West Garfield Road, Suite 160
Aurora, OH 44202
(888) 682-9696
www.akcchf.org/main.htm

American Veterinary Medical
   Association
1931 North Meacham Road, Suite 100
Schaumburg, IL 60173-4360
(800) 248-2862
www.avma.org/

Canine Eye Registration Inc. (CERF)
Veterinary Medical Data Program
South Campus Courts, Building C
Purdue University
West Lafayette, IN 47907
(765) 494-8179
www.vet.purdue.edu/~yshen/cerf.html

Centers for Disease Control and
   Prevention
1600 Clifton Road NE
Atlanta, GA 30333
(404) 639-3311 (CDC Operator)
(800) 311-3435 (CDC Public Inquiries)
www.cdc.gov

Institute for Genetic Disease/Wind
   Morgan
P.O. Box 222
Davis, CA 97617
(530) 756-6773

National Animal Poison Control Center
1717 S. Philo, Suite 36
Urbana, IL 61802
(888) 426-4435, $45 per case, with as
   many follow-up calls as necessary included. Have name, address, phone
   number, dog's breed, age, sex, and
   type of poison ingested, if known,
   available
www.napcc.aspca.org

Orthopedic Foundation for Animals
   (OFA)
2300 E. Nifong Blvd.
Columbia, MO 65201-3856.
(573) 442-0418
www.offa.org/

PennHip
c/o Synbiotics
11011 Via Frontera
San Diego, CA 92127
(800) 228-4305

U.S. Pharmacopeia
vaccine reactions: (800) 487-7776
customer service: (800) 227-8772
www.usp.org

Veterinary Medical Database/Canine
 Eye Registration Foundation
Department of Veterinary Clinical
 Science
School of Veterinary Medicine
Purdue University
West Lafayette, IN 47907
(765) 494-8179
www.vet.purdue.edu/~yshen/

Veterinary Pet Insurance (VPI)
4175 E. La Palma Ave., #100
Anaheim, CA 92807-1846
(714) 996-2311
(800) USA PETS, (877) PET HEALTH
 in Texas
www.petplan.net/home.htm

Nutrition, Natural Foods, and Treats

books...

Dog Treats, Kim Campbell Thornton
Main Street Books

Home Prepared Dog and Cat Diets,
 Donald R. Strombeck
Iowa State University Press
(515) 292-0140

Infectious Diseases of the Dog and Cat,
 Craig E. Greene, Editor
W B Saunders Company

other resources...

California Natural, Natural Pet Products
P.O. Box 271
Santa Clara, CA 95052
(800) 532-7261
www.naturapet.com

PHD Products Inc.
P.O. Box 8313
White Plains, NY 10602
(800) 863-3403
www.phdproducts.net/

Sensible Choice, Pet Products Plus
5600 Mexico Road
St. Peters, MO 63376
(800) 592-6687
www.sensiblechoice.com/

Search and Rescue Dogs

National Association for Search and
 Rescue
4500 Southgate Place, Suite 100
Chantilly, VA 20151-1714
(703) 622-6283
www.nasar.org/

National Disaster Search Dog
 Foundation
323 East Matilija Avenue, #110-245
Ojai, CA 93023–2740
www.west.net/~rescue/

Service and Working Dogs

Canine Companions for Independence
P.O. Box 446
Santa Rosa, CA 95402-0446
(800) 572-2275
www.caninecompanions.org/

Delta Society National Service Dog
    Center
289 Perimeter Road East
Renton, WA 98055-1329
(800) 869-6898
www.petsforum.com/deltasociety/dsb00
    0.htm

Guiding Eyes for the Blind
611 Granite Springs Road
Yorktown Heights, NY 10598
www.guiding-eyes.org/

The National Education
    for Assistance Dog Services, Inc.
P.O. Box 213
West Boylston, MA 01583
(508) 422-9064
www.chamber.worcester.ma.us/neads/IN
    DEX.HTM

North American Working
    Dog Association
Southeast Kreisgruppe
P.O. Box 833
Brunswick, GA 31521

The Seeing Eye
P.O. Box 375
Morristown, NJ 07963-0375
(973) 539-4425
www.seeingeye.org/

Therapy Dogs Incorporated
2416 E. Fox Farm Road
Cheyenne, WY 82007
(877) 843-7364
www.therapydogs.com

Therapy Dogs International
6 Hilltop Road
Mendham, NJ 07945
(973) 252-9800
www.tdi-dog.org/

United Schutzhund Clubs of America
3704 Lemay Ferry Road
St. Louis, MO 63125

Appendix B:
Official Breed Standard for the Yorkshire Terrier

General Appearance

That of a long-haired toy terrier whose blue and tan coat is parted on the face and from the base of the skull to the end of the tail and hangs evenly and quite straight down each side of body. The body is neat, compact and well proportioned. The dog's high head carriage and confident manner should give the appearance of vigor and self-importance.

Head   Small and rather flat on top, the **skull** not too prominent or round, the **muzzle** not too long, with the **bite** neither undershot nor overshot and teeth sound. Either scissors bite or level bite is acceptable. The **nose** is black. **Eyes** are medium in size and not too prominent; dark in color and sparkling with a sharp, intelligent expression. Eye rims are dark. Ears are small, V-shaped, carried erect and set not too far apart.

Body   Well proportioned and very compact. The back is rather short, the back line level, with height at shoulder the same as at the rump.

Legs and Feet   **Forelegs** should be straight, elbows neither in nor out. **Hind legs** straight when viewed from behind, but stifles are moderately bent when viewed from the sides. **Feet** are

round with black toenails. Dewclaws, if any, are generally removed from the hind legs. Dewclaws on the forelegs may be removed.

Tail   Docked to a medium length and carried slightly higher than the level of the back.

Coat   Quality, texture and quantity of coat are of prime importance. Hair is glossy, fine and silky in texture. Coat on the body is moderately long and perfectly straight (not wavy). It may be trimmed to floor length to give ease of movement and a neater appearance, if desired. The fall on the head is long, tied with one bow in center of head or parted in the middle and tied with two bows. Hair on muzzle is very long. Hair should be trimmed short on tips of ears and may be trimmed on feet to give them a neat appearance.

Colors   Puppies are born black and tan and are normally darker in body color, showing an intermingling of black hair in the tan until they are matured. Color of hair on body and richness of tan on head and legs are of prime importance in adult dogs, to which the following color requirements apply: BLUE: Is a dark steel-blue, not a silver-blue and not mingled with fawn, bronzy or black hairs. TAN: All tan hair is darker at the roots than in the middle, shading to still lighter tan at the tips. There should be no sooty or black hair intermingled with any of the tan.

Color on Body   The blue extends over the body from back of neck to root of tail. Hair on tail is a darker blue, especially at end of tail.

Headfall   A rich golden tan, deeper in color at sides of head, at ear roots and on the muzzle, with ears a deep rich tan. Tan color should not extend down on back of neck.

Chest and Legs   A bright, rich tan, not extending above the elbow on the forelegs nor above the stifle on the hind legs.

Weight   Must not exceed seven pounds.

Approved April 12, 1966
©1966 Yorkshire Terrier Club of America, Inc.

Index

Meet Your Yorkshire Terrier Care Experts

Author   **Elaine Waldorf Gewirtz** has been writing about dogs for the past ten years. A contributor to the *American Kennel Club Gazette, Dog Fancy, Dogs USA, Popular Dogs,* and *Dog World,* Elaine is a member of the Dog Writers Association of America (DWAA), the Independent Writers' of Southern California, the Burbank Kennel Club, and the Dalmatian Club of America. Elaine teaches conformation handling classes and is the editor of *The Spotter,* the Dalmatian national breed club publication, which received the 1999 DWAA Maxwell Award for excellence. Elaine shares a home in Westlake Village, California, with her husband and their children, as well as with her Dalmatians, which she exhibits in conformation.

Trainer   **Liz Palika** has been teaching classes for dogs and their owners for over twenty years. Her goal is to help people understand why their dogs do what they do so that dogs and owners can live together successfully. Liz says, "If, in each training class, I can increase understanding and ease frustration so that the dog doesn't end up in the local shelter because the owner has given up, then I have accomplished my goal!" She is the author of 23 books and has won awards from both the Dog Writers Association of America and the ASPCA. Liz and her husband, Paul, share their home with three Australian Shepherds: Dax, Kes, and Riker.

Series Editor   **Joanne Howl, D.V.M.,** is a graduate of the University of Tennessee College of Veterinary Medicine and has practiced animal medicine for over ten years. She currently serves as president of the Maryland Veterinary Medical Association and as secretary/treasurer of the American Academy on Veterinary Disaster Medicine. Her columns and articles have appeared in a variety of animal-related publications. Dr. Howl divides her time between family, small-animal medicine, writing, and her two dogs and six cats.